What People Are Saying About
Chicken Soup for the Kid's Soul . . .

"Kids are lucky to have a *Chicken Soup* book just for them. As a son of a preacher I was expected to know the right choices to make. I could have used examples of how other kids were dealing with the pressure of growing up."

Sinbad
actor, comedian

"*Chicken Soup for the Kid's Soul* is filled with stories that restore your faith in humanity and open your eyes to the meaningful moments in life."

Larisa Oleynik
star, *The Secret World of Alex Mack*

"A great book for kids! *Chicken Soup for the Kid's Soul* covers many tough subjects so well that every kid who reads it will be able to relate to some of the stories, and hopefully learn from the rest so that their souls—not just their bodies—will grow up big and strong."

Lori Beth Denberg
actress, star on Nickelodeon's *All That*

"The *Chicken Soup for the Soul* series has provided stories that enlighten, encourage and inspire. I believe wholeheartedly that *Chicken Soup for the Kid's Soul* will continue to reach out and provide our youth with an important motivational tool that will no doubt stimulate positive thinking."

Malcolm-Jamal Warner
actor, *Malcolm and Eddie*

"As soon as I read the book, I wanted to rush home and give it to my kids to read. The messages are so inspiring and encouraging that I'm looking forward to a second helping of *Chicken Soup for the Kid's Soul.*"

Adrienne Lopez
vice president, talent development and casting,
Nickelodeon

"Reading *Chicken Soup for the Kid's Soul* with a child will help build and strengthen the love you share. And, since the love of children is the ultimate 'Chicken Soup for the Soul,' you may even want to read it again!"

Ann Pleshette Murphy
editor-in-chief, *PARENTS Magazine*

"*Chicken Soup for the Kid's Soul* shows our children that life is an amazing journey filled with accomplishment, failure, happiness and tears, but that within us all lies the ability to beat life's challenges and to strive to achieve our dreams."

Roxanne Spillett
president, Boys & Girls Clubs of America

"As a child, I was a member of a book club. My favorite stories were those that inspired me to dream. *Chicken Soup for the Kid's Soul* is just such a book—these stories will inspire young readers not only to dream, but also to give their hearts, minds and souls to the creation of new possibilities."

Larry Jones
president, Feed the Children

"The most delicious thing about *Chicken Soup for the Kid's Soul* is kids talking to kids, sharing and relating both their joys and sorrows. Their stories will help other kids know that they are not alone in their feelings and experiences."

Sara O'Meara and Yvonne Fedderson
founders, Childhelp

"When confronted with difficult issues, it is comforting for children to know that others have been there and survived. *Chicken Soup for the Kid's Soul* does just that for readers: its stories relate to kids that they, too, can overcome hardships in their own lives."

David S. Liederman
executive director, Child Welfare League of America

CHICKEN SOUP
FOR THE
KID'S SOUL

Chicken Soup for the Kid's Soul
Stories of Courage, Hope and Laughter for Kids ages 8-12
Jack Canfield, Mark Victor Hansen, Patty Hansen, Irene Dunlap

Published by Backlist, LLC,
a unit of Chicken Soup for the Soul Publishing, LLC. www.chickensoup.com

Front cover illustration by Larissa Hise
Originally published in 1998 by Health Communications, Inc.

Back cover and spine redesign by Pneuma Books, LLC

Distributed to the booktrade by Simon & Schuster. SAN: 200-2442

Publisher's Cataloging-in-Publication Data
(Prepared by The Donohue Group)

Chicken soup for the kid's soul : stories of courage, hope and laughter for
kids ages 8-12 / [compiled by] Jack Canfield ... [et al.].

   p. : ill. ; cm.

   Originally published: Deerfield Beach, FL : Health Communications, c1998.
Interest age group: 008-012.
ISBN: 978-1-62361-060-9

   1. Children--Conduct of life--Juvenile literature. 2. Conduct of life--
Anecdotes. 3. Anecdotes. I. Canfield, Jack, 1944-

BJ1631 .C46 2012
158.1/083   2012944408

PRINTED IN THE UNITED STATES OF AMERICA
on acid free paper
21 20 19 18   08 09 10

CHICKEN SOUP
FOR THE
KID'S SOUL

Stories of Courage, Hope and Laughter for Kids ages 8-12

Jack Canfield
Mark Victor Hansen
Patty Hansen
Irene Dunlap

Backlist, LLC, a unit of
Chicken Soup for the Soul Publishing, LLC
Cos Cob, CT
www.chickensoup.com

"My teacher says I can grow up to be whatever
I want to be. I want to be a kid."

Contents

Introduction..xv

1. ON LOVE

Kelly, the Flying Angel *Louise R. Hamm* 2

The Tower *Robert J. Fern* 7

Uncle Charlie *Patty Hathaway-Breed* 10

The Game of Love *Lou Kassem*...14

"Where's My Kiss, Then?" *M. A. Urquhart* 18

The Visit *Debbie Herman*..22

The Fire Truck *Lori Moore*...26

Merry Christmas, My Friend *Christa Holder Ocker*.....................29

2. ON FRIENDSHIP

There's an Alien on the Internet *Joanne Peterson* 34

Seeing, Really Seeing *Marie P. McDougal* 39

Kim Li, the Great *Berniece Rabe* 42

Edna Mae: First Lesson in Prejudice *Sandra Warren* 46

The Connection *Joel Walker*..49

The Favorite Vase *Belladonna Richuitti*..54

A Friend . . . *Danielle Fishel and friends*...57

Best Friends *Mary Beth Olson*..63

All I Would Ever Need   *Kerri Warren* 66

My Friend Anthony   *Katie Short* 68

3. ON FAMILY

No Dad?!   *Jason Damazo* 72

Terror on Route 83   *Mary Ellyn Sandford* 75

Watching for the Miracle   *Korina L. Moss* 80

Daddy's Girl . . . At Long Last   *Candace Goldapper* 83

From the Heart   *Marcia Byalick* 85

A Brother's Love   *Diana L. James* 88

Secrets That Made Paul Special   *Judy M. Garty* 90

My Grandfather's Gift   *Rider Strong* 93

Silent Night, Crystal Night   *Lillian Belinfante Herzberg* 97

Green Salami   *Patty Hansen* 103

Going, Going, Gone   *Martha Bolton* 109

Your Name in Gold   *A. F. Bauman* 111

Father's Day   *Taylor Martini* 113

Mom's Duck   *Page McBrier* 116

4. ON ATTITUDE AND PERSPECTIVE

√ The Bobsledder's Jacket   *Tim Myers* 122

√ Things Are Not Always Black or White   *Judie Paxton* 125

What's Wrong with a B+?   *Donna M. Russell* 127

Just Ben   *Adrian Wagner* 133

The Green Boots   *Linda Rosenberg* 136

Showing Up   *Julie J. Vaughn with Tyler Vaughn Marsden* 140

The Pest   *Judy Fuerst* 144

A *Good* Reason to Look Up   *Shaquille O'Neal* 148

Close Call   *Diana Parker* 150

The Flood   *Adam Edelman* 153

The Man Who Had Plenty
    Reverend Mark Tidd as told by Jerry Ullman 156

The Perfect Dog   *Jan Peck* 158
To Be Enormously Gorgeous   *Carla O'Brien* 161

5. ON DEATH AND DYING

The Purple Belt   *Chuck Norris* 165
B. J.   *Nate Barker* 167
The Perfect Angel   *Stacie Christina Smith* 171
Someone to Hold Onto   *Ann McCoole Rigby* 174
Rebecca's Rainbow   *Tara M. Nickerson* 179
One Rainbow Wasn't Enough   *Matt Sharpe* 182
A Nightmare Come True   *Damien Liermann* 185
Lessons from God   *Jennifer Rhea Cross* 189

6. ACHIEVING DREAMS

Believe in Yourself   *Jillian K. Hunt* 194
The Little Girl Who Dared to Wish   *Alan D. Shultz* 196
The Playground   *Audilee Boyd Taylor* 200
Dreams of the Children   *Jody Suzanne Waitzman* 205
Batgirl   *Dandi Dailey Mackall* 206
G-o-o-o-a-a-a-l-l-l-l!   *Heather Thomsen* 211
With Every Footstep   *Shannon Miller* 213
The Rock Club   *Vanessa Clayton* 216
Socks for Kerry   *Barbara McCutcheon Crawford* 219
Just Ask   *David Levitt* 222

7. OVERCOMING OBSTACLES

Grandfather Learns to Read   *Karen Beth Luckett* 230
School—Moving Up   *Ben Carson, M.D.* 234
In Control   *John D. Troxler* 241
The Sandbox   *Lucas Parker* 244
What a Year   *Robert Diehl* 245
Dear God, This Is Charles   *Charles Inglehart* 250
Missy and Me   *Glenda Palmer* 253

The Miracle of Life   *Lacy Richardson* 257

8. ON CHOICES

Goodwill   *Cynthia M. Hamond*..262
Putting My Best Foot Forward   *Kathy Ireland* 267
Understanding   *Jessica Stroup*..271
Nine Gold Medals   *David Roth*...274
Without a Nightlight   *Jessica Harper* 276
Nobody Knows the Difference   *Deborah J. Rasmussen*...........279
The New House and the Snake   *Christine Lavin* 282
I Found a Tiny Starfish   *Dayle Ann Dodds* 287

9. TOUGH STUFF

Get Help Now!   *Tia Thompson*..290
The Big Director   *Kel Mitchell*..294
I Love Her More Than Ever   *Amber Foy*................................299
Dear Momma   *Darnell Hill* 303
My Dad   *Aljon B. Farin*...305
Smoking Is Cool. . . . Not!   *Valeria Soto* 306
DARE Rap   *Shelly Merkes* 308
I'm Not Dana   *Sabrina Anne Tyler*..310
No Home   *Elizabeth A. Gilbert-Bono*......................................312

10. ECLECTIC WISDOM

Baby's Ears   *Valerie Allen* 316
Kindness Is Contagious   *Kristin Seuntjens*............................320
Do You Have Your Wallet?   *Laksman Frank* 323
Small Talk   *Multiple Authors*..327
The Day I Figured Out That No One Is Perfect   *Ellie Logan* 333
The Little Notice   *Kenan Thompson* 335
Teenagers   *Melissa Mercedes*...337
My Guardian Angel   *Travis Ebel*..339

Grandpa's Bees *Barbara Allman* 341

The Flying Fish *Megan Niedermeyer with Killeen Anderson* 345

Mother Says . . . *Martha Bolton*..350

What I've Learned So Far *Multiple Authors* 353

Afterword
Reading Stories: An Act of Co-Creation
    James Elwood Conner, Ed.D...358

Who Is Jack Canfield?..359

Who Is Mark Victor Hansen? 360

Who Is Patty Hansen? 361

Who Is Irene Dunlap? 362

Contributors...363

Permissions 377

Book

Oh, look, it's a book!
I'm sure it must be
A path of adventures waiting for me,
A yellow brick road to the Wizard of Oz,
A frivolous poem without any cause.
Should I open it and peek to see what's inside?
What if it's scary I might need to hide.
I'll never know unless I dare.
I need a good laugh, a cry or a scare.
I'm sure it can wait—well, then I'll never know
Maybe it's someplace that I'll never go.
But today is the day that's been waiting for me
I'll open this book, and I will see.

Jessica McCain, age 14

Foreword

You hold in your hands a very valuable book. In it, you will find inspiring stories from celebrities and adults . . . but most importantly from people your own age! The stories will encourage you, enlighten you and maybe even make you cry . . . but hold them close. Keep the book on your bedside table and read it often—whenever you need a guiding hand or hopeful thought.

Never give up believing in yourself. With God, you hold the power and talent to achieve all of your dreams. My friends, you are our future.

Muhammad Ali
Three-Time World Heavyweight Boxing Champion,
Humanitarian

Discovery

Faraway places
Events gone by
Interesting faces
Make you laugh, make you cry.

Cities never visited
Easy to see
Mysteries unsolved
Unraveled for me.

In the chair by my bed
Tall mountains I've scaled
In the pages I've read
Seven oceans I've sailed.

Stories on pages
Picture it well
Mystical fables
Only books can tell.

Jesse Damazo, age 14

Introduction

A great man is one who has not lost his child's heart.

Mencius

I think it is funny to be writing about chicken soup for somebody's soul when you can't even see a soul. It must be a special thing inside of all of us that does something because books are written about it every day.

When I cook chicken soup, it takes a lot of ingredients to make the soup turn out right. Maybe that's why a book about chicken soup for a kid's soul will be fun—because it will take a lot of different ideas, from many different people, for the book to turn out right.

Some kids might write about happy things, and others will find that there are only sad things in their lives to write about—like when I think about my cousin Kimmy, it makes me sad because she was the first person I ever knew who died.

But then, when I play with Kimmy's baby daughter, Emilie, it makes me feel happy when she does something to make me laugh.

*Something inside of me can feel happy and sad
at the same time. Is that when you know that
you have a soul?*

Candice Hanes, age 10

Ever since the first *Chicken Soup for the Soul* was published in June 1993, we have been getting requests from kids all over the world asking for a *Chicken Soup* book just for them. So here it is, the first full-length *Chicken Soup for the Kid's Soul*, written by kids and by adults who haven't forgotten what it's like to be a kid.

When we started this book a year and a half ago, we thought we pretty much knew what issues and challenges our kids face. When our own kids—Christopher, Elisabeth, Melanie, Marleigh and Weston—went off to school every day, we assumed that they were experiencing many of the same things that we did at their age. For example, being teased because of looks or physical disabilities was a big deal. Also, making and keeping friends was important. Betrayal by a friend was guaranteed to break our hearts. Getting good grades, being accepted by our peers, and being liked and supported by our teachers were things that mattered.

In April 1997, we did a fax-mailing requesting stories from over 5,800 elementary and middle schools across the United States. We received an overwhelming response. We read every single story sent to us—over 4,000! There were an additional 3,800 stories sent from other sources, giving us a grand total of 7,800 stories submitted and read for possible inclusion in this book. What we learned from the stories was very enlightening.

You, the kids of today, face much graver issues and harder decisions than we ever did. It is not uncommon for you to be exposed to gang warfare on a daily basis, and it is not necessarily confined to inner-city or at-risk kids. Drugs, alcohol, smoking, early physical development, pregnancy, depression and suicide have found their way into our middle and elementary schools. You know about kidnappings, child abuse and violence through the media or your own experiences. Immediate family members, grandparents and friends die from accidents or from diseases like AIDS and cancer. You are frightened of losing your families through divorce or separation; even when you know it is for the best, you don't want it or like it. One of the subjects you submitted the highest number of stories about expressed your fear of and dislike of moving, and losing the home you have known all your life.

Although we celebrate the closing of the gender gap and the broader career choices that have become available to your generation, we now realize the stress that this creates for you. You are expected at an earlier and earlier age to know what you want to be and what you want out of life, and the choices can be overwhelming. We received stories that showed us that kids like you feel as if you must understand and accept all the troubles of the world. Because of the stories you have shared with us, we now have a better understanding of what you kids are going through today.

We realize that you have been requesting a *Chicken Soup* book of your own not only because you *want* one, but because you *need* one. Never has there been a time in history when kids have needed *Chicken Soup* for their souls more than now.

A book can open the door to a magical kingdom where knowledge and inspiration are available to all who read it. We hope that this book will become your best friend and nonjudgmental advisor, for a book cannot tell whether the person holding it is black or white, red or tan, young or old, a boy or a girl.

The pages in this book are meant to be read, absorbed and reread over and over again, and shared with friends and family. Within these pages are stories of heroes—kids just like you who have overcome some of the tremendous challenges that you face today. There are also stories that are funny or just plain silly. Without this side of the childhood experience, none of us can ever hope for balance and true joy in life.

This book is designed to empower and encourage you to love and accept yourself, and to believe in your dreams; to let you know that there are answers to your questions; and to give you hope for a great future.

It is our hope that any adult or teenager who picks up this book and reads it will find his or her "child heart" touched, and hopefully, reawakened. We truly believe that within each and every one of us, there is a piece of our heart and soul that we have hidden—a piece of us that perhaps still believes that there is a Santa Claus, that butterflies should be set free and that good will always prevail over evil. On a very deep level—our kid-soul level—we all want to be loved, accepted, encouraged and supported, no matter what our age. From our hearts to your hearts, we present *Chicken Soup for the Kid's Soul*.

May kids reign forever!

1

ON LOVE

Some people say love is blind, but I think love
*   is beautiful. Everything and everyone can*
*   feel love—*
Birds, humans and animals—all living
*   creatures.*
Love means caring and showing
*   understanding.*
Love means being there when someone is
*   in need.*
Love is being a friend.
You can love your pets, your doll, your favorite
*   chair,*
Your friends and family.
Love can be just about anything you want
*   it to be.*
Love is a choice.

Stephanie Lee, age 11

Kelly, the Flying Angel

Kelly and the pony met when Kelly was seven. She had gone with her father to a neighbor's farm to buy seed. The shaggy, brown and white pony stood alone in a pen. Kelly reached through the wires to touch the warm satin of the pony's nose. Kelly spoke softly as the pony nuzzled Kelly's fingers. "What's your name, pony? You seem so sad and lonely."

"She ain't got no name," the farmer grunted. "She ain't much good anymore. She's old and she's blind in one eye. I ain't got no use for her since the kids are gone." He turned back to Kelly's father, who had loaded the bags of seed onto the truck and pulled crumpled bills from his pocket. "You can have her if you pay me somethin' for the saddle."

"How much?" her father inquired, barely glancing at the pony.

"Twenty." The old man reached a callused hand toward the money. Kelly's father pulled off another bill. Gnarled fingers snatched the bills and stuffed them quickly into the pocket of well-worn, dirty overalls.

Kelly cradled the bridle in her arms as they drove home, her excitement mounting. She kept peeking into the rear of the truck to reassure herself that the pony was still there.

"Now, this pony will be your job. You have to feed her and take care of her. It'll teach you some responsibility. I don't have time to mess with her. Understand?" Her father's voice was stern.

"I'll do it, Daddy. Thank you for letting me have her. I promise I'll take good care of her."

Once they were home and the pony was safely in the stall, Kelly threw hay into the manger, then ran to the house.

"Mom, you should see our pony! She was so lonely, but she'll be happy here." Joy sparkled in Kelly's eyes. "I've named her Trixie 'cause I'm going to teach her to do tricks." Before her mother could respond, Kelly was back out the door to see that Trixie was comfortable. It was then that Kelly introduced Trixie to her angel.

When Kelly was a small child, she had been awakened by a frightening storm. She called to her mother, who reassured her by telling her, "Don't be afraid. Jesus sends his angels to protect little children." From then on, Kelly had never actually seen an angel, but she felt a presence at times when she would otherwise have been afraid or lonely.

Kelly brushed the pony's coat and trimmed her mane and hoofs. Trixie responded to the attention by nuzzling Kelly's neck, searching her pockets for treats and following her commands. As Kelly rode from the house to the back pasture, she taught Trixie to raise the latches on the gates with her nose. The gates would swing open, and Kelly would close them without dismounting.

Kelly taught Trixie a routine, trying to duplicate tricks she had seen at a circus. She rode standing up and eventually mastered the ultimate stunt of jumping through a crudely constructed hoop on each circuit of the riding ring. Kelly and Trixie became the best of friends.

When Kelly was ten, her parents divorced. Kelly and her dog, Laddie, moved with her mom to a small farm several miles away. The problems between her parents kept Kelly from seeing her father anymore, and because Trixie still lived at her father's farm, Kelly was doubly miserable.

On the day they left her father's farm, Kelly walked slowly to the pasture to say good-bye to Trixie. She had never needed her angel's help more. "Angel," she sobbed, "please stay with Trixie so she won't be lonely. I have Mom and Laddie, but Trixie will be all alone. She needs you." With her small arms around Trixie's neck, she reassured the pony, "It'll be all right, Trixie. My angel will take care of you."

Her parents' divorce, a new school, a different home and the loss of Trixie turned Kelly's life upside down all at once. Her mother encouraged her to make friends.

"Come on, Kelly, and ride with us," two of her schoolmates urged as they sat on their bicycles in the driveway.

Following the two girls down the road, Kelly felt the wind in her hair and the warmth of the sun on her face. She needed friends, she reminded herself, and pedaled faster to catch up.

During the summer, Kelly and her friends rode their bicycles to the park and around the track at the school. With her strong legs, she could match any of them when they raced.

After racing on the track one sunny day, Kelly pedaled home with her new friends. As she bounced along the bumpy, dusty road, the hard edge of the bike seat dug into her leg. She wished she were sitting in her smooth leather saddle on Trixie, gliding over the fresh green grass of the pasture.

Suddenly, the front wheel of the bicycle swerved into a rut. She turned hard to the left to get it out, but it was too late. Hurtling over the handlebars, she bounced off the edge of the road and into a ditch. The girls hurried to her.

"Her injuries are minor," the doctor informed her mother after Kelly had limped home, "but you'd better keep her quiet for a couple of days."

Though sore and scratched, Kelly returned to her bicycle in a few days. One morning, she awoke with a numb feeling in her legs. Slowly, she slid her body to the edge of the bed; but as she attempted to stand, she collapsed on the floor.

Puzzled by this development, the doctor examined her carefully.

"Her injuries have healed, but there is some psychological trauma," he said. "I've scheduled therapy, and stretching exercises should help." Kelly went home in a wheelchair.

As she sat on the porch, she hugged Laddie close and stared wistfully across the field. "Please, God, please bring Trixie and my angel back to me. I need them so."

One day a letter came from Kelly's father:

> Dear Kelly,
>
> Your aunt told me about your accident. I'm sorry to hear about it. I have made arrangements to have your pony delivered to you next week. She has been opening all the gates and letting my stock out of the pasture. I think she is looking for you. Maybe having her will help you feel better.
>
> Love,
> Dad

In a few days a truck arrived, and Trixie was led down the ramp. Nuzzling Kelly's neck and snorting at Laddie, the pony checked out her new home. Kelly petted Trixie's head and neck as far as she could reach from her wheelchair, and kissed her on the nose. "Trixie, Trixie, I knew you would come. Thank you, thank you."

Kelly awoke the next morning with renewed determination. She wheeled herself to the barnyard with a treat for Trixie. Grasping Trixie's mane, she pulled herself up from the wheelchair and stood beside the pony. Stretching to reach Trixie's back, she brushed her until the pony's coat shone.

Kelly's legs grew stronger each day. Then, eager to ride, she climbed up the wooden fence and struggled to pull herself onto the pony's back. Trixie's coat was warm and silky against Kelly's bare legs.

"Look! I'm riding. . . . I'm riding!" Kelly yelled as Trixie's slow trot bounced her up and down like a rag doll. "Go, Trixie!" Kelly dug her heels into the pony's sides, and they raced through the gate to the open pasture. Kelly squealed with delight, and Laddie ran after them, barking wildly.

When school started, an enthusiastic Kelly sprang onto the bus with a cheerful greeting. No more wheelchair for her! At home, a poster of a circus hung in Kelly's room. It showed a smiling angel. In Kelly's bold, colorful printing it read, "Kelly, the Flying Angel—Shows Nightly and Weekends."

Louise R. Hamm

The Tower

After the verb "to love," "to help" is the most beautiful verb in the world.

Bertha Von Suttner

Am I my brother's keeper? Absolutely!

James McNeil, age 17

Ten-year-old John McNeil ran barefoot out the door on a windy, cold day in February and headed straight for the 125-foot electrical tower behind the McNeil home. John didn't realize the dangers of the structure, which carries power from Hoover Dam to the southern Arizona communities. He didn't know that it carried 230,000 sizzling volts through its silver wires. He wasn't even aware that he had forgotten his shoes. John suffers from autism, a condition that separates him from reality, forcing him to live within his own thoughts. That day his thoughts were set on climbing to the top of that tower, touching the sky and feeling what it's like to fly.

He had scaled the gigantic jungle gym before, but he

had never gotten beyond the twenty-foot handrails. His seventeen-year-old brother, James, was always watching, and close by. James always made sure that no harm came to his little brother. But today was different. Today, John ran out the door unnoticed before James realized that he was missing. John had already cleared the handrails and was making his way to the sky by the time James spotted his brother. John, like most autistic children, had absolutely no fear or concept of danger. James, on the other hand, realized that he had to face his greatest fear of all—the fear of heights.

James understood the danger of the electrical tower but chose to follow his younger brother up each gray rail, trying not to look down, all the way to the top. James finally reached his brother and held him tightly with his right hand. With his left hand, he gripped a metal bar to help stabilize them both.

James was shaking. He was cold and scared, but he never released his grip on John. John struggled, wanting to fly, but James held tight. James's hands were numb, and he was afraid that if he let go, they would both fall to their death.

The minutes stretched into hours as they balanced on a three-inch rail. James sang hymns to soothe his own racing heart and to distract his brother from the rescue action taking place below.

Hundreds of people gathered at the base of the tower. They looked like ants to James, who saw them from high atop his perch. Noisy news helicopters began to circle, sending images of the two boys clinging to the tower against a bright blue sky to millions of television sets nationwide. Fire trucks and other emergency vehicles rushed to the scene. One brave firefighter from the technical rescue squad climbed up the structure to where the two brothers hung on for their lives. He quickly tied them securely to a metal beam.

Part of the equipment needed to rescue James and John was a highly specialized truck called a Condor. Luckily, one was located at a nearby construction site. The rescuers patiently awaited its arrival, and at last, it was spotted moving along the road leading toward the tower. Once positioned, a platform was raised from the truck up to the boys sitting on the top rail of the tower. Secured with a safety line, the brothers and their rescuers were then carefully lowered to the ground as the crowd below cheered and applauded.

People were telling James that he was a hero, but James didn't have any time for their praise. He wanted to be at his brother's side while they transported John to the hospital, to be treated for exposure to the cold.

Not all guardian angels have feathered wings and golden halos. Most would not be recognized. Yet, on a windy, cold day, hundreds of people caught their first—and maybe only—glimpse of one, a seventeen-year-old guardian angel named James.

Robert J. Fern

[EDITORS' NOTE: *In honor of the courage that James demonstrated during the rescue of his brother John, the Boy Scouts of America awarded him the Heroism Award with Crossed Palms. James, who is an Eagle Scout, became only the 113th person out of 100 million scouts since 1910 to receive this special award.*]

Uncle Charlie

*Where there is great love, there are always
miracles.*

Willa Cather

I remember being scared the first time I saw Uncle
Charlie. I had just stepped off the school bus, and coming
into the house from the brightness of day, I couldn't see.
When my eyes adjusted, I was surprised to see a bed in
the dining room. A strange, unshaven man, propped up
by pillows, sat in the darkened room. For a second, I
wondered whether I was in the wrong house.

"Patty, is that you?" my grandmother called from the
other room. I bolted into the kitchen.

"Nana, who's that man?"

"Remember me telling you about Charlie, about how sick
he got in the war and how they put him in the veterans'
hospital? Well, that man in there is your Uncle Charlie."

The silent man in the dining room didn't look anything
like the smiling photograph on the mantel.

"Last night, Patty, I had a dream," my grandmother
said. "In the dream, God spoke. He said, 'Go get your son.

Bring him home, and he'll get well.' That's what I did. This morning after you went to school, I took the city bus to the hospital. I walked right into that place, into Charlie's room, took him by the hand, and said, 'I'm taking you home.'" Nana chuckled. "Good heavens, how we must have looked, charging down that big ol' hospital lawn, him in that gown, open and flapping in the back. Nobody stopped us. But nobody said a word, even when we got on the bus." She paused. "It was like we was invisible."

"Nana, Charlie didn't look like he saw me. Maybe I'm invisible too."

"Charlie saw you. It's just that he's got what the doctors call catatonic. Guess that's their fancy way of saying cat's got his tongue." She stopped rocking. "Don't you worry now. Charlie will be talking. He just needs to know we love him, that he's home."

Frightened by the dark beyond the open kitchen door, I ran out the back door, leaped off the porch and raced across the field, slapping my hips, pretending I was both horse and rider.

For months, I avoided the dining room. Finally I became accustomed to Charlie's silence. After that, I played in Charlie's room. His blanket-covered knees were the "towers" of my castles.

"Charlie, you awake?" I whispered. "Today at school, I saw a picture of an enchanted prince in my teacher's book. He's got long hair, just like you."

Dust sparkled in the shaft of light streaming in under the drawn shade. I grabbed at the sparkles, making the dust whirl.

"Look, Charlie, I've caught us a handful of sun. It's got millions and billions of tiny stars in it." I held out my fist. "I've caught some for you."

"Patty, I got something for you," Nana called from outside.

Before leaving Charlie, I put my favorite doll with its

red nail-polish lips and half-bald head next to him, and tucked them both in.

"She's a princess. I'm leaving her to keep you company."

"I found this little bird under the old oak," Nana said. "Its eyes are still closed. It must have just pecked out of its shell. There's a dropper in the medicine cabinet in the bathroom. Use that dropper to feed him ground-up sunflower seeds and water."

She handed me the bird. "Empty out a shoe box and be sure to put something soft in it for a lining. What are you going to name him?"

"Little Bird. I'm calling him Little Bird, just like in the song."

I went inside and dumped the shoe box with my rock collection on the rug.

"Hey, Charlie, look what I've got!" I put Little Bird in the empty box. "Watch him for a minute. I've got to get the dropper." I put the box in Charlie's lap.

When I returned with the dropper, the box was lying on the floor, empty. Charlie had dropped him!

"Charlie," I whispered, trying not to cry, "where is Little Bird?"

Cracking open his cupped hands, Charlie smiled as he stared down at the tiny, hunger-stretched beak that peeked up between his thumbs and forefingers.

That evening, when I was mashing potatoes, I said, "You know what, Nana? Charlie's taking care of Little Bird."

"I know it. I saw him. And you know something else? He's making humming noises, like he's singing."

Nana was getting Charlie's tray ready when Charlie walked into the kitchen and sat down at the table. He was dressed in overalls and a plaid shirt. It was the first time I'd seen him in anything other than pajamas. Nana opened her eyes in exaggerated surprise. She looked so silly I started to laugh.

Then Charlie made the first sound, other than snoring and coughing, that I'd ever heard him make. He laughed! Slapping his knees, he laughed until tears ran down his cheeks. Then he reached into the big pocket of his overalls and took out Little Bird.

"Look," he said. "Isn't this the sweetest, most helpless little thing you ever saw?"

Nana almost fell off her chair. Then she started to cry. I wasn't surprised, because I knew that even though he'd been placed under a spell, the spell couldn't last. They never do.

Patty Hathaway-Breed

The Game of Love

Love is something eternal.

Vincent van Gogh

Dad brought him home from a fishing trip in the mountains, full of cockleburs and so thin you could count every rib.

"Good gracious," Mom said. "He's filthy!"

"No, he isn't! He's Rusty," said John, my eight-year-old brother. "Can we keep him? Please . . . please . . . please."

"He's going to be a big dog," Dad warned, lifting a mud-encrusted paw. "Probably why he was abandoned."

"What kind of dog?" I asked. It was impossible to get close to this smelly creature.

"Mostly German shepherd," Dad said. "He's in bad shape, John. He may not make it."

John was gently picking out cockleburs.

"I'll take care of Rusty. Honest, I will."

Mom gave in, as she usually did with John. My little brother had a mild form of hemophilia. Four years earlier, he'd almost bled to death from a routine tonsillectomy.

We'd all been careful with him since then.

"All right, John," Dad said. "We'll keep Rusty. But he's your responsibility."

"Deal!"

And that's how Rusty came to live with us. He was John's dog from that very first moment, though he tolerated the rest of us.

John kept his word. He fed, watered, medicated and groomed the scruffy-looking animal every day. I think he liked taking care of something rather than being taken care of.

Over the summer, Rusty grew into a big, handsome dog. He and John were constant companions. Wherever John went, Rusty was by his side. When school began, Rusty would walk John the six blocks to elementary school, then come home. Every school day at three o'clock, rain or shine, Rusty would wait for John at the playground.

"There goes Rusty," the neighbors would say. "Must be close to three. You can set your watch by that dog."

Telling time wasn't the only amazing thing about Rusty. Somehow, he sensed that John shouldn't roughhouse like the other boys. He was very protective. When the neighborhood bully taunted my undersized brother, Rusty's hackles rose, and a deep, menacing growl came from his throat. The heckling ceased after one encounter. And when John and his best friend Bobby wrestled, Rusty monitored their play with a watchful eye. If John were on top, fine. If Bobby got John down, Rusty would lope over, grab Bobby's collar and pull him off. Bobby and John thought this game great fun. They staged fights quite often, much to Mother's dismay.

"You're going to get hurt, John!" she would scold. "And you aren't being fair to Rusty."

John didn't like being restricted. He hated being careful—

being different. "It's just a game, Mom. Shoot, even Rusty knows that. Don't you, boy?" Rusty would cock his head and give John a happy smile.

In the spring, John got an afternoon paper route. He'd come home from school, fold his papers and take off on his bike to deliver them. He always took the same streets, in the same order. Of course, Rusty delivered papers, too.

One day, for no particular reason, John changed his route. Instead of turning left on a street as he usually did, he turned right. Thump! . . . Crash! . . . A screech of brakes . . . Rusty sailed through the air.

Someone called us about the accident. I had to pry John from Rusty's lifeless body so that Dad could bring Rusty home.

"It's my fault," John said over and over. "Rusty thought the car was gonna hit me. He thought it was another game."

"The only game Rusty was playing was the game of love," Dad said. "You both played it well."

John sniffled. "Huh?"

"You were there for Rusty when he needed you. He was there for you when he thought you needed him. That's the game of love."

"I want him back," John wailed. "My Rusty's gone!"

"No, he isn't," Dad said, hugging John and me. "Rusty will stay in your memories forever."

And he has.

Lou Kassem

"Where's My Kiss, Then?"

There once was a little girl named Cindy. Cindy's father worked six days a week, and often came home tired from the office. Her mother worked equally hard, doing the cleaning, the cooking and the many tasks needed to run a family. Theirs was a good family, living a good life. Only one thing was missing, but Cindy didn't even realize it.

One day, when she was nine, she went on her first sleepover. She stayed with her friend Debbie. At bedtime, Debbie's mother tucked the girls into bed. She kissed them both good night.

"Love you," said Debbie's mother.

"Love you, too," murmured Debbie.

Cindy was so amazed that she couldn't sleep. No one had ever kissed her good night. No one had ever kissed her at all. No one had ever told her that they loved her. All night long, she lay there, thinking over and over, *This is the way it should be.*

When she went home, her parents seemed pleased to see her.

"Did you have fun at Debbie's house?" asked her mother.

"The house felt awfully quiet without you," said her father.

Cindy didn't answer. She ran up to her room. She hated them both. Why had they never kissed her? Why had they never hugged her or told her they loved her? Didn't they love her?

She wished she could run away. She wished she could live with Debbie's mother. Maybe there had been a mistake and these weren't her real parents. Maybe Debbie's mother was her real mother.

That night before bed, she went to her parents.

"Well, good night then," she said. Her father looked up from his paper.

"Good night," he said.

Her mother put down her sewing and smiled. "Good night, Cindy."

No one made a move. Cindy couldn't stand it any longer.

"Why don't you ever kiss me?" she asked.

Her mother looked flustered. "Well," she stammered, "because, I guess . . . because no one ever kissed *me* when *I* was little. That's just the way it was."

Cindy cried herself to sleep. For many days she was angry. Finally she decided to run away. She would go to Debbie's house and live with them. She would never go back to the parents who didn't love her.

She packed her backpack and left without a word. But once she got to Debbie's house, she couldn't go in. She decided that no one would believe her. No one would let her live with Debbie's parents. She gave up her plan and walked away.

Everything felt bleak and hopeless and awful. She would never have a family like Debbie's. She was stuck forever with the worst, most loveless parents in the world.

Instead of going home, she went to a park and sat on a park bench. She sat there for a long time, thinking, until it grew dark. All of a sudden, she saw the way. This plan would work. She would make it work.

When she walked into her house, her father was on the phone. He hung up immediately. Her mother was sitting with an anxious expression on her face. The moment Cindy walked in, her mother called out, "Where have you been? We've been worried to death!"

Cindy didn't answer. Instead she walked up to her mother, gave her a kiss right on the cheek and said, "I love you, Mom." Her mother was so startled that she couldn't speak. Cindy marched up to her dad. She gave him a hug. "Good night, Dad," she said. "I love you." And then she went to bed, leaving her speechless parents in the kitchen.

The next morning when she came down to breakfast, she gave her mother a kiss. She gave her father a kiss. At the bus stop, she stood on tiptoe and kissed her mother.

"Bye, Mom," she said. "I love you."

And that's what Cindy did, every day of every week of every month. Sometimes her parents drew back from her, stiff and awkward. Sometimes they laughed about it. But they never returned the kiss. But Cindy didn't stop. She had made her plan. She kept right at it. Then, one evening, she forgot to kiss her mother before bed. A short time later, the door of her room opened. Her mother came in.

"Where's my kiss, then?" she asked, pretending to be cross.

Cindy sat up. "Oh, I forgot," she said. She kissed her mother.

"I love you, Mom." She lay down again. "Good night," she said and closed her eyes. But her mother didn't leave. Finally she spoke.

"I love you, too," her mother said. Then her mother bent down and kissed Cindy, right on the cheek. "And don't ever forget my kiss again," she said, pretending to be stern.

Cindy laughed. "I won't," she said. And she didn't.

Many years later, Cindy had a child of her own, and she kissed that baby until, as she put it, "Her little cheeks were red."

And every time she went home, the first thing her mother would say to her was, "Where's my kiss, then?" And when it was time to leave, she'd say, "I love you. You know that, don't you?"

"Yes, Mom," Cindy would say. "I've always known that."

M. A. Urquhart
Adapted from an Ann Landers column

The Visit

There isn't much that I can do,
But I can share an hour with you,
And I can share a joke with you. . . .
As on our way we go.

Maude V. Preston

Every Saturday, Grandpa and I walk to the nursing home a few blocks away from our house. We go to visit many of the old and sick people who live there because they can't take care of themselves anymore.

"Whoever visits the sick gives them life," Grandpa always says.

First we visit Mrs. Sokol. I call her "The Cook." She likes to talk about the time when she was a well-known cook back in Russia. People would come from miles around, just to taste her famous chicken soup.

Next we visit Mr. Meyer. I call him "The Joke Man." We sit around his coffee table, and he tells us jokes. Some are very funny. Some aren't. And some I don't get. He laughs at his own jokes, shaking up and down and turning red in the face. Grandpa and I can't help but laugh along with him, even when the jokes aren't very funny.

Next door is Mr. Lipman. I call him "The Singer" because he loves to sing for us. Whenever he does, his beautiful voice fills the air, clear and strong and so full of energy that we always sing along with him.

We visit Mrs. Kagan, "The Grandmother," who shows us pictures of her grandchildren. They're all over the room, in frames, in albums and even taped to the walls.

Mrs. Schrieber's room is filled with memories, memories that come alive as she tells us stories of her own experiences during the old days. I call her "The Memory Lady."

Then there's Mr. Krull, "The Quiet Man." He doesn't have very much to say; he just listens when Grandpa or I talk to him. He nods and smiles, and tells us to come again next week. That's what everyone says to Grandpa and me, even the woman in charge, behind the desk.

Every week we do come again, even in the rain. We walk together to visit our friends: The Cook, The Joke Man, The Singer, The Grandmother, The Memory Lady and The Quiet Man.

One day Grandpa got very sick and had to go to the hospital. The doctors said they didn't think he would ever get better.

Saturday came, and it was time to visit the nursing home. How could I go visiting without Grandpa? Then I remembered what Grandpa once told me: "Nothing should stand in the way of doing a good deed." So I went alone.

Everyone was happy to see me. They were surprised when they didn't see Grandpa. When I told them that he was sick and in the hospital, they could tell I was sad.

"Everything is in God's hands," they told me. "Do your best and God will do the rest."

The Cook went on to reveal some of her secret ingredients. The Joke Man told me his latest jokes. The Singer sang a song especially for me. The Grandmother showed me more pictures. The Memory Lady shared more of her memories. When I visited The Quiet Man, I asked him lots of questions. When I ran out of questions, I talked about what I had learned in school.

After a while, I said good-bye to everyone, even the woman in charge, behind the desk.

"Thank you for coming," she said. "May your grandfather have a complete recovery."

A few days later, Grandpa was still in the hospital. He was not eating, he could not sit up and he could barely speak. I went to the corner of the room so Grandpa wouldn't see me cry. My mother took my place by the bed and held Grandpa's hand. The room was dim and very quiet.

Suddenly the nurse came into the room and said, "You have some visitors."

"Is this the place with the party?" I heard a familiar voice ask.

I looked up. It was The Joke Man. Behind him were the Cook, The Singer, The Grandmother, The Memory Lady, The Quiet Man and even the woman in charge, behind the desk.

The Cook told Grandpa about all the great food that she would cook for him once he got well. She had even brought him a hot bowl of homemade chicken soup.

"Chicken soup? What this man needs is a pastrami sandwich," said The Joke Man as he let out one of his deep, rich laughs.

Everyone laughed with him. Then he told us some new jokes. By the time he was finished, everyone had to use tissues to dry their eyes from laughing so hard.

Next, The Grandmother showed Grandpa a get-well card made by two of her granddaughters. On the front of one card was a picture of a clown holding balloons. "Get well soon!" was scribbled in crayon on the inside.

The Singer started singing, and we all sang along with him. The Memory Lady told us how Grandpa once came to visit her in a snowstorm, just to bring her some roses for her birthday.

Before I knew it, visiting hours were up. Everyone said a short prayer for Grandpa. Then they said good-bye and told him that they would see him again soon.

That evening, Grandpa called the nurse in and said he was hungry. Soon he began to sit up. Finally he was able to get out of bed. Each day, Grandpa felt better and better, and he grew stronger and stronger. Soon he was able to go home.

The doctors were shocked. They said his recovery was a medical miracle. But I knew the truth: His friends' visit had made him well.

Grandpa is better now. Every Saturday, without fail, we walk together to visit our friends: The Cook, The Joke Man, The Singer, The Grandmother, The Memory Lady, The Quiet Man . . . and the woman in charge, behind the desk.

Debbie Herman

The Fire Truck

Some people give time, some money, some their skills and connections; some literally give their blood . . . but everyone has something to give.

                                                    Barbara Bush

After her parents split up, things at Tami's house changed. Her mom started working, and Tami became responsible for caring for the house and making meals for herself and her younger sister. Though money was tight, they never went without. They had a nice home in a modest neighborhood, and the girls never wanted for the necessities—food, clothing and shelter. What Tami missed most of all, though, was family.

Tami spent the summer during her ninth-grade year working at a park to earn extra spending money. Her job was to run the ball shed and organize activities for the kids who spent their summer days at the park.

The kids absolutely adored Tami. She was constantly going out of her way to do things for them. She would plan picnics, organize field trips and even buy ice cream for all of them, using her own money. She always did more than the job required, even if it did mean using her own money.

She got to know one little boy who lived in an apartment across the street from the park. His parents both worked at fast-food restaurants, and she knew that they didn't have much money.

The boy talked about his upcoming birthday and the fire truck he wanted so badly. He said he was going to be a fireman someday and needed the truck to practice. He told Tami more details about the truck than she knew a toy truck could have.

The boy's birthday came and went. The next day when Tami saw the boy, she expected to see a shiny red truck in his arms. When he arrived empty-handed, she asked about his birthday—did he get his truck?

The boy said no, his parents were going to have to wait and get it for him later, when things were better. He seemed a little sad but kept his chin up as best he could.

That week, Tami cashed her paycheck and headed for the toy store. She found the truck easily—after all, from his descriptions, she felt she knew it inside out. She used the money from her paycheck to buy the truck, then had it wrapped in birthday paper.

Early the next morning, Tami rode her bike to where the boy lived and left the wrapped truck at the door, without a note. When the boy showed up at the park that day, he was more excited than she'd ever seen him. He showed off his new truck to Tami, then played with it all day long.

That afternoon, the boy's mom came to the park. She walked over to Tami.

"Thank you," she said.

Tami tried to act confused, as though she didn't have a clue as to why this woman would be thanking her.

"I get up early in the morning, just like you do," the mother said.

Knowing that she'd been found out, Tami started to explain, but the woman stopped her.

"We want to pay you back," the woman said.

Though Tami started to say no, the woman went on to say, "We don't have the money to pay you for it, but I want you to come over for dinner tonight." Tami felt she should refuse, but the boy's mom would not take no for an answer.

After work, Tami walked over to the boy's house. She could smell dinner coming from their window, though she couldn't recognize what it was. When she entered their home, she saw that the family of four shared a small and cramped one-bedroom apartment. There were only two chairs at the makeshift table that served as the dining area. Instead of eating at the table, Tami and the family sat together on the ragged couch. They passed around collard greens and macaroni and cheese, laughing as Tami warily tried collard greens for the first time.

Tami had a great time that evening. As she left, it was Tami who was saying thank you. Though their means were modest, her hosts had given Tami something she had been missing—the warmth of a family.

She learned not only the rewards of giving, but that everyone has something to give. And that by accepting what is given to you, you complete the circle of love.

Lori Moore

Merry Christmas, My Friend

Love is the only thing that we can carry with us when we go, and it makes the end so easy.

Louisa May Alcott

"I will never forget you," the old man said. A tear rolled down his leathery cheek. "I'm getting old. I can't take care of you anymore."

With his head tilted to one side, Monsieur DuPree watched his master. *"Woof, woof! Woof, woof!"* He wagged his tail back and forth, wondering, *What's he talking about?*

"I can't take care of myself anymore, let alone take care of you." The old man cleared his throat. He pulled a hankie from his pocket and blew his nose with a mighty blast.

"Soon, I'll move to an old-age home, and, I'm sorry to say, you can't come along. They don't allow dogs there, you know." Bent over from age, the old man limped over to Monsieur DuPree and stroked the dog's head.

"Don't worry, my friend. We'll find a home. We'll find a nice new home for you." As an afterthought he added, "Why, with your good looks, we'll have no trouble at all. Anyone would be proud to own such a fine dog."

Monsieur DuPree wagged his tail really hard and strutted up and down the kitchen floor. For a moment, the familiar musky scent of the old man mingling with the odor of greasy food gave the dog a feeling of well-being. But then a sense of dread took hold again. His tail hung between his legs and he stood very still.

"Come here." With great difficulty, the old man knelt down on the floor and lovingly pulled Monsieur DuPree close to him. He tied a ribbon around the dog's neck with a huge red bow, and then he attached a note to it. *What does it say?* Monsieur DuPree wondered.

"It says," the old man read aloud, "Merry Christmas! My name is Monsieur DuPree. For breakfast, I like bacon and eggs—even cornflakes will do. For dinner, I prefer mashed potatoes and some meat. That's all. I eat just two meals a day. In return, I will be your most loyal friend."

"Woof, woof! Woof, woof!" Monsieur DuPree was confused, and his eyes begged, *What's going on?*

The old man blew his nose into his hankie once more. Then, hanging on to a chair, he pulled himself up from the floor. He buttoned his overcoat, reached for the dog's leash and softly said, "Come here, my friend." He opened the door against a gust of cold air and stepped outside, pulling the dog behind. Dusk was beginning to fall. Monsieur DuPree pulled back. He didn't want to go.

"Don't make this any harder for me. I promise you, you'll be much better off with someone else."

The street was deserted. Leaning into the wintry air, the old man and his dog pushed on. It began to snow.

After a very long time, they came upon an old Victorian house surrounded by tall trees, which were swaying and humming in the wind. Shivering in the cold, they appraised the house. Glimmering lights adorned every window, and the muffled sound of a Christmas song was carried on the wind.

"This will be a nice home for you," the old man said, choking on his words. He bent down and unleashed his dog, then opened the gate slowly, so that it wouldn't creak. "Go on now. Go up the steps and scratch on the door."

Monsieur DuPree looked from the house to his master and back again to the house. He did not understand. *"Woof, woof! Woof, woof!"*

"Go on." The old man gave the dog a shove. "I have no use for you anymore," he said in a gruff voice. "Get going now!"

Monsieur DuPree was hurt. He thought his master didn't love him anymore. He didn't understand that, indeed, the old man loved him very much but could no longer care for him. Slowly, the dog straggled toward the house and up the steps. He scratched with one paw at the front door. *"Woof, woof! Woof, woof!"*

Looking back, he saw his master step behind a tree just as someone from inside turned the doorknob. A little boy appeared, framed in the doorway by the warm light coming from within. When he saw Monsieur DuPree, the little boy threw both arms into the air and shouted with delight, "Oh boy! Mom and Dad, come see what Santa brought!"

Through teary eyes, the old man watched from behind the tree as the boy's mother read the note. Then she tenderly pulled Monsieur DuPree inside. Smiling, the old man wiped his eyes with the sleeve of his cold, damp coat. Then he disappeared into the night, whispering, "Merry Christmas, my friend."

Christa Holder Ocker

2

ON FRIENDSHIP

*Friends are there to heal the wounds
  To pull you out of saddened tunes
  To brighten up your cloudy skies
  To clear up fictitious lies*

*Friends are there with open arms
  To comfort you and block the harms
  To keep your secrets hidden away
  To entertain you when you want to play*

*Friends are there, smile or tear
  Friends are there, happiness or fear
  Friends are fun and friends are clever
  And the ties that bind friends will last forever.*

Harmony Davis, age 14

There's an Alien on the Internet

Be kind, for everyone you meet is fighting a harder battle.

Plato

Andy has never met Joey in person, even though Joey is his best friend. He met him on the Internet. At school recess he played *Star Wars* with Kevin and Rob; but it's all the neat stuff he learned about the solar system from Joey that made his *Star Wars* games fun. Joey doesn't go to school. He's home-schooled. *I wish Joey went to our school here in Portland—then I'd never get bored because he's so smart,* thought Andy.

Last week Andy's teacher, Mrs. Becker, put a big circle on the blackboard and said it was a pizza pie. "Andy," she said, "if I were to divide the pizza, would you like one-third or one-tenth?"

Ten is the bigger number, so that's what he picked. Kevin started waving his hand in the air, shouting that he chose one-third. Mrs. Becker drew lines on the circle, showing that his piece of the pie was bigger than Andy's.

"Andy's gonna get hungry," Kevin teased. Sandra, the

girl who sat behind Andy started to snicker. Then the whole class was laughing. *I wish that the recess bell would ring,* thought Andy, as he planned how he would play by himself during recess, instead of with Kevin and Rob.

Mrs. Becker's stern voice quieted the room. "Andy, do you see how the more you divide the whole pie, the smaller the pieces become?"

"Yes, ma'am," Andy lied.

The recess bell didn't ring for another half hour, and by then Mrs. Becker had assigned twenty problems in the class math book. Each problem had two fractions with an empty circle between the fractions. The students were supposed to put a sign, > greater than, or < lesser than, in each circle. Looking at all those fractions and circles made Andy dizzy. He decided he had a fifty-fifty chance of guessing which way to point the arrows, so he guessed— wrong.

After school, when Andy got on-line with Joey, he typed: "Flunked my math quiz today. I don't get fractions, how to tell which is bigger." Joey typed back: "Here's a good trick. Cross-multiply from the bottom up." Then he went to his drawing board and showed Andy how.

"Five times two equals ten. Three times four equals twelve. Ten is smaller than twelve." His trick made it a cinch, even for Andy. The next week, when Mrs. Becker gave a fractions test, Andy was the only kid who got 100 percent. The class didn't think Andy was so stupid any-more, thanks to Joey.

After Joey and Andy got to be such good pals, Andy asked Joey to send him a picture and told Joey he would send one of his in return. Andy's Little League team was having their picture taken in their uniforms, and Andy had posed for his with his bat over his shoulder, like he was up to the plate about to hit a home run. Andy thought, as he looked at his picture before he sent it to

Joey, *I look pretty cool, really athletic.* Andy mailed one to Joey in Tallahassee, and started waiting for his picture to arrive in the mail.

Each day when Andy talked on the Internet, he asked Joey if he'd received his photo yet. On the third day Joey said, "Your picture came, and it's awesome. Thanks!"

"Great!" Andy replied. "Then I should be getting yours soon." But Joey's picture never came, and each time they talked, Andy told him, "Still no picture. Maybe you'd better send another."

It was weird. No photo and no comment from Joey. He'd just change the subject. Then one day when they were talking about *Star Wars* and aliens Andy asked him, "What if there really are aliens in disguise on earth? You know, like in the TV program *Third Rock from the Sun* or the book *My Teacher's an Alien?*"

It seemed like a long time before the screen lit up with his reply. "Can you keep a secret?"

"I guess," Andy answered.

"Promise? It's really important!"

"Sure. I promise."

"I'm an alien from another galaxy. That's why I can't send you a photograph. My energy field can't be caught on film."

Andy sat there, staring at the screen. His mother was calling him to dinner, but it was Joey who signed off while he sat, staring at the computer, in a daze. *Was this one of Joey's jokes? Then why didn't he send a picture? Is this why he knew so much more than other kids about spaceships and outer space? Why was he so secretive?*

At dinner, Dad announced, "Good news! My transfer request was approved. We'll be moving to the home office in Denver at the end of this month. The company has found a rental home for us that's close to a good school for Andy and with plenty of room for Grandma to live with us."

Andy's mom was happy because her mother had been

in a Denver nursing home ever since she fell and broke her hip, and she wanted to have Grandma live with them. Andy just felt mixed up.

That night in bed, Andy thought about being a new kid in a new school. *I remember how I felt when we moved here. It was hard to make new friends. It seemed like everybody stared at me the first day, and the other kids treated me differently for a while until they got to know me.* That was the last thing he thought about before he fell asleep.

The next morning, as Andy was sitting at the kitchen table, eating cereal, his mom was watching a show on TV. A newscaster was interviewing a lady in Tallahassee, Florida. "Tell me about the role the Internet plays in Joey's life," the newscaster asked.

"Well, it has allowed him a freedom he's never known before. Not only is he able to access information from his wheelchair, but most important, he has made new friends."

The newscaster then continued, "Tell us about your Internet friends, Joey." The camera shifted to this kid in a wheelchair, sitting in front of his computer. He was kind of skinny with sort of shriveled legs. His head hung to one side, and when he answered, his words were hard to understand. He had to make a big effort to say them, and a bit of drool came out of one corner of his mouth.

"When other kids see me, they just see that I'm different. It's hard for me to talk and be understood. But when I'm on the Internet, they think I'm just another kid, because they can't see me. I've been making friends with lots of different people," Joey explained.

All day at school, Andy's mind was full of jumbled thoughts. *His Internet buddy, Joey; Joey the alien; Joey the kid on TV; making new friends in Denver; Grandma and her walker.* As soon as he got home, he ran to his room, threw his backpack on the bed and went to his computer. As Andy logged on to the Internet, he decided: *It doesn't matter where*

Joey came from—Mars, Saturn or Tallahassee. It doesn't matter what Joey looks like. I know who Joey is. Joey is my friend.

Andy typed into the computer: "Joey, guess what? We're moving to Denver. Boy, am I ever glad to have a friend who goes with me wherever I go."

Joanne Peterson

Seeing, Really Seeing

His nose was all smooshed looking, like maybe his mom had dropped him when he was a baby. His ears were two—maybe even two and a half—sizes too big for his head. And his eyes! His eyes bulged like they were ready to pop right out of their sockets. His clothes were nice, Tim had to admit. But he was still the homeliest kid he'd ever seen.

So why was the new kid leaning on Jennifer Lawrence's locker like they were best friends or something? She was a cheerleader and one of the coolest girls in school. And why was she smiling at him instead of twisting her nose all funny like she did when she looked at Tim? *Strange*, he thought. *Really strange.*

By lunchtime, Tim had forgotten about the new kid. He sat down at his usual table—in the corner, all alone. Tim was a loner. He wasn't as ugly as the new kid—just a little on the heavy side and kind of nerdy. Nobody talked to Tim much, but he was used to it. He had adjusted.

About halfway through his peanut butter and ketchup sandwich (he put ketchup on everything), Tim looked up and saw that kid again. He was holding his lunch tray and standing over Jennifer, grinning like he'd just aced a math test. And she was grinning, too. Then she moved over and made room on the bench next to her. *Strange. Really strange.*

But even stranger was what the new kid did. Tim would have plunked into that seat so fast, his lunch bag would have been left behind, just hanging in the air. But not this new kid. He shook his head, looked around and walked straight to Tim's table.

"Mind if I join you?" he asked.

Just like that. *Mind if I join you? Like the entire eighth grade was fighting to sit at my table or something,* Tim thought.

"Sure," said Tim. "I mean no. I don't mind."

So the kid sat down. And he came back, day after day, until they were friends. Real friends.

Tim had never had a real friend before, but Jeff—that was his name—invited Tim to his house, on trips with his family and even hiking. Right—Tim hiking!

Funny thing was . . . one day Tim realized he wasn't so heavy anymore. *All that hiking, I guess,* thought Tim. And kids were talking to him, nodding to him in the hallways, and even asking him questions about assignments and things. And Tim was talking back to them. He wasn't a loner anymore.

One day, when Jeff sat down at the table, Tim had to ask him. "Why did you sit with me that first day? Didn't Jen ask you to sit with her?"

"Sure, she asked. But she didn't need me."

"Need you?"

"You did."

"I did?"

Tim hoped nobody was listening. *This was a really dumb conversation,* he thought.

"You were sitting all alone," Jeff explained. "You looked lonely and scared."

"Scared?"

"Uh huh, scared. I knew that look. I used to have one, too, just like it."

Tim couldn't believe it.

"Maybe you didn't notice, but I'm not exactly the best-looking guy in school," Jeff went on. "At my old school I sat alone. I was afraid to look up and see if anyone was laughing at me."

"You?" Tim knew he sounded stupid, but he couldn't picture Jeff by himself. He was so outgoing.

"Me. It took a friend to help me see that I wasn't alone because of my nose or my ears. I was alone because I never smiled or took an interest in other people. I was so concerned about myself that I never paid attention to anyone else. That's why I sat with you. To let you know someone cared. Jennifer already knew."

"Oh, she knows, all right," Tim said as he watched two guys fighting to sit near her. Tim and Jeff both laughed. *It felt good to laugh and I've been doing a lot of it lately,* realized Tim.

Then Tim looked at Jeff. Really looked. *He isn't so bad looking,* thought Tim. *Oh, not handsome or anything like that. But he isn't homely. Jeff is my friend.* That's when Tim realized that he was seeing Jeff for the first time. Months earlier all he had seen was a funny-looking nose and "Dumbo" ears. Now he was seeing Jeff, *really* seeing him.

Marie P. McDougal

Kim Li, the Great

No one can make you feel inferior without your consent.

Eleanor Roosevelt

Dara liked school until the day Kim Li came. She didn't like Ms. Royson saying, "It's great how well you're learning English, Kim Li." Kim Li's English wasn't that great.

Dara always sat at the front of the class. But the day Kim Li came, Ms. Royson asked, "Kim Li, would you like to sit here in front? Dara won't mind." Kim Li smiled and said yes. Dara turned away.

Before Dara moved to a new seat, she whispered, "Kim Li, you're too tall to sit up front. I can't see Ms. Royson. Move! I want my seat!"

Kim Li kept smiling. "My father too tall. He tall American."

"Kim Li, you talk funny. Yuck!"

"Now, Dara," said Ms. Royson as she stood beside Kim Li's desk, "we all want new students to feel welcome, don't we?" And that very afternoon, Ms. Royson asked, "Kim Li, would you dust the erasers for me?"

As Kim Li did Dara's job, she asked Dara, "I do right?"

"No," said Dara, but Ms. Royson said, "You're doing just great."

"Don't play with Kim Li the Great," Dara told everyone at recess. Other children began to chant: "Kim Li the Great! Kim Li the Great!"

Kim Li said, "Thank you," and smiled and hung jackets on the top hooks that were too hard to reach. After school, Dara added more words to the chant: "Down with Kim Li the Great!"

The next day, Timmy pushed Kim Li really hard against the game box and said, "Down with Kim Li!"

Ms. Royson came over. "Here, here! Kim Li needs to choose."

Dara said, "Don't you choose the big blue ball, Kim Li!"

Kim Li picked an ordinary jump rope. "Thank you. I like jump."

"Kim Li sure talks funny," Dara said loudly. Everyone laughed. Then someone noticed Kim Li doing "hot peppers" with her jump rope. Kickball was forgotten. Everyone watched Kim Li do crisscrosses. And double crisscrosses! Kim Li said, "This fun doing."

Dara shouted, "Kim Li the Great, you're a show-off!" Everyone laughed so hard that Ms. Royson came running. "What happened?"

"I talk more badder. I try. Everybody laugh."

Ms. Royson's face tightened. "Recess is over. Back inside." Dara smiled and put her arms around two friends. Kim Li was not included.

Kim Li didn't know that every Friday was fire drill, room art and sharing day. *Good thing,* thought Dara. She would have come with something great.

At the next recess, Dara did her grandest somersaults, forward and backward. Kim Li did them while running. "We be friends?" she asked.

Dara thought she might quit school—until Ms. Royson said, "Dara, if you don't mind skipping workbooks, we need our mural finished." Dara didn't mind at all. When Kim Li came to help color the big mural, Dara was way too busy to get up and leave—or even argue. *Br-r-r-ring-ing-ing!* It was the fire bell. Quickly and quietly, Dara joined the line to walk outside in an orderly way. Where was Kim Li?

"For goodness sake, Kim Li, that's the fire bell!" Dara pulled her hand and didn't let go until they got outside. Kim Li threw both arms around Dara and yelled, "Dara save my life. Dara the Great!"

Everyone started laughing and dancing around the playground, chanting: "Dara the Great!"

"It was only a fire drill," said Dara.

"Will you teach me to do crisscrosses?" she asked Kim Li.

"I help you," Kim Li said.

"Say 'I will help you,'" whispered Dara to her new friend.

Kim Li said, "You will help me. I will help you."

For days they helped each other, and when Ms. Royson said, "Kim Li, you're picking up English so quickly," Dara was pleased. She thought she might even do crisscrosses during sharing time. But Kim Li got up first, smiling. Finally, she spoke. "I have good good friend. Dara!"

Dara didn't correct Kim Li. She let it go. Just this once.

Berniece Rabe

"Me 'n Jackson are exactly the same age,
only he's different. He's left handed!"

Reprinted by permission of Hank Ketcham.

Edna Mae: First Lesson in Prejudice

The chief cause of human errors is to be found in the prejudices picked up in childhood.

Descartes

Edna Mae was one of my best friends when I was in the first grade. When it came time for her birthday party, all the girls in the class were invited. Each day in school there was great excitement.

"What kind of cake you gonna have?" we'd ask.

"Are you gonna have games with prizes? And decorations? Birthday hats?"

Edna Mae would just smile and shake her head. "Wait and see," she'd say. Together we counted down the days until Saturday, the date on the invitation.

Finally the day arrived. I wrapped my gift, put on my best party dress and waited what seemed like hours for my mother to say, "Time to go!"

I was glad that I was the first to arrive because I got to help place the candy cups all around—one for each of the twelve guests. The table was covered with a special "Happy Birthday" tablecloth with matching plates and cups. Balloons were everywhere. Streamers crisscrossed the ceiling in the hallway, the living room and especially the dining room, where the table was all set. It looked like a fairyland.

"Oh, Edna Mae! Oh, Edna Mae!" was all I could say.

Edna Mae's mom sent us out to the front porch to wait for the other girls. Edna Mae lived on the edge of town, and most of the other girls had never been to her house before.

"Some might be having trouble finding us," her mother said.

We sat down on the steps and waited and waited and waited. Edna Mae began to cry. I felt so awful that I didn't know what to say. Finally her mother came out and announced, "Let the party begin!" She ushered us into the house, tied a blindfold around our eyes, put a tail with a pin in our hands and led us to the donkey taped on the wall.

"Whoever gets the tail closest to the right place wins the first super prize!" she said. My tail ended up near the donkey's nose. Edna Mae's tipped the right front hoof. We laughed and laughed.

Together, Edna Mae and I played all the games and shared all the prizes. We even got to eat two pieces of cake each.

In the car on the way home, I asked my mother, "Why didn't the other girls come? Edna Mae felt so bad."

My mother hesitated and then said sadly, "Honey, the others didn't come because Edna Mae is black."

"She's not black," I protested. "She just looks like she has a tan all year long."

"I know, honey. But Edna Mae is not like any of the other girls in the class, and some folks are afraid of those who are different from them. People are prejudiced, honey. That's what adults call it: prejudice."

"Well, those girls are mean. They made Edna Mae cry. I'm never gonna be prejudiced!" I said.

My mother put her arm around me and said, "I'm glad, honey. And I'm glad that Edna Mae has a good friend like you."

Sandra Warren

The Connection

It was the summer after fourth grade that I came to realize that the connection we have with other people is necessary for our survival.

Joel Walker, age 11

"I'm gonna die! I'm gonna die!" I was screaming over and over, hanging on for dear life. Suddenly, my toes slipped out of the crack that had been supporting me. "I'm gonna die!" I screamed again. *If I don't find a place to secure my foot,* I thought, *I'll fall in!* I felt around with my toes and found a place to steady myself. Looking up through the steam, I could see my friend Warren kneeling above the pit.

"Grab my hand!" he shouted. I stretched my hand as far up as I could without losing my balance. I couldn't get a grip on Warren's hand because of the sulfur that covered my hands.

"Don't worry. I won't leave you," he assured me. "We're gonna get you out, Joel."

Warren stayed next to the steam vent and talked to me while some of the other boys ran to get help. I knew they'd do everything in their power to save me.

Our friendships had grown out of the connection we had made, and the trust we had built with each other, while on a club soccer team called the Ameba. We had really learned how to communicate with each other while playing by saying things like "Behind you" and "Open over here."

We kept the team together for the whole year. That summer we had the chance to go to Hawaii for the Big Island Cup Tournament. It was the first time in ten years that a team from our area would have the opportunity to go. All we needed was the money to get there! Our team went door-to-door in our community, and the generous donations we received paid for our tournament costs. We were on our way to Kona for a nine-day adventure.

We got to the hotel and put in a few hours of practice the first day. The following day, we weren't scheduled to play a game, so we decided to do some sight-seeing.

We went to see the ruins of a burned-down village that had been in the path of an erupting volcano's river of molten lava. There wasn't enough time to hike up to the volcano's opening, so we went to see the steam vents at the Volcano National Park. A steam vent is a crack in the earth's surface caused by the pressure and heat of a volcano. The same steam that erupts from the volcano also comes out of the steam vent. Some vents are large and easy to spot by their steam, which rises into the air. Others are small and difficult to see, so we had to be careful where we walked because they are sort of hidden in the grass throughout the park.

I wanted to take some pictures, so I went exploring with Warren in search of a steam vent to photograph. Just as I heard Warren call out, "Joel, you're walking past one," I turned too sharply and tripped over some weeds. The next thing I knew, I found myself wedged into a steam vent that was just large enough for me to have fallen into.

That's when I began screaming for my life. Warren tried to rescue me, but the slippery brown sulfur that is a by-product of volcanoes burned my hands and made it impossible for us to connect.

My mind sent screaming panic signals all through my body. I pushed against the sides of the steam vent with my hands, which were being burned so badly by the smoldering sulfur that the blisters rose two inches high on my fingers and palms. I felt that if I slipped down any farther, I'd surely die from the deadly heat of the steam. Or worse, fall into the mysterious black passageway that led to the volcano's boiling lava center.

Somehow my shoes slipped off my feet. I don't know how that happened because I had socks on, and the socks should have kept my shoes on. Losing my shoes saved the soles of my feet from having rubber melt into my skin. The hot sulfur, which smelled like rotten eggs, still burned my soles right through my socks.

I tried to look up through the scalding, rising steam. This time, I saw a man—a stranger—calling down to say that help was on the way. Warren, reassuring me, added, "They're coming, Joel. Hang on!" The team chaperones got there and quickly made a human chain, so that the person pulling me up wouldn't fall in with me. One of our team chaperones reached down and finally made the connection that saved my life.

The instant that our grip was locked, she pulled as hard as she could. I landed on the ground, just outside of the steaming vent. Without hesitation, the adults stripped me of my scalding hot clothes before the burns got any worse. I didn't even care that I was naked in front of everyone! I was shivering and shaking all over, and in the most terrible pain I'd ever experienced. But I was just glad to be alive!

The stranger who had come to help quickly carried me to my coach's car. We headed for the visitor's center, where they could call the paramedics. A park ranger passed us in his truck. We flagged him down, and he had us follow him to the park office. The first thing he did was to put me into a sink of cold water, to keep the burns from getting any worse. The paramedics arrived not long after that. Halfway to the hospital, after the paramedics had taken my blood pressure and temperature, I had to be transferred to a second ambulance because of some crazy territory line or something. I kept pleading with the driver, "Just go! Please, don't stop." I was in so much pain; all I wanted to do was get to the hospital. The paramedics in the second ambulance had to do all of the same tests again! It seemed to take forever.

It wasn't until I had finally reached the hospital and had been treated for my burns that the initial shock began to wear off. I realized how important friends are—people are—to all of us. They saved my life! If I had been alone, I would have died.

The news of my accident spread over the television stations from Hawaii to California. My mom flew to Hawaii on the first plane she could catch, to bring me home. On the plane, and even at the airport in Los Angeles, people recognized me as "the boy who had fallen into the steam vent." They'd stop to talk to me, and I felt that they honestly cared. Many people told me that they had been praying for me.

My family and friends were there for me throughout my painful recovery. My parents took me for treatment to a hospital near my home, and I had to go there every day for four weeks to have whirlpool therapy. Either my mom or dad would go with me every single time. Getting into that water was the most painful thing that I've ever had to go through. I would kiss my mom or dad's hands over and over again, to keep my mind off the pain. That seemed to make the pain less unbearable.

I have learned a lot since that summer day, which came so close to being my last. The experience has changed my relationships with my friends. We talk a lot more, about anything and everything. I am more interested in being there for my family, too, just as they were there for me. When my mom got stitches in her thumb, I stayed with her in the emergency room the whole time and held her hand. I understand the importance of moral support, of just being there for people. I reach out to others more than I used to.

Once that summer was over and all of the therapy was behind me, I got right back out there to play soccer again. I had really missed the sport. But mostly I had missed my friends, the people—the connection.

Joel Walker, age 11

The Favorite Vase

My younger brother and I were home watching cartoons while my father slept and my mother was out shopping. I left my brother in the living room and went to get something to drink. As I was pouring some orange juice, I heard something break. First, I looked in to see if my father had woken up, and he hadn't. Then I quickly ran to see what had happened. When I went into the living room, I was shocked. My brother had broken my mother's favorite vase.

"What did you do?" I gasped.

"I broke it!" my brother answered. "It was an accident!"

Knowing that he was freaked out, and not wanting him to get in trouble, I did what any friend would do. I tried to help him. I quickly ran and got some glue. I didn't know what time my mother was going to be back or when my father was going to wake up, so I tried to hurry. I frantically gathered up all of the broken pieces and started to glue them together. It took me an hour but I *finally* fixed the vase. Then came the real disaster.

"Oh my gawd! Oh my gawd!" I screamed.

I had fixed the vase, but I had accidentally glued my hair to it!

While my brother looked at me like I was some kind of idiot, I carried the vase—with my hair attached to it—into the bathroom. I looked in the mirror.

"My beautiful hair," I cried. Realizing that there was no way to pull my hair from the vase, I grabbed a pair of scissors. With every single strand of hair that I cut, I cried again. My hair was ruined and the vase looked like a wig was attached to it! As I was leaving the bathroom with my ridiculous new hairdo, I heard a key turn in the front door. "Hey guys, I'm back!"

My mother was back! My brother ran to his room and quickly pretended to be asleep leaving me to deal with her all by myself. Before I could explain, my mother yelled at me and grounded me because she thought I had broken the vase. I went to my room to think about what had happened. I was grounded and I was also going to have to go to school looking like an idiot!

While I was lying on my bed looking up at the ceiling, I realized that what I had done for my brother was an act of friendship. I knew that even though my brother and I fight a lot, I had made a sacrifice for him. This was a huge sacrifice though—my hair and my freedom!

"Knock, knock," sounded someone at my door.

"Who is it?" I asked.

My brother walked in and gave me a hug.

"Thank you," he said.

"You're welcome," I replied. "I guess that's what a big sister is for, to be a friend when you need one."

Belladonna Richuitti, age 12

"My mom's not a big believer in accidents."

A Friend . . .

Friendships multiply joys and divide grief.

Thomas Fuller

Recently, one of my best friends, whom I've shared just about everything with since the first day of kindergarten, spent the weekend with me. Since I moved to a new town several years ago, we've both always looked forward to the few times a year when we can see each other.

Over the weekend we spent hours and hours, staying up late into the night, talking about the people she was hanging around with. She started telling me stories about her new boyfriend, about how he experimented with drugs and was into other self-destructive behavior. I was blown away! She told me how she had been lying to her parents about where she was going and even sneaking out to see this guy because they didn't want her around him. No matter how hard I tried to tell her that she deserved better, she didn't believe me. Her self-respect seemed to have disappeared.

I tried to convince her that she was ruining her future

and heading for big trouble. I felt like I was getting nowhere. I just couldn't believe that she really thought that it was acceptable to hang with a bunch of losers, especially her boyfriend.

By the time she left, I was really worried about her and exhausted by the experience. It had been so frustrating, I had come close to telling her several times during the weekend that maybe we had just grown too far apart to continue our friendship—but I didn't. I put the power of friendship to the ultimate test. We'd been friends for far too long. I had to hope that she valued me enough to know that I was trying to save her from hurting herself. I wanted to believe that our friendship could conquer anything.

A few days later, she called to say that she had thought long and hard about our conversation, and then she told me that she had broken up with her boyfriend. I just listened on the other end of the phone with tears of joy running down my face. It was one of the truly rewarding moments in my life. Never had I been so proud of a friend.

Danielle Fishel

A Friend . . .

Won't allow you to self-destruct.

Will take all the time that's needed, no matter what time of day, to listen to your problems and give you her best advice.

Is someone who can open up and be herself around you.

Will swallow her pride to take your advice.

Will never write you off.

Danielle Fishel

Is someone who keeps promises, tells the truth, makes time for you and is someone to laugh with.

Leah Hatcher, age 14

Is a person who knows what you are saying, even if you're not talking.

Understands what you're feeling, even if you don't understand your own feelings.

Will always forgive you, usually before you forgive yourself.

Sarah Bennett, age 13

Will do something for you and not ask for a favor in return.

Comes and cheers for you at your games.

Roman Zaccuri, age 12

Will always say that you look great—even if you don't.

Will tell you if you have something in your teeth.

Katie Adnoff, age 13

Doesn't talk bad about you.

Martina Miller, age 12

Has a special place in your heart and is always there when you need them.

Meghan Gilstrap, age 14

Is someone who will hold in a laugh when you make a fool out of yourself.

Stays after school when you get in trouble, to help you write 250 sentences.

Danielle Uselton, age 12

Is someone that you respect, who respects you and shares their feelings.

Jorge Prieto, age 11

Makes you feel good about yourself.
Encourages you to reach for your goals.
Never gets jealous of you.

Megan Preizer, age 12

Shares the good times and helps out by listening during the bad times.

Molly Oliver, age 9

Never tells a secret they promise not to tell.
Doesn't talk about you to other friends.
Is forever and for life.

Angie Porter, age 12

Is there for you even when you feel like the world is against you.

MeShelle Locke, age 13

Will open the door for you no matter how late it is.
Would never betray you.
Helps you make new friends.

Eun Joo Shin, age 13

Might get in fights with you but will always forgive you.

Gina Pozielli, age 12

Is someone who will share lunch with you if you forgot yours.

Hayley Valvano, age 12

Doesn't laugh when someone makes a mean joke about you.

Brittany Miller, age 12

Likes you for who you are and not what you look like, because that is what really matters.

Marleigh Dunlap, age 11

Never makes fun of anything you have or do.

Jessica Ann Farley, age 10

Helps you get up when you fall at the roller-skating rink.

Elisabeth Hansen, age 12

Is not about beauty or popularity, but it is someone who likes your personality.
Is with you to the end.

Renny Usbay, age 12

Doesn't always think the way that you do.
Is a person who will tell on you when you are doing drugs or smoking.
Is someone that tells you when you are wrong, but not in a bad way.

Stephanie Lane, age 12

Is someone that your own mom trusts, too.

Mike Curtis, age 13

Is not afraid to be seen with you.
Will laugh at your jokes, even if they're bad.

Geoff Rill, age 12

Never blames everything on you.

Tania Garcia, age 13

Will give you the last bite of their candy bar.
Is a present that you can open again and again.

Natalie Citro, age 12

Is someone who believes you when nobody else will.

Ashley Parole, age 12

Best Friends

We're swallowed up only when we're willing for it to happen.

Nathalie Sarraute

"Please stay," I begged.

Ann was my best friend, the only other girl in the neighborhood, and I didn't want her to go.

She sat on my bed, her blue eyes blank.

"I'm bored," she said, slowly twirling her thick red pigtail around her finger. She had come to play a half hour ago.

"Please don't go," I pleaded. "Your mother said you could stay an hour."

Ann started to get up, then spotted a pair of miniature Indian moccasins on my bedside table. With their bright-colored beads on buttery leather, the moccasins were my most cherished possession.

"I'll stay if you'll give me those," Ann said.

I frowned. I couldn't imagine parting with the moccasins. "But Aunt Reba gave them to me," I protested.

My aunt had been a beautiful, kind woman. I had really

adored her. She was never too busy to spend time with me. We made up silly stories and laughed and laughed. The day she died, I cried under a blanket for hours, unable to believe that I would never see her again. Now, as I cuddled the soft moccasins in my hands, I was filled with fond memories of Aunt Reba.

"Come on," prodded Ann. "I'm your best friend." As if she needed to remind me!

I don't know what came over me, but more than anything, I wanted someone to play with me. I wanted someone to play with so much that I handed Ann the moccasins!

After she stuffed them in her pocket, we rode our bikes up and down the alley a few times. Soon it was time for her to go. Upset at what I had done, I didn't feel like playing anyway.

I pleaded "not hungry" that evening and dragged off to bed without dinner. Once up in my room, I began to really miss those moccasins!

When my mom had tucked me in and turned out the light, she asked me what was wrong. Through my tears, I told her how I had betrayed Aunt Reba's memory and how ashamed I felt.

Mom hugged me warmly, but all she could say was, "Well, I guess you'll have to decide what to do."

Her words didn't seem to help. Alone in the dark, I began to think more clearly. *Kids' code says you don't give, then take back. But was it a fair trade? Why did I let Ann toy with my feelings? But most of all, is Ann really my best friend?*

I decided what I would do. I tossed and turned all night, dreading daylight.

At school the next day, I cornered Ann. I took a deep breath and asked for the moccasins. Her eyes narrowed, and she stared at me for a long time.

Please, I was thinking. *Please.*

"Okay," she said finally, producing the moccasins from her pocket. "I didn't like them anyway." Relief washed over me like a wave.

After a while, Ann and I stopped playing together. I discovered the neighborhood boys weren't half bad, especially when they asked me to play softball. I even made girlfriends in other neighborhoods.

Through the years, I have had other best friends. But I have never again begged for their company. I have come to understand that best friends are people who want to spend time with you, and they ask nothing in return.

Mary Beth Olson

All I Would Ever Need

Lots of people want to ride with you in the limo, but what you want is someone who will take the bus with you when the limo breaks down.

Oprah Winfrey

I had always felt like I was a misfit in school. My friends, although good and true friends, were not in the crowd of popular kids in school. Besides, I was sure I was funny looking. I just didn't fit the mold.

Parading constantly before my eyes was "the fun group"—the popular kids—always laughing and whispering, never sad or depressed, skipping their way through school, the best of friends. Teachers loved them, boys loved them, the whole school loved them. I worshipped them and wanted to be just like them. I dreamed of the day that they would accept me.

My dream came true when I turned fourteen and I tried out for the cheerleading squad. To my surprise, I was chosen. Almost instantly, I was thrust into the "in crowd." I felt like a butterfly coming out of a cocoon. I changed my hair and the way I dressed. Everyone thought the change in me was fantastic—new clothes, a new group of friends and a new outlook on life.

Almost overnight, the whole school knew who I was, or at least they knew my name. There were parties and sleepovers, and of course, cheering at the games. I was finally one of the popular kids. Everyone I had hoped to know, I knew. Everything I had wanted to be, I was.

Something strange was happening to me, however. The more I was included with the "in crowd," the more confused I became. In reality, these people were far from perfect. They talked behind each other's backs while they pretended to be best friends. They rarely had a truly good time but smiled and faked it. They cared about what I was wearing and who I was seen with. But they didn't care about who I was, what I believed in, what my dreams were or what made me who I was. It was a shock to see them as they really were, instead of as I had *thought* they were.

I began to feel a huge sense of loss and disappointment. But worst of all, I realized that I was becoming just like them, and I didn't like what was happening at all. I had to get my life back in order.

I concentrated first on finding out who my real friends were—the ones who listened and who really cared about me. They were the only ones who really mattered. I stayed with cheerleading because I really enjoyed it. But I stopped hanging around with only the popular kids, and I widened my circle of friends. I found out that my real friends had never left me. They were simply waiting for me to come to my senses. I finally realized that my original friends were all I would ever need.

Kerri Warren

My Friend Anthony

Whenever I think back to third grade, I think of my friend Anthony. He had blond hair and big, brown, expressive eyes. I had been surprised to see that he was in my class because he was older than I was.

Although Anthony had AIDS and knew his days were limited, he was always eager to come to school and try to lead a normal life. Some days, he got tired and had to leave early. His mother usually came every day to eat lunch with him or just to be with him. It seemed like he always had a positive outlook on things even though he knew everything wasn't okay. He came to school with what appeared to be a medicine pouch attached to his waist. Many times I felt sorry for him because I knew he must have been in pain.

In June of that year, Anthony died. I clearly remember that he wore a Charlotte Hornets windbreaker outfit in his coffin, and lying beside him was his Cabbage Patch doll, along with a small bag of toys. After that, I sometimes lied awake at night, afraid to go to sleep because I was afraid of dying.

I knew Anthony had left his body to go to a better place, a place without pain, but I felt bad for his family because they would always feel empty without Anthony.

During the year that I had gone to school with Anthony, I had grown to respect him and his mother, too. Through her love and compassion, she taught Anthony, as well as others such as myself, to be brave, and to love, care for and respect everyone. Anthony had taught me to live life to the fullest, and I intend to do just that.

Katie Short, age 12

3

ON FAMILY

Thank you
For teaching me wrong from right and
encouraging me to keep my dreams in sight
For showing me to not let obstacles keep me
down
And for creating a smile from of my frown
For saying that you care about me
And for showing just how special love should be
For wiping my tears away when I'm feeling sad
And for calming me down when I tend to get mad
For helping others with the good that you do
And for teaching me that I should help others, too
For hugging me when I am feeling blue
And whispering into my ear "I love you"
Thank you, family, for all that you do
I don't know where I would be if it weren't
for you.

James Malinchak

No Dad?!

It was early on a stormy winter morning in Northern California. We were making our way along icy roads to the airport, and from there to our weeklong vacation in the warm Hawaiian sun. My dad had worked the night shift at our local hospital, and he was tired from his long hours of work. He was sleeping in the backseat of our van. This was a typical occurrence as we often tried to maximize vacation time by having Mom drive and allowing Dad to sleep en route to our destination.

My younger brother and I were half asleep. My older brother, Jesse, was absorbed in his latest book. He spends most of his waking moments reading. Whenever Jesse reads, he loses touch with everything except whatever he is reading. He could probably read right through a bomb dropping on us.

After several hours on the road, Mom pulled the car into a rest stop. We could hear Dad snoring as we all got out to stretch and yawn—well, everyone except Jesse and Dad. Dad was still asleep in the back, under the blankets, and Jesse was right in the middle of a "very interesting chapter."

When we had all done the usual business that you do at a rest stop, we hopped back into the car and drove on. The time went by slowly, and I kept peeking at my watch and then at the sky. Would we ever get to the airport?

After about thirty minutes, I stretched my arms and caught a glimpse of the seat behind me. I looked again. I pulled back the blankets and even looked under the back-seat. *That's funny,* I thought. *Where's Dad?* I glanced back again, expecting to find him where we had left him. Still no Dad. Certain that there was an explanation for all of this, I questioned my mother.

"Do you know where Dad is?"

"Yeah, he's in the back."

I sat in bewilderment and glanced back one last time, but he simply wasn't there.

"In the very back, with the luggage?"

"No, just the ba . . . "

Screeeech!

The car roared to a sudden stop, followed by a 180-degree turn that sent us back the way we'd come. Mom had looked in the back and confirmed my suspicions. Dad was missing!

Mom frantically questioned each of us about whether we knew the location of our missing father—first my younger brother, then me, then Jesse. Jesse had been reading through all this excitement, but he suddenly awakened to the panic.

Calmly he remarked, "Don't worry. He told me to tell you he was going to the bathroom and he'd be right back." My mother pointed out that we had left the rest area half an hour ago. Jesse just blinked.

An hour after we had left the rest stop, we picked up our now freezing father. He had been trying to keep warm by pressing the blow-dryer in the bathroom over and over again.

Dad spent the rest of the trip wide awake.

And did we make it to the airport on time for our flight? Absolutely. The plane had been delayed because of a bomb threat. Were we shocked or surprised? Naaaw. It was all part of our typical family vacations.

Jason Damazo, age 12

Terror on Route 83

"*Rodney!* Where is Aunt Emily?" Jenny asked for the third time as she walked into the living room drying her hair.

Rodney kept his eyes glued to the video screen. "How am I supposed to know? *Jennifer!*" He really hated it when his sister called him "Rodney." That's why he had ignored her the first two times when she had asked him about Aunt Emily.

"C'mon, Rod!" Jenny was getting concerned enough to plead a little. "I asked you to watch Aunt Em while I took a shower."

"You did?" he asked, offering her his best "who, me?" look.

"Rod, please! When I got into the shower, she was in the kitchen cleaning the sink—like she does at least ten times every day. Now she's gone!" Jenny was moving around the room looking out all the windows.

"Honest, I dunno, Jen," Rod answered, pulling himself up off of his elbows. "I don't remember you asking me to watch her."

"I can't find her anywhere and Mom should be home from the dentist in less than an hour," Jenny wailed.

"Where do you think she would go?" he asked.

"I don't know!" Jenny said. "But we have to find her. She could get hurt or something." Now Jenny was sounding borderline frantic.

Rod raced to the back door. Aunt Emily's blue fall coat was hanging on a hook right next to his faded jean jacket. "Jenny, look!" he said. "We'd better take her coat."

As he opened the back door, a gust of cold November wind whooshed into the house. "Aunt Em could get really sick if she's outside too long," Jenny said.

"You check the yard and the garage. I'll go down the block. She might have tried going to the beach again," Rod said as he took off running.

Rod and Jenny lived five miles from the closest beach, but Aunt Emily grew up living only a block away from Rainbow Beach in Chicago. A few months ago she had slipped out of the back door with her bathrobe on. She said that it was her beach jacket and that she was going for a little dip.

Aunt Emily was Grandma Berniece's oldest sister. Rod used to have fun with Aunt Emily because she had been an elementary school teacher for forty years. She definitely understood kids. Whenever she used to come to visit, they would play Monopoly. Aunt Emily had been the best Monopoly player Rod had ever met. Lately though, she hadn't been able to play Monopoly at all because she couldn't remember the rules, and then she would get upset.

Aunt Emily forgot things on a regular basis—like where she was or what day it was. The doctor said she had Alzheimer's disease. She didn't look sick or anything, but she said weird things and sometimes she didn't know who Rod and Jenny were. One day when Rod came home from school, she had locked the door. She kept shouting and asking him who he was.

"Rodney," he said.

"Rodney who?" she asked.

"Rodney Schuler; I'm your sister's grandson."

"Grandson!" Aunt Emily said with a laugh. "Don't be ridiculous! Berniece is only twelve years old!"

"Yeah, that would be pretty funny wouldn't it." Rod laughed, too, because that was the only way to handle Aunt Emily when she said things like that.

Last Christmas, Aunt Emily went to live with Grandma and Grandpa. Every Tuesday, she would come to stay at Rod and Jenny's house for the day—to give their grandmother a rest. Most of the time their mom was there to watch Aunt Em, but on this day Mom had to go to the dentist.

Rod and Jenny's house was on a dead-end street, so checking their block for Aunt Emily didn't take long. Jenny was in the front yard holding Aunt Emily's coat. She looked like she had just swallowed a whole red pepper. Her eyes were red and watery.

"Rod, Joey Nicholas said he saw Aunt Em about five minutes ago. She was headed toward Devon Road."

A huge lump formed in Rod's throat and stuck there when he tried to swallow. He could hardly squeak out the words, "Let's go!"

They sprinted about ten steps when Jenny grabbed Rod's arm. "Rod, we should pray about this."

"You're right, but I think today we pray while we run," he answered.

It was only three blocks to Devon Road, but Rod had plenty of time to pray. He asked God to please protect Aunt Emily and to help them find her.

As they turned the corner onto Devon Road, Rod could see Aunt Emily about a block away. She was standing on the cement island in the middle of the four-lane highway. Cars were whizzing by at fifty-five miles per hour on both sides of her. She had her hand up as if she thought the cars would stop.

Rod was just about to yell when Jenny grabbed his arm. "Rod, don't yell! And pray she doesn't see us. She might just step off the island right in front of a car."

"What are we going to do?" he asked.

"I don't know," Jenny said. She covered her face with her hands, crumpled into a heap, and started to sob.

Rod stood there looking at her for a second, dumbfounded and desperate. "Aunt Em belongs to you, Lord," he reminded God again. "Please, help us!"

He snatched Aunt Emily's blue coat and rushed along the roadside. When he got directly across from her, he crouched down. He was praying she wouldn't see him.

Then Rod waited. It seemed like forever. Cars, vans, pickup trucks and huge semitrailers zoomed past, between Aunt Emily and him. She just kept standing there with her hand up. In spite of the cold wind, warm air from the heavy traffic swirled around Rod's legs. He licked his lips. They tasted like exhaust.

Finally Rod saw a break in the traffic. He lunged across the highway and grabbed Aunt Emily firmly by the arm.

Rod said as calmly as he could, "Boy, Aunt Em, you must be cold. Here's your coat."

Aunt Emily looked at him with a blank expression on her face. Inside of his head he was crying, *Please God, make her know me!*

Slowly a familiar smile stretched across her face.

"Why thank you, Rodney. It is getting chilly out."

A feeling of relief and gratefulness rushed through his entire body. Rod took Aunt Emily's arm, trusting God to help him with the next step. "This is a really busy road, Aunt Em. Can you help me cross and get home?"

"Hold my hand, Rodney," she said with a confident smile. "I'll take care of you."

Aunt Emily clutched his hand tightly as they waited for a break in the heavy traffic. "Be careful, Rodney; this is a very busy street, Dear."

When they had safely reached the other side of the street, Jenny was anxiously waiting for them. "Jennifer, what are you doing here?" Aunt Emily asked. "I had better get both of you home before your mother finds out you have been near this busy road."

As they walked home, Aunt Emily chattered away happily. Jenny leaned behind her and whispered, "Thanks, Rod."

"Don't thank me, Jenny," he said, pointing one finger toward heaven. "Thank him."

Mary Ellyn Sandford

Watching for the Miracle

All things are possible until they are proved impossible.

Pearl S. Buck

Cindy Plumpton's brother had been missing now for almost nine months.

The Plumpton family, which included Cindy, then twelve, her fourteen-year-old brother, Kirk, and their parents, were spending their traditional summer vacation at their cabin in the Colorado mountains. The cabins were fairly secluded, separated from each other by trees. Because they knew all the families who had cabins close by, Cindy and Kirk had many friends there. Kirk's best friend lived in the cabin next door. As he often did, Kirk had dinner at his friend's place one evening. Just before dusk, he began to walk the hundred yards back to his family's cabin. He never made it.

The state police, volunteers and his family combed those mountains for any trace of what might have happened to Kirk, but when winter came and fresh snow blanketed the earth, they had to halt the search.

It was shortly after that when I met Cindy at our church. Although she was quiet at first, there was something special that drew me to her. We became Sunday-school friends. It wasn't until she invited me over to her house several weeks later that she told me about her brother. She and I didn't go to the same school, but we saw each other every weekend after that. Sometimes I slept over at her house, although her parents wouldn't let her sleep over at mine.

On a warm, sunny Saturday in April, I called her to say that my mom had agreed to drive us to the park. We could pack a lunch and take our bikes and make a day of it. Cindy sounded as excited about the day as I was, so when I got to her house an hour later, I was puzzled when she said she couldn't go. She said that she was sorry and hoped I would understand, but there was a rainbow today and she had to stay home and wait for the news.

"What news?" I asked.

"About my brother," she said, almost too excited to speak. "He's going to come home today."

"What? They found him?" I asked excitedly.

"Not yet, but they will." Then she explained. "Instead of wishing on stars, my brother used to wish on rainbows. He used to say that stars were nothing special; you could see them any old night. But when you saw a rainbow, that was a miracle. Seeing this rainbow means a miracle is going to happen today. Kirk's coming home. So you see, I have to stay home and wait for him. You understand, don't you?"

I saw only hope in her large brown eyes, and I nodded yes, I understood. We hugged, and together we stared out the window at the rainbow, with hope in our hearts.

Cindy and her family weren't at church the next day. The reverend announced that the Plumptons had received a call from the police in another county telling them that they had found a boy who fit Kirk's description. He had been wandering the street, severely bruised and only semiconscious. Cindy was right! The rainbow had brought Kirk home. Cindy's family immediately drove the three hours to the hospital where the boy was staying.

That night on the TV news, we found out that the boy the police had found was not Kirk. Although his face was swollen purple, the minute the Plumptons entered his hospital room, they knew he was not their son. The news report said that the boy was still unidentified and in a coma.

Even though the boy in the coma wasn't Kirk, the Plumptons stayed by his bedside every day. They did not want him to be alone when he awoke from his coma, which he did five days later. It turned out the boy was a runaway. The Plumptons notified his parents, who lived in another state and had no idea that their missing boy had been found. The parents were overjoyed, and the Plumptons left only after a tearful reunion between the boy and his parents.

When Cindy finally returned home, I was afraid to visit her. I was afraid because I didn't want to see the disappointment that I knew would be on her face. When I finally went to her house and entered her room, she was staring out the window.

"I'm sorry it wasn't Kirk." The words barely got past the lump in my throat.

"Me too," she said. "But there'll be another rainbow. I just know it."

"How can you still believe in rainbows? It didn't bring your brother home."

"The boy they found is my brother's age. His name is Paul, and he has a sister, too. I knew the rainbow would bring a miracle. It just wasn't our miracle this time. But I'll see another rainbow. I just know it."

Together, we stared out the window, with hope in our hearts.

Korina L. Moss

Daddy's Girl . . . At Long Last

Have you ever felt like nobody?
Just a tiny speck of air.
When everyone's around you,
And you are just not there.

Karen Crawford, age 9

Daddy wanted a boy. He was so disappointed when I was born. And when Momma found out she couldn't have any more children, Daddy was devastated.

He never tried to hide his disappointment from me. He was brutally honest. I guess I understood his feelings, living on a small farm in Iowa. He had hoped a boy would help him with the farm and eventually step into his shoes. But a girl . . .

I tried to do everything just to please Daddy. I could shimmy up a tree in the blink of an eye, throw a ball farther than any boy my age and look the town bully straight in the eye.

But still Daddy didn't seem to notice. I would bring home straight As from school and other achievement awards. He was unmoved by that as well.

I was determined that I would win his love and admiration, no matter what.

I worked twice as hard doing my chores by getting up extra early in the morning. I milked our cows and gathered the eggs from our hens. Then I went to school.

Still Daddy seemed so unappreciative. Momma always tried to ease some of the frustration and hurt. "He'll come around one day," she'd say.

The year I turned thirteen was the one hundredth anniversary of the founding of our town. The town council decided to hold a parade, and they wanted a young lady to sit on a float and lead the parade. The families in the area were asked to send pictures of their children. Every parent in the area hoped that their daughter would be selected. Every parent except Daddy.

Momma sent in a picture of me. I was always so busy being the boy Daddy always wanted that I had never considered trying for the honor of leading the parade. I had no idea that Momma had sent in a picture of me, so it was quite a surprise when the selection committee stopped by one evening to tell us I'd been chosen. Momma was thrilled. As I expected, Daddy showed no interest in the matter.

The day of the big parade finally arrived. I was dressed in a beautiful white dress. At first I felt awkward—I'd hardly ever worn dresses. But soon I felt like a princess in a fairy tale.

As the parade passed down the main street of our town, I saw Momma and Daddy standing on the side. Momma was waving an American flag. But Daddy . . . well, he was just something else! There he stood, smiling like I'd never seen him smile before! As I passed him, I thought I saw tears in his eyes. At that moment, I knew I had finally gained his admiration—not as a replacement for the boy he'd always wanted, but as the young lady I really was.

Candace Goldapper

From the Heart

Jimmy was five when he and his parents adopted Neil. He still remembers that day in court when the judge called him up to the bench, all by himself, and said, "Today, it's not just your mom and dad who accept the responsibility of raising another child. I'm counting on you, too, to share that obligation. Being a big brother means that this baby is going to look up to you and depend on you. Are you ready to take on that job?" Even though he was only in kindergarten at the time, Jimmy took the judge's words very seriously.

Neil grew up thinking that being "adocted," as he called it, was the coolest thing. His parents must have read every book in the library about how to explain such a complicated issue to a child, and they did a great job. Not only did he not feel bad about it, he felt even more special than if he weren't adopted. At every opportunity, whether it be current events or a talent show or even a holiday celebration, he'd proudly stand up and tell the immediate world how he had a "tummy mom" and a "heart mom." Sometimes it got to the point where Jimmy felt a little neglected.

When Neil was in second grade, he came across someone who had a different idea about what being adopted meant. Andy, a fifth-grader who rode the bus with Neil, didn't have a lot of friends in school. He acted like a big shot with the younger kids on the school bus. One day, for no reason at all, he yelled out from the back of the bus, "Hey, Neil, you know what being adopted really means?"

Neil was nervous because Andy had never spoken directly to him before. Andy sounded mad, as if Neil had done something to make him angry. Neil knew better than to go into his show-and-tell routine, so he didn't answer.

Then Andy snarled, "It means your real mother threw you in the garbage." The bus got very quiet. "That's right, the garbage. You were lucky someone came along and got you out before the trucks came and ground you up."

Neil felt as if his heart had moved up to his throat. He tried to get off the bus at the next stop, even though it was blocks away from his house, but the driver wouldn't let him. Everyone was talking, but he didn't hear a word. The second the doors opened in front of his house, he ran out of the bus and through the front door.

Jimmy was already home from school. He and his mom were sitting in the kitchen. Neil's milk and Oreos were waiting on the table.

"What's wrong?" his mother asked sharply, in that way mothers have of knowing before they're told that something bad has happened to their child.

Neil told them what Andy had said. His mother slumped in her chair, without any comforting phrases about "tummies and hearts" to offer. She knew that all the advice in all the books couldn't erase the devastation on Neil's face. When she reached out to hug him, he moved away. Instinctively, she sought her own comfort and grabbed the phone to call their dad.

Suddenly, Jimmy stood up. He walked around the table to where Neil was sobbing with his head in his hands.

"Neil," he said quietly, "just think about what's true. Babies aren't adopted because nobody cares about them. Babies are only adopted when they are loved. Very much."

Their mom stopped dialing the phone. Neil picked up his head. Some people say the truth hurts. But sometimes it cures, when it comes from the heart.

Marcia Byalick

A Brother's Love

She pulled back on the ropes, making the homemade swing fly higher and closer to the leafy branches of the tall sycamore tree. The breeze swished cool against her cheeks. She was five years old, and, at that moment, stomping mad at her eleven-year-old brother, David.

How could he have been so mean? she asked herself, remembering how he had made a face and called her a "big baby" at the breakfast table. *He hates me,* she thought, *just because I took the last muffin out from under his nose. He hates me!*

The swing carried her up so high that she could see for miles. It was fun looking down at the farmyard below. Her red sweater flashed brightly in the morning sunlight. She stopped thinking about being mad at her brother and started to sing a swinging song.

On a distant hill behind the swing, a huge bull with long, sharp horns watched the red sweater flashing in the sunlight. The bull had broken out of his pasture. He was cranky and ready to charge at anything that moved. He snorted and scraped the ground with his hoof. Then he lowered his massive head and began lumbering across the field toward the red sweater he saw swinging back and forth beneath the sycamore tree.

Meanwhile, David was in the barnyard, feeding the chickens. He looked out and saw his little sister on the swing. *Sisters are a pain in the neck,* he thought. Then suddenly he saw the bull charging across the field, heading straight for his sister. Without a second thought, David screamed as loudly as he could, "Look out behind you! Get out of there! *Run!*"

His sister didn't hear him; she just kept singing and swinging. The bull was halfway across the field and closing in fast. David's heart pounded. It was now or never. He ran across the chicken yard, jumped the fence and dashed toward his sister. He ran faster than he had ever run before.

Grabbing one of the ropes, David jerked the swing to a stop, tumbling his sister sideways to the ground only a second before the snorting bull charged at the place she had been. She let out a terrified yell. The bull spun around, scraping the ground again with his hoof. He lowered his head to charge again.

David yanked on one sleeve of the red sweater and then the other. Pulling it off of his sister, he flung the sweater as far away as he could. The bull followed it. With horns and hooves, he ripped it into a hundred shreds of red yarn, while David half dragged, half carried his frightened sister to safety.

I was that little girl, and ever since that day, I just laugh when my brother calls me a "big baby." He can't fool me— I know he loves me. He doesn't have to face a charging bull to prove it. But I'll never forget the day he did.

Diana L. James

Secrets That Made Paul Special

*The optimist sees the doughnut, the pessimist,
the hole.*

McLandburgh Wilson

Paul was my little brother, and he was special. He was
different from me because he was blind, and he sat in a
wheelchair. Lots of people knew he was different because
he had his own school bus and had to go to a special
school. But that's not really why he was special.

Paul was special for the things just our family knew
about—like introducing us to new friends. Lots of times
when we walked with Paul, other kids came over and
asked us why he was in his chair. They wanted to know
why Paul couldn't see, and I would tell them to shake
Paul's hand. Then we'd talk about other stuff.

Paul was a good listener. I could tell him all kinds of
things, and he never got tired of listening to me. He
laughed when I told him something funny, and he was
the only one in our family who could keep a secret.

Paul helped me exercise. Sometimes when we'd go for
a walk, we'd have to go uphill. Paul liked to feel the sun

and wind on his face, and he liked to listen to the birds. When I pushed his chair to the woods at the top of the hill, I was really getting my exercise!

Paul helped us carry things. He never minded if I hung my backpack on the back of his chair or if Mom put her purse there. Sometimes he carried the packages we'd get when we went shopping. I think he felt like the driver!

Paul helped me hear small noises. When I was with him, I'd have to be quiet as a stone to hear the munching chipmunks and the talking trees that he heard.

Paul let me practice my reading. When I was his reader, I read at my own speed. Sometimes I had to stop to figure out a difficult word, but Paul didn't mind. His favorite stories were about animals, especially worms.

When there was a special day in town, like the circus in summer or the one time when the president came in his helicopter, Paul would let me share his front-row seat.

In winter, Paul helped me keep my feet dry. When Paul went somewhere he had to use ramps instead of stairs. The snow was usually shoveled off the ramps, so we both kept our feet dry! Inside buildings, Paul gave me free elevator rides. Paul's chair didn't fit on the escalator, and boy, was I glad. I don't like escalators!

Paul hardly ever complained. He went along with whatever the rest of us wanted to do. One time when he had a fever, he got crabby, but he never yelled or fought or asked me to switch the TV channel.

Paul let me put things in his lap. We played a kind of feel-and-tell game. Sometimes I put different toys there for him to feel, or I'd surprise him with our dog, Muffin. Once I put a crawly worm in his lap. He was always surprised when I let him hold something new. He made faces and sounds to let me know his guess.

Paul let me come with him on the rides at the fair. They have a handicapped-ride day, and all the kids in wheelchairs get to go on the rides for free. Since Paul couldn't sit up by himself, I got to sit on one side of him so he wouldn't fall over.

Paul was my friend. He couldn't talk to me like most of my friends, and he couldn't run outside or play hide-and-seek. But he was there for all the quiet times, and he had the best smile in the world.

Paul died in his sleep five years ago. Growing up as his sister was a blessing. He helped me to see that there is a positive side to every situation, if we simply make the choice to find it.

Judy M. Garty

My Grandfather's Gift

A child's life is like a piece of paper on which every person leaves a mark.

Chinese Proverb

When I was a child, storytelling was an active part of my upbringing. My parents fostered any activity that might exercise my imagination. As a result of this encouragement, I have indeed become the modern version of a storyteller—an actor.

Surprisingly, not one relative on either side of my family has ever taken up this profession before. The only person to whom I can trace a "storytelling gene" is my grandfather on my mother's side. This grandfather, in the great tradition of grandfathers everywhere, has always been a source of wisdom in my life.

When I was younger, my entire family would go camping, and as it grew dark, we would roast marshmallows around a fire and listen to my grandfather recite a poem. It was always the same poem that my grandfather would recite from memory.

When my grandfather was fourteen, he discovered the

poem in a book of verse. He was working with horses at the time, and he had read the poem only two or three times when one of his horses had gotten loose. He was forced to chase the horse for miles, and somewhere in the course of the chase, he lost the book after only committing the first half of the poem to memory.

He tried for years to find another copy of the poem, but not knowing the author's name, he gave up his search, content to having memorized only the beginning. "My First Cigar" is a poem about a child's first attempt at smoking. Neither my grandfather nor I have ever smoked, but the poem contains such an endearing quality of innocent introspection that I was always thoroughly entertained by it.

It was not just the poem that got to me—it was the light in my grandfather's eye, the lilt in his speech, and the sweeping movements of his arms that passionately involved me in the verse. Each one of these performances would be cut short when my grandfather would shrug and say, "That's as far as I memorized," and we would all nod and be left wondering how the poem ended. We accepted his inability to finish because we all knew why he could not.

Last year, about seventy years from the time my grandfather had originally found the poem, he installed a computer system in his local library, free of charge. As a return favor, he asked the library researchers to try to find "My First Cigar." Several months later, one of them sent him the poem through the mail. I remember reading the rest of it for the first time with joy.

My grandfather has never recited the poem since, and I have never asked him to. Perhaps now that my grandfather knows the poem's ending, his personal involvement with it is complete. For me, the story was better when it was incomplete . . . when it still had a future. I

have since become actively involved in poetry, both reading and writing, and I credit my interest to my grandfather entirely.

There was a wonderful moment not long ago, when I
was memorizing Wordsworth's poem "My Heart Leaps
Up" aloud, and my grandfather surprised me when he
said, "I know that poem," and was able to recite it with
me. He had enjoyed the poem many years ago—I was
memorizing it myself—and it was here that our two generations were bridged.

After seventeen years of knowing my grandfather better than most people I know in my life, every now and
then he still decides to open the treasure chest that is his
mind, and surprise me with a gift of wisdom.

Rider Strong

My First Cigar

'Twas just behind the woodshed,
One glorious summer day.
Far o'er the hills, the sinking sun
Pursued its western way;
And in my safe seclusion
Removed from o'er the jar
And dim of earth's confusion
I smoked my first cigar.

It was my first cigar!
It was my worst cigar!
Raw, green, dank, hidebound and rank,
It was my first cigar!

Ah, bright the boyish fancies
Wrapped in smoke-wreath blue;
My eyes grew dim, my head was light,

The woodshed round me flew!
Dark night closed in around me—
Black night, without a star—
Grim death methought had found me
And spoiled my first cigar.

It was my first cigar!
A six-for-five cigar!
No viler torch the air could scorch—
It was my first cigar!

All pallid was my beaded brow,
The reeling night was late,
My startled mother cried in fear,
"My child, what have you ate?"
I heard my father's smothered laugh,
It seemed so strange and far,
I knew he knew, I knew he knew
I'd smoked my first cigar!

It was my first cigar!
A give-away cigar!
I could not die—I knew not why—
It was my first cigar!

Since then I've stood in reckless ways.
I've dared what men can dare,
I've mocked at danger, walked with death,
I've laughed at pain and care,
I do not dread what may befall
'Neath my malignant star,
No frowning fate again can make
Me smoke my first cigar!

Robert J. Burdette

Silent Night, Crystal Night

As we walked, my grandfather said, in a voice tinged with sadness, "This month is very meaningful to me. Three highly significant events occurred in our family in November. Do you know what they are?"

"You mean our birthdays on the same day and Thanksgiving?"

He shook his gray, balding head. "*Kristallnacht* also happened in November."

"Is that what happened when you were a boy? You've never talked about what happened to you growing up."

With a hint of a German accent he said, "Well, you're getting older, and it's time you heard a bit of history by someone who lived it."

This is the story he told to me during my thirteenth year.

"By 1935, when I was very young, the Nazis had gained great strength throughout Germany. In my city of Magdeburg, their symbols were everywhere. Nuremberg Laws deprived Jews of the right of citizenship. We could no longer have telephones, businesses or personal relationships with non-Jews. Non-Jews could not hire us, nor could we have them work for us.

"Soon after those statutes were enacted, store windows and buildings were plastered with signs saying *Juden Verboten'* (Jews Forbidden) in huge letters, blaring like trumpets their malicious message. During the 1936 Olympics in Berlin, these signs disappeared, only to return after the games. On the last day that I was allowed to attend school, a Nazi schoolmate threw a rock at my head, hitting me.

"Locating medicines and food had become difficult unless a Jewish-owned business was still in operation. Prominent Jewish doctors, banned from hospitals, worked from their homes; professors, banned from universities, taught classes in secret.

"My parents spoke little about the situation to my younger brother and me. I did overhear them saying that they hoped this madness would soon pass.

"'After all,' my father said, 'our families have lived in Germany for generations.'

"My parents warned us to remain as invisible as possible, to avoid crowds and any commotion in the streets. Can you imagine how I felt as a teenager?

"My mother wrote to her American relatives in Maine, requesting they sign a required affidavit without delay, guaranteeing the four of us freedom in America. This document would also permit us to leave Germany.

"A year later, my country's situation worsened, becoming extremely dangerous. Jews were required to wear the Star of David on their sleeves, becoming targets for open harassment.

"Around the first of November in 1938, my mother left for Munich to learn fancy hotel cooking in hopes of finding work in America after we received permission to emigrate. My father stayed home to try to run what little business he had left.

"During the night of November 10, while we slept, uniformed Nazi hoodlums organized demonstrations all over

Germany. They hurled rocks and firebombs at Jewish-owned businesses and property. People trying to escape the flames were shot. Millions of pieces of glass shattered all over the streets. Desecrated and torched synagogues were blown up. The noise and smell woke me. The stifling smell of burning buildings saturated the air. I jumped out of bed, peeked through the curtain and thought I was in hell. My father came into our room, closed the curtain, and told me to go back to bed and keep the lights off. I finally went back to sleep.

"Throughout that night, countless Jewish men as well as boys my age, natural-born German citizens, were arrested and sent to concentration camps. Some of these men had previously earned medals while bravely serving their country during World War I. Survivors, rounded up the next day, were forced to march to the nearest government office, and received papers demanding payment to the German government for damages to their own businesses and homes. This catastrophe later became known in German as *Kristallnacht*, meaning the night of broken glass.

"When the alarm woke us in the morning, my father wasn't home. We assumed he had gone out early on business. So I got your Uncle Fritz and myself ready for school. As we were about to leave, a family friend rang our doorbell. When we opened the door, he looked around to make sure that no one else was around to hear what he had to say.

"'Your father may not be home for a while, and he wants you and your brother to stay in the apartment, and not go to school,' the friend told us.

"For our protection, he didn't reveal that my father had gone into hiding to avoid the mass arrest of all Jewish adult males. The friend left. Scared, I remained at home with a terrified eight-year-old brother.

"An hour later, someone pounded on the front door. Opening it, I saw a tall stranger dressed in a dark leather overcoat. He nearly filled the doorway. Intimidated by his size, I looked up shyly as he looked down arrogantly, both of us staring for a moment. Then the six-foot-plus intruder pushed his way inside and announced, 'Gestapo!' I can still hear that cold, sharp voice demanding, 'Where is your father?'

"Scared, I answered, 'I don't know where he is or when he'll return.' The agent left, threatening to come back.

"Two or three hours later I heard that familiar, dreaded banging at the door. I shivered. I assumed the first caller had returned.

"Upon opening the door, I saw two different Gestapo agents who looked like clones of the first man.

"'So! Has your father returned?' one snarled. Then, without waiting for an answer, both pushed me aside, entered our home, started opening bureau drawers, emptying them on the floor, looking into all the closets and searching under the beds. Fritz and I shook with fright. We tried to hide our terror by jamming our cold, clammy hands into our pockets. Not finding whatever they were looking for, they turned without saying a word and left. Fritz and I nearly collapsed with relief.

"A short time later, these same two goons returned, demanding that I accompany them to Gestapo head-quarters immediately. I told Fritz to go directly to our family's friends. I got my coat. Then, sandwiched between the two tall, robotic Nazis who accompanied me, rode a public streetcar, believe it or not, and was delivered to Gestapo headquarters.

"Shoved into a scary-looking office, the first thing I noticed was a uniformed official seated behind a large, highly polished, wooden desk. On the mahogany wall behind him hung a huge color portrait of Hitler, whose eyes seemed to follow the administrator's every move. Barely looking up from his papers, he shouted in a deep, menacing voice, 'Wait outside the office until your father turns himself in!' One of the aides pushed me into a large marble anteroom and ordered me to sit on a bench at the other end of the room.

"'How long will I have to wait?' I asked.

"'For as long as it takes!'

"Only then did I realize that I was being held as a hostage. Shivering from fright and cold, I wrapped my coat around me and kept very still to avoid being noticed. I had no idea how long I had been sitting there before I saw my father pass through the doorway at the other end of the anteroom, disappearing into what must have been another office. Evidently, friends who had watched the apartment had told him of my arrest. He gave himself up in exchange for my release. The Nazis often took children hostage, knowing their fugitive parents would turn themselves in. It was a very effective tactic.

"I sat there for a long time, numb, not knowing what to do. No one paid any attention to me. After what seemed like hours, I got up some courage and approached the deputy who was seated down the hall.

"'Excuse me.'

"'What?' he snapped.

"'My father has already arrived, and I would like to go home.'

"Verifying my father's arrival, the uniformed official behind the desk dismissed me with a flick of his pen, warning, 'It will be your turn next time.'

"My father never discussed his experiences in the camp after his release. If anyone asked, he would address the question with a distant stare and silence.

"Five months before the start of World War II, the necessary papers came through, allowing us to sail to America."

As we returned for our turkey dinner, Opa, as I called my grandfather, came to the end of his story.

"When the United States entered World War II, I automatically became a citizen, joined the Army and was ordered to Europe as an interpreter for German prisoners of war. I don't dwell on my boyhood experiences, but today I felt that I wanted you to know. I guess it's okay to remember those things once in a while."

"Well, something good came out of all that tragedy, Opa," I told him.

"Yah? What's that?"

"Me," I said, putting my arms around him, planting a kiss on his cheek.

My grandfather never spoke of this again.

Lillian Belinfante Herzberg

Green Salami

That is the best—to laugh with someone because you both think the same things are funny.

Gloria Vanderbilt

Sometime during the seventh grade two things happened to me. The first was that I got hooked on salami. Salami sandwiches, salami and cheese, salami on crackers—I couldn't get enough of the salty, spicy sausage. The other thing was that my mom and I weren't getting along really well. We weren't fighting really badly or anything, but it just seemed as if all she wanted to do was argue with me and tell me what to do. We also didn't laugh together much anymore. Things were changing, and my mom and I were the first to feel it.

As far as the salami went, my mom wouldn't buy any because she said it was too expensive and not that good for me. To prove my emerging independence, I decided to go ahead and eat what I wanted anyway. So one day I used my allowance to buy a full sausage of dry salami.

Now a problem had to be solved: Where would I put the salami? I didn't want my mom to see it. So I hid it in the only place that I knew was totally safe—under my bed. There was a special corner under the bed that the upright Hoover couldn't reach and that my mom rarely had the ambition to clean. Under the bed went the salami, back in the corner—in the dark and the dust.

A couple of weeks later, I remembered the delicious treat that was waiting for me. I peered beneath the bed and saw . . . not the salami that I had hidden, but some green and hairy object that didn't look like anything I had ever seen before. The salami had grown about an inch of hair, and the hair was standing straight up, as if the salami had been surprised by the sudden appearance of my face next to its hiding place. Being the picky eater I was, I was not interested in consuming any of *this* object. The best thing I could think of to do was . . . *absolutely nothing.*

Sometime later, my mom became obsessed with spring cleaning, which in her case meant she would clean places that had never seen the light of day. Of course, that meant under my bed. I knew in my heart that the moment would soon come when she would find the object in its hiding place. During the first two days of her frenzy, I watched carefully to judge the time when I thought she would find the salami. She washed, she scrubbed, she dusted . . . she *screamed!* She screamed and screamed and screamed. "Ahhhhhh . . . ahhhhhh . . . ahhhhhh!" The screams were coming from my room. Alarms went off in my head. She had found the salami!

"What is it, Mom?" I yelled as I ran into my room.

"There is *something* under your bed!"

"What's under my bed?" I opened my eyes very wide to show my complete innocence.

"Something . . . something . . . I don't know what it is!" She finally stopped screaming. Then she whispered, "Maybe it's alive."

I got down to look under my bed.

"Watch out!" she shouted. "I don't know what it is!" she said again. She pushed me to one side. I was proud of the bravery she was demonstrating to save me from the "something" in spite of her distress.

I was amazed at what I saw. The last time I had looked at the salami, the hair on it was about an inch long and fuzzy all over. Now, the hair had grown another three inches, was a gray-green color and had actually started to grow on the surrounding area as well. You could no longer tell the actual shape of what the hair was covering. I looked at my mom. Except for the color, her hair closely resembled the hair on the salami: It was standing straight up, too! Abruptly she got up and left the room, only to return five seconds later with the broom.

Using the handle of the broom, she poked the salami. It didn't move. She poked it harder. It still didn't move. At that point, I wanted to tell her what it was, but I couldn't seem to make my mouth work. My chest was squeezing with an effort to repress the laughter that, unbidden, was threatening to explode. At the same time, I was terrified of her rage when she finally discovered what it was. I was also afraid she was going to have a heart attack because she looked so scared.

Finally my mom got up her nerve and pushed the salami really hard. At that same exact moment, the laughter I had been trying to hold back exploded from my mouth. She dropped the broom and looked at me.

"What's so funny?" my mom asked. Up close, two inches from my face, she looked furious. Maybe it was just the position of having her head lower than her bottom that made her face so red, but I was sure she was about to poke me with the broom handle. I sure didn't want that to happen because it still had some pieces of gray-green hair sticking to it. I felt kind of sick, but then another one of my huge laughs erupted. It was as if I had no control over my body. One followed another, and pretty soon I was rolling on the floor. My mom sat down—hard.

"What is so funny?!"

"Salami," I managed to get out despite the gales of laughter that I had no control over. "Salami! Salami!" I rolled on the floor. "It's a salami!"

My mother gazed at me with disbelief. What did salami have to do with anything? The object under the bed did not look like any salami she had ever seen. In fact, it did not look like *anything* she (or I) had ever seen.

I gasped for breath. "Mom, it's a salami—you know, one of those big salami sausages!"

She asked what any sane mother would ask in this situation. "What is a salami doing under your bed?"

"I bought it with my allowance." My laughter was subsiding, and fear was beginning to take its place. I looked at her. She had the strangest expression on her face that I had ever seen: a combination of disgust, confusion, exhaustion, fear—and *anger!* Her hair was standing on end, perspiration beaded on her flushed face and her eyes looked as if they were going to jump out of her head. I couldn't help it. I started to laugh again.

And then the miracle of miracles happened. My mom started to laugh, too. First just a nervous release, a titter really, but then it turned into the full-on belly laugh that only my mom's side of the family is capable of. The two of us laughed until tears rolled down our cheeks and I thought I would pee my pants.

When we finally were able to stop laughing, my mom shoved the broom into my hands.

"Okay, Patty Jean Shaw, *clean it up,* no matter what it is!"

I had no idea how to clean up something and not look at it or touch it. So, of course, I got my little sister to help me. I could get her to help with anything, as long as I bribed or threatened her. Since she didn't know what the object was supposed to look like to begin with, she didn't have much fear attached to helping. Between the two of us, we managed to roll it onto the evening newspaper (my dad never knew what happened to it). I *carefully*, carefully carried it outside and put it into the trash. Then I had my sister remove the remaining fuzz from the carpet. I had convinced her that I was too large to get into the small corner where it had grown. I ended up owing her my allowance for two weeks.

My mom never got mad at me for buying the salami. I guess she thought I had already paid a price. The salami provided a memory of shared, unrestrained laughter. For years to come, all I had to do was threaten to buy salami to make my mom laugh.

Patty Hansen

©Lynn Johnston Productions, Inc. Distributed by United Feature Syndicate, Inc.

Going, Going, Gone

"They're going to give us twenty bucks for it?" I asked my sister, Melva, in disbelief. "Are you sure?"

"They said twenty," my sister repeated. "Thirty if we throw in the old cabinet radio."

"Sold!" we exclaimed in unison, giving each other a high five. We couldn't believe what was happening. All we did was post a sign that said "Garage Sale," and our yard was swarming with shoppers. We sold the baby crib I'd long since outgrown, clothes, jewelry, dishes, antique records—whatever we could find around the house that was old and seemingly useless.

Mom and Dad were away on vacation, and we were determined to surprise them with more money than they could ever make in one weekend. Each time the stock on the front lawn ran low, one of us would excitedly return to the house to find more items to sell. On one trip, we weren't quick enough, and a few of the customers came in after us.

"How much would you take for that two-piece sofa set?" one woman asked.

My sister and I looked at each other. It certainly wasn't new, and Mom had been talking about replacing it. Still, it was our living room furniture. If we sold it, what would the family have to sit on?

"We don't really know if we can sell that. . . . " we hedged.

"I'll give you ten bucks for each piece," she coaxed.

Ten dollars? That would be twenty bucks for the whole set! We had no idea how much it would cost to replace, but we did know another twenty bucks would bring our day's total to over three hundred dollars! Mom and Dad were going to be so proud of us. They were going to be thrilled. They were going to be . . .

"You did *what?*" Mom said as she walked into the house and saw the empty spaces where the furniture used to be.

"But we made over three hundred dollars!" we said, handing her the wad of bills.

"Do you have any idea what the things you sold were worth?"

Her tone of voice made it hard to tell whether she was laughing or crying.

"More than three hundred dollars?" we asked meekly.

By our calculations, we'll be allowed to come out of our rooms in just three more years.

Martha Bolton

Your Name in Gold

Anne sat at the breakfast table, eating her cornflakes and reading the print on the cereal box in front of her. "Tastee Cornflakes—Great New Offer!" the box read. "See back of box for details."

Anne's older sister, Mary, sat across from her, reading the other side of the cereal box. "Hey, Anne," she said, "look at this awesome prize—*your name in gold.*"

As Mary read on, Anne's interest in the prize grew. "Just send in one dollar with proof-of-purchase seal from this box and spell out your first name on the information blank. We will send you a special pin with your name spelled in gold. (Only one per family, please.)"

Anne grabbed the box and looked on the back, her eyes brightening with excitement. The name *Jennifer* was spelled out in sparkling gold. "That's a neat idea," she said. "A pin with my very own name spelled out in gold. I'm going to send in for it."

"Sorry, Anne, I saw it first," said Mary, "so I get first dibs on it. Besides, you don't have a dollar to send in, and I do."

"But I want a pin like that so badly," said Anne. "Please let me have it!"

"Nope," said her sister.

"You always get your way—just because you're older than me," said Anne, her lower lip trembling as her eyes filled with tears. "Just go ahead and send in for it. See if I care!" She threw down her spoon and ran from the kitchen.

Several weeks passed. One day the mailman brought a small package addressed to Mary. Anne was dying to see the pin, but she wouldn't let Mary know how eager she was. Mary took the package to her room. Anne casually followed her in and sat on the bed.

"Well, I guess they sent you your pin. I sure hope you like it," Anne said in a mean voice. Mary slowly took the paper off the package. She opened a little white box and carefully lifted off the top layer of white cotton. "Oh, it's beautiful!" Mary said. "Just like the cereal box said, *your name in gold.* Four beautiful letters. Would you like to see it, Anne?"

"No, I don't care about your dumb old pin."

Mary put the white box on the dresser and went downstairs.

Anne was alone in the bedroom. Soon she couldn't wait any longer, so she walked over to the dresser. As she looked in the small white box, she gasped. Mixed feelings of love for her sister and shame at herself welled up within her, and the pin became a sparkling gold blur through her tears.

There on the pin were four beautiful letters—her name in gold: A-N-N-E.

A. F. Bauman

Father's Day

When I was six years old, I never thought I would feel happy inside again. My father had just died. He had been sick for a very long time and never could play with me. The Father's Day after my father died, we had to make cards for our dads at school. I made mine for an angel. No one seemed to understand how sad I was inside not to have a dad, and not to have anyone to make a card for.

Then the most wonderful thing happened. My mom met Michael. On New Year's Eve, we all sat down together and said our thanks for the past year and our wishes for the New Year. I told Michael that my wish was that he would be a dad to me. Michael's eyes filled with tears, and he said yes—but only if he could really be a father to me, not just do all the fun stuff. I said yes. Of course, Mom thought this was all pretty wonderful, too.

I want to thank Michael for being my dad, for being there for me and for taking away much of the sadness. I want to thank Michael for getting Mom to say yes to a lizard, for throwing a baseball with me and for being at *all* of my soccer games. But mostly I want to thank

Michael for teaching me that parents can come to us in many different ways, and that a person who did not help to create you can be as much or more of a parent to you as someone who did. Happy Father's Day, Dad!

Taylor Martini, age 8

Mom's Duck

*God could not be everywhere, and therefore he
made mothers.*

Jewish Proverb

My mother always had a soft spot for those less fortu-
nate than she was. Mom would find a stray dog and take
it to the pound, only to return with three more. She'd
shun luncheon invitations with other housewives, prefer-
ring instead to become fast friends with the house painter
or her beautician. She'd troll the church congregation
every Sunday for anyone unattached who might be in
need of a dinner invitation, or worse yet, a place to stay.

The fact was that Mom opened her heart and our home
to anything that breathed. She was the Dolly Madison of
the downtrodden, and by the time I was thirteen, we had
eight pets, five foster children and several other unofficial
kids and/or adults living with our family. My sister,
brother and I came to call ourselves "The Three Originals."

I admit, my sister and I felt slightly displaced by all this.
We referred to these recipients of Mom's generosity as
her "basket cases." And although in later years I came to

admire and even emulate the compassion Mom taught us to have for others, there was one time when all of us agreed that Mom had carried her kindness too far. This was the day she allowed a duck to follow her home.

As she tells the story, she was out walking the dogs in the woods near our house one afternoon when a large white duck with a huge red wart-like growth on his bill "happened" upon them. Mom claims only to have shown concern for a poor, lost duck out of water. All we knew was that by the time the hiking party reached home, the duck was in love with Mom, and our household would never be the same.

The duck, whom we named Harry, had such a thing for Mom that it was embarrassing. Whenever he saw her, he'd fly over, sit on her lap and make low quacking noises or nibble at her hair. Like a faithful dog waiting for its master, he'd sit outside on the deck all day, loyally watching for her arrivals and departures.

Not that he didn't try to get inside the house. An open door to Harry meant an open invitation. Any chance he could, he'd rush in and waddle around in an agitated state, annoying cats, dogs and humans until he'd located Mom.

His peskiness aside, all that attention Harry showered on Mom would have been okay with the rest of us except for one unfortunate fact: While Harry adored my mother, he hated the rest of us.

Being a family of mostly strays ourselves, we tried to get along with him. It was pointless. Harry considered us threats and would hiss, poke and chase us at every opportunity.

Our yard became unsafe for visitors. Whenever anyone approached the house, Harry would swoop over and try to scare them off. We started referring to Harry as our "watchduck." He particularly hated flapping trousers, and would hang on to pant legs with the determination of a pit bull. He could nip, too, and many of us had red welts on our arms to prove it.

One afternoon, my father became particularly upset with Harry after he kept interfering with Dad's attempts to mow the lawn. In desperation, Dad turned an empty garbage pail on top of Harry and promptly forgot about him until the next morning, when Mom noticed him missing. "Albert, how could you?" she cried after he'd confessed. She rushed outside and pulled the garbage pail off Harry, who staggered onto the lawn, still with us, but barely.

"Honey, we've got to do something about that duck," Dad said. "He's a nuisance."

"But he's happy here," Mom answered. "He's found a home." Not long after, Harry committed his final act of treason.

My future brother-in-law, Maurice, was living with us for the summer while putting himself through college. He had a job selling vacuum cleaners door-to-door. One afternoon, Maurice returned home early and realized that he was locked out of the house.

After unsuccessfully trying all the doors, he noticed an open window on the second floor, directly above our driveway. Being a smart guy, he decided to park his car underneath the window, then stand on the roof of his car and pull himself up through the window.

Maurice was hanging by his arms from the window ledge when he heard a loud flapping noise behind him. He turned and saw Harry flying toward him with the speed of a fighter-bomber.

Maurice screamed and let go. He bounced off his car roof and onto the driveway.

The next morning, my dad drove Harry to a large pond several miles from our house and dropped him off. He told Mom that this pond had a lot of ducks and that Harry would be happy there. Mom reluctantly agreed, but not before cruising past the pond to check it out. She reported back that Harry seemed happy, even though he was by himself on the far side of the pond.

For about a month, our house returned to normal. Then one day, Mom decided to go visit Harry and see how he was doing.

When we drove up to the pond, we saw lots of ducks, but no Harry. Mom quickly jumped out of the car. "Where could he be?"

On the far side of the pond, up on a muddy section of the hill, one of my sisters noticed Harry, dirty and bedraggled. "There he is!" she pointed. Mom gasped and stretched out her arms. "Harry!" she called out.

Harry wearily lifted his head. When he saw Mom, he let out a squawk and started hobbling toward her.

"Oh, you poor thing!" Mom cried.

Harry and my mother raced into each other's arms like long-lost lovers. They kissed; they hugged; they made small talk.

After their reunion, Mom checked Harry over. "What's happened to you?" she asked. "You're so thin!"

My sister, who had been standing quietly with the rest of us, nodded wisely. "Even ducks don't like him," she observed. "They kicked him out of the pond."

"Then he's coming back with us," Mom declared. "Everyone deserves a loving home."

No one said much in the car, not even Harry. I think he was feeling apologetic.

We tried to make the best of it, and for the next few days, Harry was on his best behavior. By the end of the week, though, he was back to his old habits. Even Mom could see that we had to do something.

Within days, one of my brothers came home with exciting news. He'd just seen a pond with ducks in it that looked exactly like Harry—big, white and with ugly red growths across their bills.

We couldn't believe it. All this time we'd thought Harry was an original. Would he be happy among his own kind?

Trying not to expect too much, we loaded Harry into the car (he sat on Mom's lap) and drove him to the new pond. Mom gently carried him over to the area where the other ducks were nibbling on weeds and paddling around. She launched him into the water. Right away, Harry began clucking and chatting and making friends.

We left him there. On the way home, we couldn't stop talking about how easily the other ducks had accepted Harry. Was it because he looked like them? Probably. But that still didn't explain Harry's affection for Mom.

We guessed that Harry had once lived with these ducks but had somehow become separated from them. Then Mom had discovered him wandering in the woods, lost and alone. No wonder he fell in love with her. She had rescued him.

On our next visit, Harry had a new girlfriend. This one had feathers and a red, warty face. Harry hardly gave Mom a second glance. I don't think she minded, though. There were plenty more souls in the world to rescue. Besides, as Mom had said, Harry deserved a loving home. To everyone's relief, he'd finally found one.

Page McBrier

4

ON ATTITUDE AND PERSPECTIVE

Attitudes are self-created. You are free to choose to be victimized by circumstance or people, or you can choose to look at life with an open mind and be victorious. No one else can choose your attitude for you. Your perspective and choice of attitude gives you the power to be in control.
That is the essence of true freedom.

Irene Dunlap

The Bobsledder's Jacket

For as long as he could remember, Jack had dreamed of being in the Olympics. For years he'd worked hard to become a good bobsledder, training and practicing, always getting better. Now he and his partners were in Sapporo, Japan, for the Winter Olympics—as the American bobsled team!

They were on their way to the opening parade. Athletes from all over the world were gathering to march into the Olympic stadium. Jack and his partners were laughing and joking, and their hearts were beating with joy. Everything was perfect—well, almost everything. The sleeve of Jack's Olympic jacket had been torn. He loved the red, white and blue jacket, with "USA" on the front and the Olympic rings on the back, but earlier that day he'd torn it climbing a fence.

"Too bad about your jacket," his friend Bill told him.

"Oh well," Jack said. "I don't think anyone will notice."

"They'll notice it," said Bill. "Japanese people notice things like that. They'll probably laugh at us."

Jack didn't answer. Bill's father had been killed by Japanese soldiers in the island battles of World War II. Jack knew Bill felt uneasy about being in Japan.

Suddenly a little Japanese girl came up to Jack and pointed right at the tear in his sleeve. Jack smiled at her, not knowing what to do. So he said, "Uh . . . *Ohayo* . . . Good morning!" The little girl said *ohayo* back to him—and a lot more. She kept speaking words that he couldn't understand and was pointing to his torn sleeve. Jack looked at his friends and shrugged. "I don't know what she wants," he said.

The little girl began to tug at his jacket. Her eyes were very bright and her straight black hair fell over the back of her winter coat.

"What are you doing?" Jack asked, but he knew she couldn't understand him. Suddenly she started taking off her own coat. Then she looked up at him.

"She wants you to take off your jacket!" Bill said.

"Oh—I get it," said Jack. "She wants to try it on. Sure, kid—here you go." He slipped off the jacket and handed it to the girl. She took it and bowed. He bowed too. But when he raised his head again, she was running off with his jacket! "Hey!" he cried.

"The little thief!" Bill shouted. "She's stealing it!" Jack ran a few steps after her, but in an instant she'd disappeared along the crowded street.

"I'm telling you, Jack—you can't trust these people!" Bill said in a loud voice, his eyes blazing.

"Be quiet, Bill! Some of them may speak English!" one of the other bobsledders said. Bill said nothing, but his face was still red with anger. "So now what do I do?" Jack asked. "I need my jacket for the parade."

"Don't hold your breath, Jack," another bobsledder said. "You'll just have to go as you are."

Twenty minutes later, they were standing with the other American athletes, waiting to start. Bill stood next to Jack. He could sense that Jack was worried. "It's okay, buddy," he said. "You're with us—everyone can see that. I just wish I could get my hands on that kid."

Suddenly Jack felt a tugging, this time on his shirt sleeve. He looked down. It was the Japanese girl. "You!" Jack burst out, and he put his hands on her shoulders so she couldn't run off. But she only smiled at him. In her hands was his jacket. She held it up to him. Jack took it— and then he understood. The long rip in the sleeve was gone. It had been sewn so perfectly that he couldn't even see the thread. He had to hold it up close to see the stitches. Bill was looking at the little girl with his mouth open. She smiled at him, and at Jack, and bowed again.

"Bill!" Jack said. "She didn't steal it! She took it to be *fixed!*"

"She must have run to her mother or someone—and they fixed it just like that!" said another bobsledder. "Holy cow, Jack—they didn't want you to be embarrassed in the parade!"

The music began and the parade started. Along the streets of Sapporo, thousands of athletes marched together, proudly wearing the colors of their countries. Moving with the same rhythm and the same joy, each was determined to be the best that he or she could be.

There was an extra marcher in the parade on that proud day. A Japanese girl who spoke no English rode for a while on the shoulders of an American bobsledder named Jack—and then on the shoulders of another named Bill.

Tim Myers

Things Are Not Always Black or White

Teachers are those who use themselves as bridges,
Over which they invite their students to cross;
Then having facilitated their crossing, joyfully collapse,
Encouraging them to create bridges of their own.

Nikos Kazantzakis

When I was in elementary school, I got into a major argument with a boy in my class. I have forgotten what the argument was about, but I have never forgotten the lesson I learned that day.

I was convinced that *I* was right and *he* was wrong—and he was just as convinced that *I* was wrong and *he* was right. The teacher decided to teach us a very important lesson. She brought us up to the front of the class and placed him on one side of her desk and me on the other. In the middle of her desk was a large, round object. I could clearly see that it was black. She asked the boy what color the object was. "White," he answered.

I couldn't believe he said the object was white, when it was obviously black! Another argument started between my classmate and me, this time about the color of the object.

The teacher told me to go stand where the boy was standing and told him to come stand where I had been. We changed places, and now she asked me what the color of the object was. I had to answer, "White." It was an object with two differently colored sides, and from his viewpoint it was white. Only from my side was it black.

My teacher taught me a very important lesson that day: You must stand in the other person's shoes and look at the situation through their eyes in order to truly understand their perspective.

Judie Paxton

What's Wrong with a B+?

Reality isn't the way you wish things to be, nor the way they appear to be, but the way they actually are.

Robert J. Ringer

It seemed to take forever, but I finally turned thirteen last Saturday. I felt warm and happy inside, and would have spent the day with my friends, but alternating sleet and rain kept me at home. I decided to hang around my room and junk a bunch of kid stuff. By midafternoon, three bulging garbage bags leaned against my door. As I grabbed the first bag and began dragging it down the stairs, a snapshot fell to the floor. The face staring up at me was Jane's. We had been friends in the fourth grade and probably would have been friends forever if her father hadn't been transferred to Japan. He was vice president of some big hotel chain.

Jane Farmer was the smartest girl I'd ever known. She almost always got straight A's, and she was pretty, too. Part of me wanted to hate her, but I couldn't. She was too nice. Instead, I envied her and longed with all my heart to be just like her.

Her hair was the color of honey. She had a zillion corkscrew curls, usually held back by a satin headband that matched our school uniform. When she walked, the curls bounced up and down and reminded me of my pogo stick. My hair was straight, wispy and braided every morning into pigtails.

She was a little plump, but that didn't matter. Like the other popular girls, Jane was short. That's what really mattered since most of the boys in our class were also short. I was tall and skinny. Even Jane's freckles were the cute kind, and the dimples on either side of her mouth made her look like she was always smiling.

My grandfather often called me "funny face" to get me to smile. He wasn't being mean. He just didn't understand that my face was the serious sort. My mother didn't understand either. "Stand in front of your bedroom mirror, Donna," she'd say. "Practice for five or ten minutes each day, and before long, you'll have a lovely smile, too." I tried it a few times, but I felt dumb, and it didn't work anyway.

Jane was an honor student and got to sit in the front of the class. My desk was in the back, on the side of the room that had no windows. I'd watch Mrs. Schnell, our teacher, pace back and forth in front of us. She was short and stout with wiry red hair and a smile she turned on and off like a water faucet.

I always slumped way down in my desk, desperately hoping to hide myself behind Stanley, the kid who sat in front of me. It was difficult. Stanley was a head shorter than I was, and he often also scrunched down, trying to hide from Mrs. Schnell. There I would wait, terrified that the next name I heard would be my own. Sometimes my heart thumped so loudly that I was sure her ears would find me even if her mean eyes didn't.

Day after day, she strutted up and down the aisles, her right hand clutching a sheet of paper that listed every one of us alphabetically. She pretended to study it for a moment, and then her eagle eyes, searching out their prey, would dart from kid to kid. "Who shall it be this time?" she'd crow.

Each time she called out a name, the victim would have to rise, stand straight as a broomstick, shoulders squared, and with a book resting across open palms, read to the entire class. Sometimes the person was lucky and only had to read a few sentences or a short paragraph. Other times, it would be a page or two. Once in a while, a whole chapter would be read before she called out the next name.

More than anything, I hated to stand and read aloud to the class, a feat so easily accomplished by Jane. Unlike me, she never slurred her words or stuttered, and she rarely made a mistake. And if she did, she was never made to feel ashamed. Mrs. Schnell would flash a pleasant smile and patiently guide her toward the correct answer. I wasn't good at reading and could tell that Mrs. Schnell was often not at all pleased with me. If only she had treated me the way she treated Jane, I would have done much better. But she was always correcting me too soon, never giving me a chance to say the words.

One day after soccer practice, Jane and I were standing together waiting for our mothers. All of the other kids' parents had come for them and taken them home. Jane leaned against one of the stone columns that supported the wrought-iron gate at the front of the school. I leaned against the other and watched Jane read a textbook. We weren't friends yet. I wanted to ask her if she liked movies and if her parents ever let her go to weekend matinees, but I changed my mind when I looked at her face. I just stared at her instead. She seemed to feel my eyes.

"What are you looking at?" she asked. Her voice was soft and kind, not what I expected.

"You," I said, unable to stop staring.

"Why?" she asked.

"Because you look so sad," I said. *It's rude to stare.* My mother's words played over and over in my head.

"I got a B+ on the history test," she said, sounding like she had committed some awful crime.

"That's why you're sad?" I asked. It didn't make sense to me. *What's wrong with a B+?* I wondered. Before I knew it, I was talking so fast I couldn't stop myself.

"Gosh, Jane, a B+ isn't exactly the end of the world, you know. I'd love to get your grades, read and spell like you, have the teachers like me for a change—and you're worried about a B+? You must be nuts! What'll happen to you anyway?"

She looked at me for a moment, maybe deciding if she should trust me. Then she leaned over and whispered in my ear as if we were best friends sharing a secret.

"Promise me you won't tell anyone. Promise."

The fact that Jane wanted to share her secret with me made me feel good, important like the popular girls she hung around with. But it surprised me, too. She grabbed my arm when I didn't answer her right away, and I felt her fingernails dig into my skin.

"Promise me," she demanded. I nodded, and she released my arm.

"My dad uses a leather strap on me," she said, her voice so low that I could hardly hear her. Tears had welled up in her eyes, but she kept talking. "Straight A's are all he wants to see. I have to get straight A's."

I was sure I had misunderstood what she said. "You mean he takes off his belt and hits you with it? He hits you because you get a B+ and not an A?"

"Yes," she cried, hanging her head as if she were ashamed to show her face. "He will tonight, just as soon as he gets home from work."

"He hits you?" I asked again, not wanting to believe her, not wanting to believe a dad would do such a thing or be so cruel.

"Yes. He says there's no excuse for poor grades. He always got straight A's in school, and since I'm his daughter, I must do the same."

She lifted her head and looked at me, but I knew she wasn't seeing me.

"It's expected," she said, in a tone that was as flat and cold as the stone floor in our basement.

"What about your mother?" I asked.

"Oh, she leaves the room. But she comes back later, after he's gone. She hugs me and tells me how much Daddy loves me, how he's only doing it for my own good." Jane shrugged her shoulders as if it didn't matter. "Besides, it only hurts for a little while. You see, Donna, grades are very important. Doesn't your dad think so?"

"My dad is always saying that my brother and I must have a good education. When we get home from school, we're not allowed to play outdoors or have friends over until all of our homework is done. He's pretty strict about that, and it sure doesn't make him happy when we get bad grades. But he never hits us."

"But doesn't he punish you when you mess up?"

"Well, not really," I said, "at least, not the way your dad does."

"What do you mean?" she said.

"If you knew my dad, you'd understand. He just stands there, straight as an arrow, his gray eyes locked onto yours. Then he says your first name very slowly, in a very low, stern voice. Then he says your middle name very slowly, and in the same low, stern voice. That's all he does, and believe me, my brother and I know he means business."

"And then what?" Jane asked. She seemed to shiver, and I saw fear in her eyes. I knew she expected to hear a truly horrid thing, some sort of gruesome punishment far worse than being beaten with a leather strap.

"And then what?" she repeated, impatient for my answer.

"We fix the problem real fast," I said. "We work harder the next time and do a better job."

Just then, we saw Jane's mother coming up the circular drive in a big, white, shiny car.

"That's my mom. Gotta go now. Bye, Donna," she said and dashed to the car. She opened the door, then suddenly looked back at me and whispered, "Remember, Donna, you promised."

I nodded and watched her climb into the passengers side of the front seat.

"Bye, Jane." Their car cruised around the drive, then sped away down the long, narrow, tree-lined street. I watched Jane's big car get smaller and smaller until it disappeared around the corner at the end of the lane.

Jane and I became best friends after the day she shared her secret with me, but from then on I never again envied Jane Farmer.

Donna M. Russell

Just Ben

*Children: much more than just little people.
Young kids are definitely special people. There
are no other people like them in the world.*

Adrian Wagner

It was late August and quite chilly outside. I was coaching a soccer team for kindergarteners and first-graders, and it was the day of our first practice.

It was cold enough for the kids to be bundled up in extra sweatshirts, jackets, gloves and mittens.

I sat the kids down on the dugout bench—soccer in Austin is played on the outfield grass at the softball complex. As was normally the case any time I was coaching a new team, we took the first few minutes to get to know one another. We went up and down the row a few times, each kid saying his or her name and the names of all the kids sitting to the left.

After a few minutes of this, I decided to put the kids to the ultimate test. I asked for a volunteer who thought he or she knew the names of all eleven kids on the team and could prove it to all of us right then. There was one brave six-year-old who felt up to the challenge. He was to start at the far left end of the bench, go up to each kid, say that kid's name and then shake his or her right hand.

Alex started off and was doing very well. While I stood behind him, he went down the row—Dylan, Micah, Sara, Beau and Danny—until he reached Ben, by far the smallest kid on the team. He stammered out Ben's name without much trouble and extended his right hand, but Ben would not extend his. I looked at Ben for a second, as did Alex and the rest of the kids on the bench, but he just sat there, his right hand hidden under the cuff of his jacket.

"Ben, why don't you let Alex shake your hand?" I asked. But Ben just sat there, looking first at Alex and then at me, and then at Alex once again.

"Ben, what's the matter?" I asked.

Finally Ben stood up, looked up at me and said, "But coach, I don't have a hand." He unzipped his jacket, pulling it away from his right shoulder.

Sure enough, Ben's arm ran from his right shoulder just like every other kid on the team, but unlike the rest of his teammates, his arm stopped at the elbow. No fingers, no hand, no forearm.

I'll have to admit, I was taken aback a bit and couldn't think of anything to say or how to react, but thank God for little kids—and their unwillingness to be tactful.

"Look at that," said Alex.

"Hey, what happened to your arm?" another asked.

"Does it hurt?"

Before I knew it, a crowd of ten players and a bewildered coach encircled a small child who was now taking off his jacket to show all those around him what they all wanted to see.

In the next few minutes, a calm and collected six-year-old explained to all of those present that he had always been that way and that there was nothing special about him because of it. What he meant was that he wanted to be treated like everybody else.

And he was from that day on.

From that day on, he was never the kid with one arm. He was just Ben, one of the players on the team.

Adrian Wagner
Submitted by Judy Noble

The Green Boots

Don't compromise yourself. You are all you've got.

Janis Joplin

On Monday morning I wore my green platform boots to school for the first time since I had started at Edison Middle School.

It was the day of the poetry festival, and I was excited. At my old school, I had won the poetry ribbon every year. I'm horrible at sports, too shy to be popular and I'm not cute—but I do write good poetry.

The poem I wrote for the Edison Festival was about my dad. I had a good feeling about sharing how special he was to me, even if it was just with the fifth grade and Mrs. Baker.

English class was not until after lunch period on Mondays, so by the time we started poetry, I was so nervous my mouth was dry as toast. When Mrs. Baker called on me, I had to clear my throat, take a breath and swallow about ten times before I could speak. I didn't even bother to look at my paper. I'd spent so much time perfecting the rhymes, and counting the beats, that I knew the poem by heart.

I had just started the third verse when I noticed Mrs. Baker was glaring furiously at me. I stopped in the middle of a word and waited for her to say something.

"Linda, you are supposed to be reading an original work, a poem you made up yourself, not reciting something you learned. That is called plagiarism!"

"Oh, but it's not. I mean . . . I did make it up; it's about my dad." I heard a "Yeah, right!" from somewhere behind me, and someone else giggled.

I felt as if I'd somersaulted off the high dive and then, in midair, realized that there was no water in the pool. I opened my mouth to explain, but no words came out.

"You will leave the room and will not return until you are ready to apologize," said Mrs. Baker. "Now. Go!"

My last thought was a flash of understanding as to why the kids had nicknamed her "Battle-Ax Baker"—then my brain just fizzled out, and I turned and left the room.

I'd been standing outside for about half an hour when Joseph, the school janitor, came over to ask me what heinous crime I'd committed to be banished for so long. He loved using unusual words.

We'd made friends one morning before school, when he saw me sitting alone, pretending to do homework. He invited me to help open up the classrooms, and after that, it sort of became my job. He always talked to me as we wiped down the chalkboards and turned on the heat. Just that morning he'd been telling me that Mark Twain once said that the difference between the right word and the almost right word is like the difference between lightning and a lightning bug. I liked that. My dad would have liked it, too.

Now as Joseph waited for me to answer, he looked so kind and sympathetic that I poured out the whole story, trying not to cry. A tightness flashed over his face, and he jerked an enormous yellow duster out of the pocket of his gray overalls. "So what are you going to do?" he asked, rolling up the duster into a tight ball.

I shrugged, feeling helpless and sad. "I don't know."

"Well, you are not going to stand here all day, are you?"

I sighed. "I suppose I'll do what she said. You know . . . say I'm sorry."

"You'll apologize?"

I nodded. "What else can I do? It's no big deal. I'll just never write anything good in her class again."

He looked disappointed with my response, so I shrugged once more and turned away from him.

"Linda." The tone of his voice forced me to look back. "Accepting defeat, when you should stand up for yourself, can become a very dangerous habit." He twisted the duster around his fingers. "Believe me. I know!"

He was staring right into my eyes. I blinked and looked down. His eyes followed mine, and we both noticed my green boots at the same time. Suddenly his face relaxed and creased into a huge smile. He chuckled and said, "You're going to be just fine. I don't have to worry about you. When you put on those boots this morning, you knew you were the only Linda Brown in the whole world." As if he didn't need it anymore, he cheerfully dropped the duster back into his pocket and folded his arms across his chest. "Those are the boots of someone who can take care of herself and knows when something is worth fighting for."

His eyes, smiling into mine, woke up a part of me that had been asleep since I'd come to this school, and I knew that he was right about me. I'd just lost direction for a while. I took a deep breath and knocked on the classroom door, ready to face Mrs. Baker—ready to recite *my* poem.

Linda Rosenberg

Showing Up

Any guy who can maintain a positive attitude without much playing time certainly earns my respect.

Earvin "Magic" Johnson

My son's first season of playing basketball was when he was ten years old. Often, when I picked him up from his father's house, he was shooting hoops. On one such day, he came running over to my car and said, "Mom, can I *pleeease* get another basketball?"

"Why do you need two basketballs, Tyler?" I asked.

"Because then I could have a basketball at my mom's house and at my dad's house," he replied.

I thought that was a fine idea, especially since all Tyler could talk about was basketball. Sometimes he'd ask me to take him to the gym an hour before practice began. He enjoyed meeting his new teammates and thought the basketball drills were fun. I often had to convince him to leave the gym after practice was over. He usually wanted to hang around and shoot baskets.

Tyler and I have always had our most special talks

when I go into his room to say good night. One night, he expressed some concern over his basketball shoes. He told me that maybe he needed better ones. I closed my eyes tightly, wishing that his last sentence would just go away. Being a single mom, the topic of new shoes was always difficult for me. I looked over at his "broken-in" shoes sitting next to his perfectly folded uniform. They looked just fine to me. I quickly changed the subject.

Finally, the first game of the season arrived. The gym was surprisingly crowded. Tyler's team, the Hornets, was playing the Magic. I saw the happy look in my son's eyes when he saw his dad sitting in the stands a few yards down from me.

There was a look of determination on Tyler's face as he joined his teammates. As I watched the other kids running up and down the court, I saw my son sitting on the bench. By the fourth quarter, Tyler hadn't even touched the ball, and his team had won the game.

The games that followed were pretty much the same. The team kept winning, but Tyler barely touched the ball. He ran so hard when he was on the court, but when he got the ball, he would quickly throw it to a teammate. I would sit there with my heart pounding out of my chest.

On the way home from one of his games, I asked, "Tyler, do you still enjoy basketball?"

He replied, "I like basketball a lot. But I know that some of the kids play better than me, so when I get the ball, I just throw it to them."

The next day, I ran into an old friend of mine who used to play basketball when we were younger. I shared with him how I thought that Tyler played somewhat cautiously.

"Does he have good shoes?" he asked. I remembered how earlier in the season, Tyler had mentioned that he thought he needed better shoes. My friend must have noticed the look on my face as I thought about Tyler's worn-out shoes. Before I knew it, we were shoe shopping. He insisted on buying Tyler a pair of beautiful, high-quality basketball shoes. It was the kind of gesture that inspires deep gratitude for any single mom, especially the mother of a son.

As I put Tyler to bed, he told me that he had wanted new basketball shoes for a long time. He loved them. They were awesome. He hoped that his new shoes would help him with his game.

Weeks of Tyler's unending enthusiasm and devotion to basketball flew by. Once more, Tyler told me that he knew he wasn't the best player on his team but that it was okay because he liked basketball so much. He played hard and kept practicing. I watched him improve. He never became discouraged. He said that he felt more comfortable in his new shoes and once more thanked me for them. He gave me detailed descriptions of new plays he had thought of. He told me how he was proud to be on such a good team. So far, they were undefeated.

The team made it to the play-offs. In front of a standing-room-only crowd, Tyler scored eight points at the end of a very close and exciting game.

The season came to a close, and the time for the awards ceremony was coming up. Tyler was guessing which kids would be getting awards for Most Valuable Player, Best Defense, Most Improved and Best All-Around Player. Tyler's team had come in second place, and each player received a trophy. Toward the end of the ceremony, the director got up and thanked everybody. Then he said, "We aren't finished yet. We have one last, special award for a very special player. He shows up for every game with a positive attitude. He has never argued with a referee or another player, never been late and never missed a practice or a game. He knows his place while playing, and his teammates speak highly of him. He plays because he obviously loves the game, and he always runs hard and tries his best. The Sportsmanship Award goes to Tyler Marsden!"

Suddenly, all the attention was on Tyler. His teammates and friends were giving him high-fives and slaps on the back. I felt tears welling up in my eyes. I looked a few yards down into the stands and saw his father with the same tears in his eyes. We actually smiled at one another.

The other kids were still congratulating him when Tyler walked over and picked up his second trophy. I overheard other parents saying, "He got the most impressive award of the evening."

Tyler proudly said, "Now I have a trophy for my mom's house *and* a trophy for my dad's house!"

Julie J. Vaughn
with Tyler Vaughn Marsden

The Pest

Ellen was a pest. When we met in kindergarten, she hogged all the clay. When we were seniors in high school, she made fun of the art college I was planning to attend. During the years in between, we each grew up in our own way. She was loud and made sarcastic remarks. I remained skinny and shy, with a reputation as the artist of the class. Every other year or so, there she was in my class again— loud, insulting and so unpopular. I wasn't popular either, but I always had a little circle of friends to keep me safe.

So our two paths muddled along throughout school, occasionally crossing for short, always irritating, episodes. When I discovered her in my seventh-grade gym class, I knew I was in for a really bad year. I was always the light-weight in gym class, the girl who was trampled on during a hockey game or beaned with a basketball. Ellen, on the other hand, was the one who did the trampling. Clearly, we were on a collision course this time.

I managed to survive the field hockey unit by employing my dodging skills. I wasn't much at scoring goals, but boy, could I dodge! I was relieved when our teacher announced that the next unit of study would be gymnastics. That was one of the few things I was fairly good at, and it was definitely not a contact sport.

On the first day of gymnastics, we chose partners to work with on a floor routine. My best friend, Chris, and I were of similar size and strength, and we made a good team. Together we practiced balancing over each other on the mats, doing Chinese sit-ups and spotting each other for handstands. Ellen never really had a partner. She would be paired off with whoever was left over that day. She was so clumsy and rough that her unfortunate partners often wound up with bumps and bruises. Luckily, Chris and I never missed a class, and so were spared the terror of working with her.

After three weeks of practicing, it was time to perform for the teacher and receive our grades. When our turn came, Chris and I went through the routine. We were well rehearsed and even received a smattering of applause along with our A's. As we returned to our friends along the mats, we laughed with relief that it was over.

When it was time for Ellen to stand up, we all wondered who her partner would be. She'd never practiced the routine with anyone more than once. To my horror, I heard her give the teacher my name. I had never been paired with her at all, so why me?

I stood up, outraged, with my friends murmuring their disapproval. The popular girls were giggling among themselves. This was a good chance for them to have their revenge on me for being a better artist than they were. I wondered if I should challenge Ellen's right to pick me, since we'd never practiced together. But when I looked into her eyes, I could see that she was thinking the same thing and praying that I wouldn't humiliate her.

I walked to the center of the mat, anxious to get the whole thing over with. I held her ankles for the sit-ups and got a foot in my chin when she did her handstand.

But we got through the mat work all right, and the fact that she was fifty pounds heavier than I was didn't seem to matter much. When it came time for the horizontal balance though, I felt a shiver of fear and rebellion. How could I ever support her weight over me with just my outstretched arms and legs?

As I flopped onto my back on the mat, I heard the other girls giggling and whispering together. If Ellen collapsed onto me, it would be the end of my self-respect as well as the end of all my internal organs. I rested my feet against her hipbones and reached out to grasp her hands. As her fingers interlaced with mine, I was struck by how small they were. They were short and soft, like a baby's. My hands were always rough from scrubbing paint and ink off them. Slowly straightening my legs, I shifted her weight over me as she raised her own legs out behind her. Her fingers clutched mine, and I was looking directly into her frightened eyes.

Is she worried about crushing me to lifeless jelly, I wondered, *or is she just worried about her grade?*

We held our position for the required length of time, our eyes locked in mutual fear, our fingers grasping until they turned white at the tips. I was surprised to feel that, as long as we held that delicate balance, I was able to support her weight fairly easily. When I slowly lowered her back to her feet, there was no sound of applause. But I could hear a general murmur of amazement that we had actually done it. The teacher said "Good!" in a voice that betrayed her own surprise. Ellen glanced at me, and I could see that the fear in her eyes had turned to relief and pride. *Did I do that?* I wondered, returning to my place.

"How did you do it?" my friend Barbara whispered as I sat down.

"*Why* did you do it?" Chris asked, as some of the other girls continued to snicker.

"I don't know," I replied, and it was the truth. But it was beginning to dawn on me that when someone reaches out with small hands and frightened eyes, the only possible answer is "Yes, I'm here." That day with Ellen the Pest seemed to help me grasp other hands when they needed me. I learned that, together, people of all sorts can find that safe little point of balance, if they just have faith in each other.

Several weeks after Ellen earned her first B in gymnastics, she was absent from school for a few days. I heard that her father had just died after a long illness. Although I wasn't there to see it, I knew how tightly her fingers had interlocked with her mother's on the day he was buried.

Judy Fuerst

A *Good* Reason to Look Up

Much is required from those to whom much is given, for their responsibility is greater.

Luke 12:48

When I was in junior high school, what my friends thought of me was real important to me. During those years I grew much taller than most of my peers. Being so tall made me feel uncomfortable. In order to keep the focus off of me and my unusual height, I went along with the crowd who would play practical jokes on other kids at school. Being one of the class clowns gave me a way to make sure that the jokes were directed at others, and not at me.

I would pull all kinds of pranks that were hurtful, and sometimes even harmful, to others. Once before gym class, my friends and I put Icy Hot in the gym shorts of one of the kids on the basketball team. Not only was he terribly embarrassed, but he also had to go to the school nurse's office. I thought it was going to be funny, but it ended up that no one thought it was—least of all my father.

My parents didn't always think that my behavior was funny. They reminded me about The Golden Rule: to treat others as I would like to be treated. Many times, I was disciplined for the hurtful way that I was treating others. What I was doing was hurting other kids, and in turn hurting my reputation as someone to be looked up to. My friends were looking up to me because I was tall, but what did they see?

My parents wanted me to be a leader who was a good example to others—to be a decent human being. They taught me to set my own goals, and to do the best at everything that I set out to do. During the lectures I got from my father, he told me over and over again to be the leader that I was meant to be—to be a big man in my heart and actions, as well as in my body. I had to question myself whether or not it was important to be the kind of leader and person my father believed I was inside. I knew in my heart that he was right. So I tried my best to follow my father's advice.

Once I focused on being the best that I could be at basketball and became a leader in the game, I took my responsibility to set a good example more seriously. I sometimes have to stop and think before I act, and I make mistakes occasionally—everyone is human. But I continue to look for opportunities where I can make a difference, and to set a good example because of my father's advice. I now pass it on to you.

"Be a leader, Shaq, not a follower. Since people already have to look up to you, give them a *good* reason to do so."

Shaquille O'Neal

Close Call

A few years ago, my mom went to the doctor to ask him about her neck. "Lately it's been a little swollen," she told him. He looked at her and then told her she needed to see a hematologist. It turned out there was something wrong with her lymph glands, and she would have to have a biopsy. Soon they had scheduled her for surgery on the seventh of September.

As soon as I found out, I was furious. September 7 is my birthday. I screamed and yelled at her and everyone else, too. I even yelled at the dog. I started begging her to reschedule. She gave me this look like she was about to cry and said, "I'm sorry, but I've done everything I can. There's nothing else I can do." Finally, I just yelled, "I hate you!" and ran into my room, crying. I sat on my bed thinking, *Why do things always have to happen to me? What did I do to deserve this?* I didn't even think about how my mom, the one who was actually going to get cut open, was feeling.

For the next couple weeks, all I did was sulk. Deep down I knew I shouldn't act that way, but I did anyway. Anyone could see how miserable I was making my mom. I knew it wasn't her fault, but I had to have someone to blame.

Finally, my birthday came. My parents left early in the morning for the hospital in Salt Lake City, and my aunt came to look after my brother and me. All day we played games, opened presents and had a picnic in the yard. Everyone pretended to have fun, but the tension in the air was as thick as peanut butter, and you could tell no one was really having a good time. *This isn't fair,* I thought. *This was supposed to be* my *day.*

My parents came home late that night. My mom walked in with a bandage on her neck. She sat down and rested her head on my dad's shoulder. It hurt so badly, she couldn't even talk. My dad had to tell us what had happened. They had left the hospital all right, but after they had driven for just half an hour, the car broke down. My mom had to sit in a cold car while my dad walked to get help.

Later that night, Mom was in her room. She pulled out a bag and handed it to me. It was my birthday present, a Walkman.

"I'm sorry it's not wrapped," she said in a quiet, raspy voice. "And we didn't have time to get batteries, but I'll get some soon."

"Thank you," I said. That was all I could say.

About a week later the doctor called. It turned out that my mother's condition was nothing serious. Everyone seemed relieved. Later my dad told me that the doctors had thought she might have cancer. I couldn't believe it. My legs turned to Jell-O, and I had to sit down. Even though I knew she was all right, when I thought of what I had said and done, I felt sick. If she had gotten cancer, nothing in our lives would have ever been the same.

Less than a year later, my dad's cousin, Nathan, was diagnosed with cancer. He had four kids and his wife was about to have another. He stayed alive just long enough to see his new baby's birth, and then he died. Now his son will never be able to see or know his dad.

It's scary to think how close I was to having the same thing happen to me and how selfish I had been. I will always regret the things I said. It is really true that you don't appreciate something until you come close to losing it.

Diana Parker, age 12

The Flood

I woke up to the crash of thunder and the pitter-patter of rain. It was 3:43 A.M. *Boom! Boom!* Thunder was crashing as loud as a stereo with the volume turned up to the limit and the speaker held up to your ear. This didn't alarm me, though, and I fell back to sleep. At 5:16 A.M., my father rushed into my room.

"Adam! Adam! Get up! We're flooding! The basement is flooding!" he shouted.

Still groggy, I tried to ignore him, but he shook me by my shoulders. That got me up! Since I didn't have time to change, I ran downstairs in my pajamas to the basement. It was a devastating sight.

The water had risen six inches already. My mother and I immediately started to pick things up off the floor and take them upstairs. I had no shoes on, and my feet were absolutely freezing.

My parents were quite upset, and they had a right to be. Within half an hour, the water was eighteen inches deep. Things would only get worse.

Within the next hour, we had moved everything that we could to the first floor. The computer, big-screen television and heavy boxes filled with our most valuable possessions were taken to safe ground. However, our piano, Ping-Pong table, sleeper sofa, laundry machine, dryer, furnace and water heater were all still down there—being destroyed.

During our final trip to the basement, we smelled a disgusting odor coming from the water near our bathroom. Our toilet downstairs looked like a geyser. Water was shooting out of the bowl at great speed. I rushed upstairs to try to call our neighbors, but the phones were dead. My mother waded over to their house, but soon returned, saying there was nothing we could do.

That was the hard part. Knowing that part of your home is being destroyed is bad enough, but realizing that you can't do anything to stop it feels even worse. Most people don't know how sickening the feeling of being totally helpless is. For the record, it's horrible.

We all went out on the front porch. The water was rising outside, too. It was about four inches away from coming through our front door. When my parents saw this, they ran back inside. My mother told me to pack an overnight bag of clothes and valuables. With a lump in my throat, I knew what was happening.

I packed my stereo, CDs, baseball cards and a change of clothing. My mother rolled up her Oriental rugs and packed her china dishes. We carried everything out and put it on higher ground. My father was frantic. He had only enough time to pack clothes. It was really bad.

By the time we were ready to leave, water had come in our front door. Rescue rafts were floating in our streets. The basement was like a swimming pool—six feet of water, we would later learn. My parents weren't crying, but they *were* praying. About half an hour later, our prayers were answered. It finally stopped pouring. We learned that the National Weather Service had declared the storm a flash flood.

When it was finally safe to walk outside, all the people in the neighborhood gathered at the street corner. The only positive thing that day was the corner gathering. Everybody bonded. Acquaintances became friends, friends became like family. People comforted each other. Everyone was saying, "We have suffered enough!" That was definitely true.

For the next month, my family had to live at our friends' houses, where we could shower, eat, do laundry and have a good time together.

I really have learned something from this flood. I've learned what devastation is. I've learned what family is. During the past few weeks, I've learned what true friends are. In the future, when I watch people's lives affected by natural disasters, I will not laugh. Instead, I will pity them. I will feel more compassion. I will relive my own sadness and remember the flood.

Adam Edelman, age 12

The Man Who Had Plenty

Remember, happiness doesn't depend on who you are or what you have; it depends solely upon what you think.

Dale Carnegie

Once there was a family that was not rich and not poor. They lived in Ohio in a small country house. One night they all sat down for dinner, and there was a knock at the door. The father went to the door and opened it.

There stood an old man in tattered clothes, with ripped pants and missing buttons. He was carrying a basket full of vegetables. He asked the family if they wanted to buy some vegetables from him. They quickly did because they wanted him to leave.

Over time, the family and the old man became friends. The man brought vegetables to the family every week. They soon found out that he was almost blind and had cataracts on his eyes. But he was so friendly that they learned to look forward to his visits and started to enjoy his company.

One day as he was delivering the vegetables, he said, "I

had the greatest blessing yesterday! I found a basket of clothes outside my house that someone had left for me."

The family, knowing that he needed clothes, said, "How wonderful!"

The old blind man said, "The most wonderful part is that I found a family that really needed the clothes."

Reverend Mark Tidd
As told by Jerry Ullman

The Perfect Dog

During summer vacations, I would volunteer at the vet's, so I'd seen a lot of dogs. Minnie was by far the funniest-looking dog I'd ever seen. Thin curly hair barely covered her sausage-shaped body. Her bugged-out eyes always seemed surprised. And her tail looked like a rat's tail.

She was brought to the vet to be put to sleep because her owners didn't want her anymore. I thought Minnie had a sweet personality, though. *No one should judge her by her looks,* I thought. So the vet spayed her and gave her the necessary shots. Finally, I advertised Minnie in the local paper: "Funny-looking dog, well behaved, needs loving family."

When a young man called, I warned him that Minnie was strange looking. The boy on the phone told me that his grandfather's sixteen-year-old dog had just died. They wanted Minnie no matter what. I gave Minnie a good bath and fluffed up what was left of her scraggly hair. Then we waited for them to arrive.

At last, an old car drove up in front of the vet's. Two kids raced to the door. They scooped Minnie into their arms and rushed her out to their grandfather, who was waiting in the car. I hurried behind them to see his reaction to Minnie.

Inside the car, the grandfather cradled Minnie in his arms and stroked her soft hair. She licked his face. Her rat-tail wagged around so quickly that it looked like it might fly off her body. It was love at first lick.

"She's perfect!" the old man exclaimed.

I was thankful that Minnie had found the good home that she deserved.

That's when I saw that the grandfather's eyes were a milky white color—he was blind.

Jan Peck

The little woman who lived in a
plain old sneaker.

To Be Enormously Gorgeous

My dad says I am ENORMOUSLY GORGEOUS. I wonder if I really am.

To be ENORMOUSLY GORGEOUS . . . Sarah says you need to have beautiful long, curly hair like she has. I don't.

To be ENORMOUSLY GORGEOUS . . . Justin says you must have perfectly straight white teeth like he has. I don't.

To be ENORMOUSLY GORGEOUS . . . Jessica says you can't have any of those little brown dots on your face called freckles. I do.

To be ENORMOUSLY GORGEOUS . . . Mark says you have to be the smartest kid in the seventh-grade class. I'm not.

To be ENORMOUSLY GORGEOUS . . . Stephen says you have to be able to tell the funniest jokes in the school. I don't.

To be ENORMOUSLY GORGEOUS . . . Lauren says you need to live in the nicest neighborhood in town and in the prettiest house. I don't.

To be ENORMOUSLY GORGEOUS . . . Matthew says you can only wear the coolest clothes and the most popular shoes. I don't.

To be ENORMOUSLY GORGEOUS . . . Samantha says you need to come from a perfect family. I don't.

But every night at bedtime my dad gives me a big hug and says, "You are ENORMOUSLY GORGEOUS, and I love you."

My dad must know something my friends don't.

Carla O'Brien

5

ON DEATH
AND DYING

Death.
What a great teacher you are.
Yet few of us elect to learn from you,
About life.
That is the essence of death's teaching,
Life.
Death is not an elective.
One day we all will take the class.
The wise students audit the class in early years
And find enlightenment.
They are prepared when graduation day comes.

Bernie S. Siegel, M.D.

The Purple Belt

A few years ago, I organized the Kick Drugs Out of America Foundation. It is an organization designed to work with high-risk, inner-city children. The idea is to teach the kids martial arts, to help raise their self-esteem and instill discipline and respect for themselves and others. Many of the kids, boys as well as girls, come from broken homes and are having trouble in school and in their lives in general. I'm pleased to say that the program has been working phenomenally well. Most young people quickly adapt to the philosophy of the martial arts.

After more than thirty-five years in the martial arts, competing and training thousands of young people, there is one story that is engraved in my memory. It was told to me by Alice McCleary, one of my Kick Drugs Out of America Black Belt instructors.

One of her young students showed up for karate training without his purple belt. Alice reminded him that part of his responsibility as a student was to have his karate uniform and belt with him at all times.

"Where is your belt?" she asked.

The boy looked at the floor and said he didn't have it.

"Where is it?" Alice repeated. After pressing the boy to answer, he quietly lifted his head and looked at her and replied, "My baby sister died and I put it in her coffin to take to heaven with her."

Alice had tears in her eyes as she told me the story. "That belt was probably his most important possession," she said.

The boy had learned to give his best, unselfishly.

Chuck Norris

B. J.

You don't get to choose how you're going to die. Or when. You can decide how you're going to live now.

Joan Baez

"Phhhhh." The whistle blew, and everybody started tackling each other. It was football practice, on a cool August evening.

Bam! I hit somebody. I looked down into the face of one of my best friends, B. J.

"You were just lucky that time, Nate," he teased.

"Yeah, right! It's just that I'm good at football," I joked back.

I had met my friend B. J. when we ended up on the same football team in sixth grade. Although everyone on our team liked B. J., he grew to be someone special to me. When we had to pick partners for things like tackling, it would always be B. J. and me. He was funny and fun— everything was always "Cool!" to him.

B. J. got back up and tackled me. We laughed, and then we heard our coach calling us.

"Come here, guys." We all went over to him. "At our game tomorrow, I want you to play as hard as you can."

"Okay," we said in unison.

"That's it for tonight. Don't forget to finish your homework," our coach hollered as we left the field.

"See you at the game tomorrow," I screamed to B. J. He was going to his church youth group meeting. B. J. walked away with his dad, who was our assistant coach, as my mom pulled into the parking lot.

"Mom, after the game tomorrow, can B. J. come over?" I asked, hopping into the front seat.

"I don't know. We'll see," she replied.

The next day, I went to the game, pads on, ready to go. We reviewed the plays that we had learned the night before. Then we stretched out. B. J. was late, and I was starting to wonder where he was. It was always easy to spot him right away because he was taller than anyone else on the team. I said to myself, *B. J. would never miss a game*. That was when I realized his dad wasn't there either. He had never missed a game since he had started coaching us.

Something is wrong, I thought. Our coach called us over. Now I was really wondering what was going on.

"Guys, we need to win this game today." Then he stopped talking. Everything was silent. "I've got some bad news. B. J. had an accident last night," he told us.

I shut my eyes and started to cry to myself. I knew it was going to be really bad. My coach kept on talking.

"He was on his way back from his church youth group with a bunch of other kids. B. J. was swinging a nylon rope outside the car window when the rope got caught on the wheel axle. The rope jerked out of his hands, and he must have stuck his head outside the window to see what had happened. The rope whipped up and wrapped around his neck. It strangled him to death. And after the . . . " My coach's voice started to drift off. I couldn't even concentrate on what he was saying anymore. All I could think about was how I had just seen him last night.

All the kids on our team were standing with their helmets in their hands, crying. "Let's win this game for B. J.," my coach shouted.

Through the whole game, I kept thinking about B. J. and looking into the sky. I wondered if he could see us playing our hearts out for him. We played our best game ever, and we won.

At our next practice, we took the blue stripe off our helmets and replaced it with a black stripe. We all put the number eighty, B. J.'s jersey number, on the backs of our helmets.

B. J.'s father came back to help coach our games again. He would have his hat on crooked, like he just didn't care anymore. I felt really sad for him—he never looked happy and I never saw him smile again, even when we won. I know it was extra terrible for both B. J.'s mom and dad because he was their only child.

We wore our helmets with B. J.'s number to our next four games. We won every single game, and we played them for him. We made it to the championships, and there we tied for first place.

I know we couldn't have done it without B. J. I feel as if he was with us. Sometimes I would look around, expecting at any moment to see him—in his favorite red T-shirt, with that blond buzzed hair sticking up every which way, his face with that great smile on it.

Although B. J.'s death hasn't made me stop doing the things that I love, like football, in-line skating and snow skiing, I'm not the daredevil I used to be. I stop and think about what I am doing before I do it—not only about the fun I will have, but also about the dangers that could be involved. I used to stick my hand out the car window when my dad or mom was driving, to catch leaves or something. Now I don't.

I couldn't go to B. J.'s funeral. It was too hard for me. All of us took it really hard, but I just couldn't stop thinking about him. I really miss him.

Nate Barker, age 12

The Perfect Angel

When someone dies, they still live on in you and me, and everyone else who loved them.

Jessica Ann Farley, age 10

When I was seven years old, I met a new little girl who had just moved to my street. Kiki was a year older than I was. She had a brother, Sam, who needed to go to a special school, which is why her family had moved to Boston.

It was the summertime when we met, and the weather was very hot. Kiki and her mother came over to my house to get to know their new neighbors. Once Kiki and I saw each other, we knew that we would become great friends. That day, Kiki and I played outside and laughed together every minute. As the years progressed, Kiki and I became better and closer friends.

There is one day that I will never forget. I was in the fourth grade when this happened. I had noticed that Kiki had been getting a lot of really big bruises everywhere. I will not forget that night when the telephone rang and it was Kiki's mother. When my mother got off the phone, she looked really upset. My mother and father called me into the dining room. My mother said, "Stacie, Kiki has a bad kind of cancer called leukemia."

The first words I said were, "Is she going to die, Mom?" My mom said, "I don't know, Stacie."

At that moment, I knew that she meant "yes" in a nicer way. I ran up to my room and started crying and crying until I fell asleep.

The next day, I didn't get to see Kiki at all. When a few days went by, I got a call from Kiki telling me that she was in the hospital. She told me that she had to go in for a bone marrow test with her brother, Sam. If this test matched, she would have a good chance of surviving. Sadly, there was no match.

Because we felt so helpless with the situation, my two sisters and I decided to do something to try to help. We called the Children's Leukemia Center, and asked for some banners and money jars to use for a bake sale to try to raise funds for the center. We sold lemonade and cookies and made over sixty dollars. It made us feel like we were at least making a small contribution. What we really wanted was for Kiki and the other children to get well.

Months went by, and Kiki was still not getting any better. She had lost all of her hair. It was very hard for me to see her as sick as she was. But I went to see her almost every day.

The day before Kiki died, I was in school and got a message to come to Kiki's house to say my final good-bye to my best friend. My mother came to the school to drive me to Kiki's house. She told me that Kiki wanted to see me really badly. In the car, I was crying a lot.

I got to Kiki's house, and I went up to her room, and everyone left so that we could talk together. We talked about everything, and I think it made Kiki feel better. Kiki seemed so brave and so unselfish, because her biggest concern was for her family. She asked me (and later, we found out, many people who knew them) to be sure to take care of her mom and dad and Sam. My last words were "I love you," and she said, "I love you, too."

That night I could not sleep, so I went downstairs. I had prayed every night that Kiki would get better and not die. My wishes and my praying did not help because Kiki died on that Thursday in January. It was six in the morning when my mom came down and said to me, "Stacie, she is gone." I cried more than I ever had in my life. I could not believe that my best friend was gone. Days later, I went to Kiki's funeral and cried even more.

One year passed, and we were having an anniversary memorial service. I have a pretty good voice, so Kiki's mother asked me if I would sing a song from *The Lion King* at the service. I said yes and that I would sing "Can You Feel the Love Tonight" by Elton John.

I sang it, and everyone thought it was really good. I felt that when I sang that song, Kiki was singing it with me. The first movie Kiki and I saw together was *The Lion King*. That was our favorite movie. When I went to say my final good-bye to her, I was wearing my *Lion King* sweatshirt.

Two years have passed, and I still remember Kiki. I can remember very special things about Kiki: her warmth, her big heart, and her cute laugh and smile.

I sing a lot at talent shows and plays, and every time I sing, I know that Kiki is with me. I will never, ever forget Kiki because she was so special to me. I feel that she watches over me and that she is my guardian angel. I would call her the Perfect Angel, wouldn't you?

Stacie Christina Smith, age 12

[EDITORS' NOTE: *For support in dealing with the illness or loss of a loved one due to an illness, call Kids Konnected at 800-899-2866.*]

Someone to Hold Onto

The friend who can be silent with us in a moment of despair or confusion, who can stay with us in an hour of grief and bereavement, who can tolerate not knowing, not curing, not healing—and face with us the reality of our powerlessness—that is the friend who really cares.

Henri Nouwen

Strange that I can still remember the doorbell ringing late that afternoon. I was twelve years old, and the everyday sound of that two-tone chime interrupted the gray February day.

Mom wiped her hands on the bleached dish-towel, throwing it over her shoulder as she left the kitchen. I abandoned my math homework somewhere in the "hundreds" column and raced my younger brothers to the door. We came to the required halt just as Mom entered the living room.

Waiting by our heavy front door, I could feel the wet Missouri cold pressing in from outside. I was tall enough to see through the top half where the window was. Standing on our red cement porch, just one pane of glass away, was Barb Murphy—the teenager I most admired in the whole neighborhood and in the entire world!

But Barb's usually vibrant cheeks were drained, her perfect skin pulled tightly across her strong jawline. She kept her lapis blue eyes on my mom, who opened the door enough to greet her, but not enough to let the dog out.

There were whispered words, quick, jerking glances toward my brothers and me, and then Barb was spelling a word. It didn't sound like any word I knew. Bits and pieces of my mother's conversation with Barb kept distracting me, jumbling the letters. I struggled to make sense of that word. S-u-i-c-i- . . .

"Oh no, dear, not Bruce Garrett. When? Where did they find him?" And finally, the part I was straining to hear: "How did he do it?"

The mysterious letters became a black-hearted word that hit my stomach hard. I knew this word *suicide*, after all. Mr. Garrett, Cindy Garrett's father, was dead. He had killed himself.

Cindy and I had played together every possible day of every summer, for all the years we had both lived in the neighborhood—since kindergarten. Mr. Garrett had built a playhouse for us, and when he made wooden stilts for Cindy, he made a second pair for me. When we were older, he bought real canvas bases for our neighborhood softball games. He drew a chart and showed us how to keep score, with all nine innings and each person's name listed in his strong, black printing.

I think that Mr. Garrett really wanted to be accepted by us kids. If he drove up during one of our dodgeball games in the street, he would turn his radio to a rock 'n' roll song, as loud as it would go, and wave at us as we stood by the curb. There'd be a dozen high-pitched voices overlapping one another, chorusing back, "Hi, Mr. Garrett!" as he drove by.

I tried to picture his tan face, straight nose and the shiny black hair that made him look like an Indian—without seeing the bloody mess that a bullet had made. I couldn't do it, so I tried to stop seeing him at all.

My mom turned to me. "Annie, get your shoes and coat on, and go up there."

What could my mom possibly mean? I stared at Barb, wondering if she would translate for me.

Mom's voice came again. "Go stay with Cindy, and ask Mrs. Garrett if there is anything I can do. Tell her we are praying. . . ."

Finally hearing Mom's words, I obeyed. Under my brothers' silent stares, I got ready fast enough to catch up with Barb as she was leaving our house. But when we reached the sidewalk, she turned the other way, toward our next-door neighbors'.

"I have to tell the Parkers," Barb told me. It sounded like she was talking to herself. She pulled a pair of knitted gloves from the pocket of her camel-hair coat and simply walked away.

Left with no alternatives that I could think of, I headed toward the Garretts' house. I don't remember walking up the street. I only remember following the sidewalk to the white police car and turning in there.

I went up the dark green steps to Cindy's screened porch door and opened it as I had hundreds of times before. I stepped onto the rug made of scratchy straw squares, all woven together. I wanted my walk across that rug to the front door to last forever so I would never have to arrive within arm's reach of the doorbell.

But the full-length glass of the Garretts' storm door somehow came to meet me. I looked away to avoid my reflection. With the thumb of my left mitten, I punched at the doorbell twice before it actually rang. When it did, my stomach felt like Alka-Seltzer dropped into a glass of water.

What will I say to Cindy? Why am I here, anyway? What am I supposed to do?

I hadn't thought to ask my mom about any of this. For a moment, my bewilderment outweighed my panic. I heard slow footsteps on the other side of the white colonial door. Terrified, I watched the brass doorknob turn and tried to remember how I normally greeted my best friend.

Struggling to see through my own reflection in the glass, I didn't even recognize her at first. In the widening space inside stood not Cindy, but Mrs. Garrett. She pushed open the storm door with a force that belied her small frame. Her eyes were wild and red, and there was a desperate sagging to her face, with lines I had never seen.

"Annie!" she cried, as she grabbed me and clutched me to her bony, collapsing chest. It was the first time that I realized Mrs. Garrett was not much bigger than I was. I let her surround me with her shaking arms, until her sobs finally quieted. She held onto me for what seemed a long time.

I didn't know what to say or do next, but I knew this woman's life was broken apart, shattered now like the windshield of Mr. Garrett's blue station wagon. I was just twelve years old, but I was someone to hold onto.

During the long months that followed, I would be with them often. I learned to spend more time greeting Mrs. Garrett and to use a softer voice. I remembered to have tissues on the floor next to every board game Cindy and I played, and I knew that if my dad walked into the room, Cindy would cry harder.

More than a year later, I explained to the librarian why Cindy had walked out in tears, leaving her application for a new library card unfinished at the section that said "Father's Occupation."

Knowing how to be with a family in pain never became easy. But from those first moments in Mrs. Garrett's arms, I learned that my awkwardness didn't matter. I was there, and that's what counted.

Ann McCoole Rigby

Rebecca's Rainbow

O Christ, that it were possible
For one short hour to see
The souls we loved, that they may tell us
What and where they may be.

Alfred Lord Tennyson

From the time she was a small girl, eleven-year-old Rebecca loved to paint rainbows. She painted rainbows on Mother's Day cards, rainbows on valentines, rainbows on drawings she carried home from school. "You're my Rainbow Girl," her mother would laugh, as she stuck another picture on the refrigerator with a big rainbow magnet.

Each bright band of color reminded Rebecca of something special in her life. Red, the color at the top, was like the sweet red ketchup she dumped on top of her favorite thing to eat, french fries—and anything else she could think of. Red was also the color of her other favorite food, lobster, which her mother rewarded her with at the end of every school year for a good report card. Orange made her think of pumpkins and the holiday she liked best,

Halloween, when she could dress up and be whatever she chose. Yellow was the color of her hair—long, straight, fairy-tale princess hair that hung down her back like Rapunzel's. Green meant the tickle of grass under the palms of her hands as she turned cartwheel after cartwheel, stretching her long legs toward heaven. Blue was the color of the morning sky, which she glimpsed from the skylight over her bed. Blue was also the color of her eyes, and the color of the ocean she lived near. And purple, the band at the heart of each rainbow, was her mother's favorite color and always reminded Rebecca of home.

It was the last weekend in May, and Rebecca was looking forward to all her end-of-school-year activities. In a few days, she would be center stage, making all her friends laugh as "the nerd" in the school play. Shortly after that, she would be doing arabesques in her annual dance recital. Her father was about to host his famous Memorial Day weekend cookout. The only unhappy note was that Rebecca's mother was going on vacation for a few days. It was the first time her mother had been away from home since Rebecca's parents had divorced. Rebecca was unusually anxious about the separation and cried when they had to say good-bye. Perhaps she sensed something was about to happen.

Coming home late one night over the Memorial Day weekend, Rebecca, her father and his new wife were killed when a drunk driver traveling the wrong way down the highway hit their car. Only Rebecca's nine-year-old brother, Oliver, survived the crash, protected by his sister's body.

Rebecca's funeral was held on the day that she was to have starred in the school play. It was a beautiful spring day, as bright and sunny as Rebecca herself. Rebecca's mother closed her eyes and prayed. "Rebecca, I need to know that you are at peace. Please send me a sign. Send me a rainbow."

After her funeral, Rebecca's grieving friends and relatives were gathered with her mother at her grandparents' house when, unexpectedly, it began to rain. It rained hard for a while. Then all at once it stopped. Suddenly, from the front porch of the house someone shouted, "Hey, everybody! Look! Look what's out here!"

Everyone ran outside. Out over the ocean, a rainbow had appeared. It was a great big, magnificent array of colors that came down out of the clouds as if by magic. Every hue was bright and vivid and true.

As aunts wept and uncles jostled each other to get a better look, Rebecca's mother gazed up at the beautiful picture her Rainbow Girl had painted in the sky and whispered, "Thank you."

Tara M. Nickerson

One Rainbow Wasn't Enough

Think of him still as the same, I say,
He is not dead; he is just—away.

James Whitcomb Riley

The day that Grandpa came to school to pick me up, I knew something was wrong because Mom was supposed to be there. We were all supposed to go out to dinner that night to celebrate our friend Sherry's birthday. When Grandpa told me that you had a heart attack, I thought he was just kidding. When I could see that he was serious, I thought I was going to die. I was too shocked even to cry. I felt so numb and helpless. I just sat there, thinking, *Why? You were so big, strong and healthy. You worked out every day.* I thought you would be the last person, ever, to have a heart attack.

Being in the hospital was terrifying. You were in a coma. You had so many tubes and machines all around you. You didn't look at all like yourself. I could feel myself shaking. I just wanted you to wake up from this horrible nightmare and take me home.

The whole hospital was filled with many people who came to see you. They treated me very nicely. I never knew you had so many kind friends. Sherry was there, too, but we didn't celebrate her birthday.

That first day was followed by a couple of days of restless sorrow, sleepless nights, and lots and lots of praying. None of it worked. On February 26, the most tragic thing of my entire ten years of life, and for probably the rest of my life, happened to me. The one person I looked up to more than anyone else in this world died. I don't even know if you heard me tell you good-bye.

I had never been to a funeral before. I was astonished to see that over a thousand people came. All our family and friends were there, and a lot of people I didn't even know. I figured out afterward that you must have treated them the same special way you treated me. That's why they all loved you. Of course, I always knew you were so special, but you were my dad. On that day, I found out how special you were to so many other people.

Even though it has been over a year, I still think about you all the time and miss you very much. Some nights I cry myself to sleep, but I try not to get too downhearted. I know I still have a lot to be thankful for. You gave me more love in ten years than a lot of kids probably ever get in their whole lives. Sure, I know you can't play ball with me anymore on the weekends, take me to Denny's for breakfast, tell your corny jokes or sneak me doughnuts. But I also know that you are still with me. You're in my heart and in my bones. I hear your voice inside my head, helping to guide me through life. When I don't know what to do, I try to think about what you would tell me. You are still here, giving me advice and helping me figure things out. I know that whatever I do, I will always love you and remember you.

I've heard that whenever someone dies, God sends a

rainbow to take the person to heaven. The day you died, a double rainbow appeared in the sky.

You were six foot four. I guess one rainbow wasn't enough to carry you all the way to heaven.

I love you, Daddy.

Matt Sharpe, age 12

A Nightmare Come True

"Sticks and stones may break my bones, but words can never hurt me!" Words can never hurt me? During my life I've wondered—is that myth or reality? Now I know the answer.

When I was born, my dad and mom were very young. All they wanted to do was party, and they based their lives on alcohol and drugs. As I began to grow up, I spent most of my time with my grandmother because my parents weren't able to help raise me.

Finally, when I was about five, my dad stopped doing drugs. He went to a place to get detoxed so he could be a real father to me. My mom tried to do the same thing, but she couldn't stop drinking.

For years I lived happily with my dad. I saw my mom off and on. It made me sad when I stayed with her because she was always crying or making promises she couldn't keep. It was rare to see my mom without a beer in her hand. Sometimes she had this blank look in her eyes. I knew that when she looked that way, she was trying to block out all her feelings. It was the way that she hid her pain.

One day I was in the front yard when my uncle Tommy drove up. I was excited to see him, and I went up to him to give him a hug. My uncle sort of pushed me away and told me he needed to talk to my dad. Later, he left without saying good-bye to me.

I tried not to think about what he and my dad might have discussed, but after that day I started having nightmares. I was dreaming really crazy stuff, trying to figure out what my uncle had said. Night after night it went on. My dad would wake me up, telling me it was just a dream, but the dreams felt like reality to me.

Two weeks before Halloween, my uncle Tommy came over again. He looked so pale—he could have been a walking dead man. I gave him a wave and a faint hello. Then I walked away because I could tell he wanted to talk to my dad. After he left, my dad went into the house to talk to his girlfriend.

I was getting very worried. I went into the house and asked, "What's wrong with the two of you?"

Then my dad told me something about my mom that I wasn't ready for. She was in the hospital.

The very next day, I went to the hospital to visit her. I was expecting to see the same beautiful face of my mom that I was used to, but it wasn't that way. I couldn't believe the person lying there was really my mom. She had drunk so much beer that it had destroyed her liver. She looked like she had yellow cover-up all over her body. Then it hit me. My mom was dying.

For one week, my mom lay in the hospital, and I felt completely lost. I visited her so often that it was like I was living there.

Then one day, when I was at home, my dad received a phone call. His smile disappeared, he started to frown—and in my heart I knew what it was. There would be no more pain or suffering for my mom, and my nightmares had come true. The one in pain, the one I loved—my mom—was dead. Those three little words, "She is gone," will hurt me forever. Sticks and stones would be easier to bear.

Damien Liermann, age 14

Lessons from God

One cannot get through life without pain . . .
What we can do is choose how to use the pain
life presents us.

Bernie S. Siegel, M.D.

There was a time in my childhood when I believed that
God was punishing my family by making us watch my
only brother die.

My brother Brad was a hemophiliac. If a person has
hemophilia, his blood doesn't clot in a normal way; so, if
he gets a cut, it is very difficult to stop the bleeding. When
too much blood is lost, he has to have his blood replen-
ished to keep him going.

Even though Brad couldn't be as active as other kids
because of the hemophilia, we had many common interests and spent a lot of time together. Brad and I rode bikes
with the neighborhood kids, and we spent most of our
summers swimming in our pool. When we played football
or baseball, Brad would throw the ball, and the rest of us
would do all the rough playing. Brad picked out a puppy
for me when I was seven, and I named her PeeWee. My

brother, Brad, was my protector and my best friend.

When Brad was ten, he received blood from someone who didn't realize, or was too selfish to admit, that he or she was carrying the AIDS virus.

I had just entered the sixth grade when my brother began to have serious symptoms, and was diagnosed with AIDS. He was a freshman in high school and had just turned fifteen. At that time, many people were not educated about how you "catch" AIDS and were very afraid of being around people who had it. My family worried about how people would act when they found out.

Our lives changed when Brad's symptoms became obvious. I couldn't have friends over to spend the night. Whenever I had a basketball game, only one, never both of my parents, could come to watch because someone had to stay with Brad. Often, my parents would need to be with Brad during the times he was hospitalized. Sometimes they were gone for a week at a time while I stayed at a neighbor's or an aunt's house. I never knew where I'd be from one day to the next.

Through all the sadness and confusion, I grew resentful about not being able to lead a normal life. My parents weren't able to help me with my homework because they had to tend to Brad's needs. I began having problems in school. The emotional part of slowly losing Brad, my best friend, made things even worse. I became very angry and needed to blame someone, so I turned my blame toward God.

It was a burden to keep his condition a secret, yet I knew how cruel kids could be. I didn't want anyone to see my brother not looking at all like his former self, and lying in diapers. I wasn't going to have him be the subject of their jokes at school. It wasn't my brother's fault that his twelve-year-old sister had to change his diapers or feed him through a tube.

The AIDS virus caused damage to Brad's brain and destroyed the person that he had grown to be. Eventually, he became like a very young child again. Instead of listening to current music or talking about things that kids in junior high or high school would be interested in, he wanted us to read childhood books to him. He wanted me to help him color. I felt like I had lost my brother while he was still alive.

I remember the day that Brad died, just like it was yesterday. The old musty room was filled with recognizable faces. There was my brother's worn-out body in the bed. The body was now empty, and the pain could no longer be felt. That was the end of my only brother's life—two weeks before his eighteenth birthday.

Between 1980 and 1987, over 10,000 hemophiliacs like Brad received blood that was infected with the AIDS virus. Ninety percent of these severe hemophiliacs who were infected are either living with AIDS or have died from it. If the blood that they received had been tested before they gave it to them, their early deaths could have been avoided. As I see it, my brother was basically murdered.

The experimental drugs used to battle AIDS only made him worse. Even some of the doctors seemed to have a what's-the-use attitude. Some of these things made losing him even more painful.

Since his passing, I've searched for some reason for his life and death. Although there may not be a complete answer to my question, I believe that there was a purpose. Brad taught us many things. He is still teaching people, even now, with the story of his life. I told his story to someone just the other day, and that person learned something.

Brad was a person who always fought for what he believed in. He taught his friends and family members not to give up. He never gave up, and he never gave in to his hemophilia. Although Brad was special because of it, he never wanted to be treated special. He would play basketball with the heart of Larry Bird, but the body of a hemophiliac. Those who watched him play for his elementary school team would see him limping up and down the court, trying his hardest.

Out of respect for his memory, we have not given up. My family and I have taken an active part in helping to make a difference in the way that people with hemophilia and AIDS are treated. We have been interviewed on the television program, *60 Minutes*. We have gone to Washington D.C. twice, fighting for the Ricky Ray Bill to be passed by Congress. This bill would help families who have been through similar or worse situations. The bill was named for a boy who was taken out of school because he had AIDS. People who were afraid of AIDS and thought they could get it from him burned down his family's home. The people didn't understand that people can get AIDS from tainted blood donations.

My brother gave so much love and happiness to so many people while he was alive, that his death left us feeling empty and sad. Before he was infected with AIDS, my big brother, Brad, was my protector and the person I would tell all my secrets to. Brad can no longer protect me, or even talk to me, and I miss him every day.

Since Brad's death I've come to realize that God was not punishing my family for anything. He simply had given us a gift of love—my brother, Brad—that had to be taken back. With these lessons from God, I can continue with my journey—this journey called life—with the hope that everyone with whom I share Brad's story will learn exactly how precious life is.

Jennifer Rhea Cross

[EDITORS' NOTE: *If you would like information about hemophilia and/or AIDS, call the COMMITTEE OF TEN THOUSAND hotline at 800-488-2688.*]

$\overline{6}$

ACHIEVING DREAMS

A dream is a seed
The seed of a tree
A tree full of life
And the things you can be
Your dreams are the windows
Through which you can see
A hint of your future
And the things you will be
Each night when you sleep
You're feeding the seed
The seed of the tree
Of who you will be.

Jennifer Genereux Davis

Believe in Yourself

Set your standards high
You deserve the best.
Try for what you want
And never settle for less.

Believe in yourself
No matter what you choose.
Keep a winning attitude
And you can never lose.

Think about your destination
But don't worry if you stray
Because the most important thing
Is what you've learned along the way.

Take all that you've become
To be all that you can be.
Soar above the clouds
And let your dreams set you free.

Jillian K. Hunt

The Little Girl Who Dared to Wish

As Amy Hagadorn rounded the corner across the hall from her classroom, she collided with a tall boy from the fifth grade running in the opposite direction.

"Watch it, squirt," the boy yelled as he dodged around the little third-grader. Then, with a smirk on his face, the boy took hold of his right leg and mimicked the way Amy limped when she walked.

Amy closed her eyes. *Ignore him*, she told herself as she headed for her classroom.

But at the end of the day, Amy was still thinking about the tall boy's mean teasing. It wasn't as if he were the only one. It seemed that ever since Amy started the third grade, someone teased her every single day. Kids teased her about her speech or her limping. Amy was tired of it. Sometimes, even in a classroom full of other students, the teasing made her feel all alone.

Back home at the dinner table that evening, Amy was quiet. Her mother knew that things were not going well at school. That's why Patti Hagadorn was happy to have some exciting news to share with her daughter.

"There's a Christmas wish contest on the radio station," Amy's mom announced. "Write a letter to Santa, and you might win a prize. I think someone at this table with blonde curly hair should enter."

Amy giggled. The contest sounded like fun. She started thinking about what she wanted most for Christmas.

A smile took hold of Amy when the idea first came to her. Out came pencil and paper, and Amy went to work on her letter. "Dear Santa Claus," she began.

While Amy worked away at her best printing, the rest of the family tried to guess what she might ask from Santa. Amy's sister, Jamie, and Amy's mom both thought a three-foot Barbie doll would top Amy's wish list. Amy's dad guessed a picture book. But Amy wasn't ready to reveal her secret Christmas wish just then. Here is Amy's letter to Santa, just as she wrote it that night:

Dear Santa Claus,

   My name is Amy. I am nine years old. I have a problem at school. Can you help me, Santa? Kids laugh at me because of the way I walk and run and talk. I have cerebral palsy. I just want one day where no one laughs at me or makes fun of me.

Love,
Amy

At radio station WJLT in Fort Wayne, Indiana, letters poured in for the Christmas wish contest. The workers had fun reading about all the different presents that boys and girls from across the city wanted for Christmas.

When Amy's letter arrived at the radio station, manager Lee Tobin read it carefully. He knew cerebral palsy was a muscle disorder that might confuse the schoolmates of Amy's who didn't understand her disability. He thought it would be good for the people in Fort Wayne to hear about this special third-grader and her unusual wish. Mr. Tobin called up the local newspaper.

The next day, a picture of Amy and her letter to Santa made the front page of the *News Sentinel*. The story spread quickly. All across the country, newspapers and radio and television stations reported the story of the little girl in Fort Wayne, Indiana, who asked for such a simple yet remarkable Christmas gift—just one day without teasing.

Suddenly the postman was a regular at the Hagadorn house. Envelopes of all sizes addressed to Amy arrived daily from children and adults all across the nation. They came filled with holiday greetings and words of encouragement.

During that unforgettable Christmas season, over two thousand people from all over the world sent Amy letters of friendship and support. Amy and her family read every single one. Some of the writers had disabilities; some had been teased as children. Each writer had a special message for Amy. Through the cards and letters from strangers, Amy glimpsed a world full of people who truly cared about each other. She realized that no amount or form of teasing could ever make her feel lonely again.

Many people thanked Amy for being brave enough to speak up. Others encouraged her to ignore teasing and to carry her head high. Lynn, a sixth-grader from Texas, sent this message:

"I would like to be your friend," she wrote, "and if you want to visit me, we could have fun. No one would make fun of us, 'cause if they do, we will not even hear them."

Amy did get her wish of a special day without teasing at South Wayne Elementary School. Additionally, everyone at school got another bonus. Teachers and students talked together about how bad teasing can make others feel.

That year, the Fort Wayne mayor officially proclaimed December 21 as Amy Jo Hagadorn Day throughout the city. The mayor explained that by daring to make such a simple wish, Amy taught a universal lesson.

"Everyone," said the mayor, "wants and deserves to be treated with respect, dignity and warmth."

Alan D. Shultz

The Playground

I always tried to turn every disaster into an opportunity.

John D. Rockefeller

"Carlos, we're going to the store to get a soda. You wanna go?"

Carlos joined his friends as they walked the few blocks to the store, crossing the railroad tracks, kicking cans and tossing rocks as they went.

It was a Sunday afternoon in January, and they were especially carefree. Monday would be a holiday honoring Martin Luther King Jr.'s birthday, and they wouldn't have to go to school.

Carlos was eight years old, a second-grader living with his mother in the housing project, just blocks from the train tracks. He was the sixth of her eight children. His father lived in Florida.

Carlos had lived in the country most of his life. Their little town of Millen was like a giant playground to him. He and his friends loved to wander and explore. Freight trains were a part of everyday life in their little town. The trains would drop off and pick up boxcars and tank cars at the loading yards, then continue on their way to Savannah. It was a given that since the tracks were between home and the church, as well as the store and their neighborhood, Carlos and his friends often had to jump over them.

Carlos was good at sports and always included anyone who was left out or said to someone who needed cheering, "Come on, buddy; let's play." When anyone called to him, "Carlos, come help us," he always helped them. Upon meeting him, he seemed quiet. He would drop his head; but the look in his eye was playful, and his face had an easy smile. The children liked Carlos because he was fun. He could make playtime out of most any situation. Carlos was not afraid of anything.

It was a cold day, warming slightly in the afternoon from the sun. Carlos hated to wear his jacket, so on this particular afternoon, he was only wearing a short-sleeved shirt with his jeans and tennis shoes. On the way home from the store, he and his friends began to play on a freight train that had stopped to drop off and pick up boxcars, moving back and forth on the tracks in the process. They were near the middle of the freight train, having great fun climbing the ladders and hopping on and off the train. It was exciting to feel the moving train, to hear the squealing of the wheels as it came to a halt and the whistle blowing, to experience the sounds and smells of the engine as the train moved back and forth.

The train began to travel forward on the tracks, and all the boys jumped off—all except Carlos. He held on, yelling to them, "I'll get off at the next stop. Meet me there." Just outside of town, there was a dirt railroad crossing. He would get off there. It wasn't too far away. It was very exciting to ride the train. They would all have a good laugh at his feat.

The sun was beginning to go down, and the wind became cold. Carlos held on to the ladder at the rear of the freight car. He watched for the dirt crossing. As the train moved out of town, it began to pick up speed. He began to wonder if it would stop. He decided he might have to jump off. By the time he saw the crossing, the train had passed it. They were going too fast, and he had missed his chance.

A chill from the cold wind went up his spine. Perhaps it was a chill of fear as he became aware of what had happened. This was more adventure than he had bargained for. He decided to hold on very tightly and look for the lights of the next town. The train would stop there, and he could get off and ask for help to get back home. It was very cold now, and Carlos said out loud to himself, "If I had my jacket, I'd put it on for sure. That's how cold I am."

It was hard work holding on to the moving train. The cold was making it even harder. Carlos felt like his hands were freezing. He had not realized the weather would be this cold. The area they were traveling through was very wooded with lots of bushes. He was glad to finally see houses and lights, and got ready for the train to stop . . . but the train kept going!

Carlos felt his first real fear. He had counted on the train stopping, but it was not going to stop! He was getting farther and farther from home. *What should I do? Can I hold on until the train reaches its destination? Can I hold on that long? Should I try to jump?* It looked too dangerous to do that. His mind was in turmoil as he tried to think of what to do. He decided that his best course of action would be to hold on until the train finally stopped. Surely it would stop somewhere along the way.

He decided to talk to himself, to build up his courage. *Come on, buddy, you can do it. Hold on tight, now. I know you're tired and freezing cold, but you can put on your jacket as soon as you get home. Hold on, buddy, you can do it!*

As time went on, the cold and fear kept him holding tightly to the ladder, pressing himself as closely as he could to the freight car to block the wind. The bushes and trees seemed to fly by as they traveled the rails. After a time, Carlos saw lights in some of the houses by the side of the tracks. But they passed through another small town without stopping!

Terror filled his heart as he clutched the ladder; tears of anguish flowed from his eyes as he fully realized his danger. He continued to hold his grip as tightly as he could, but it was getting harder all the time. He was exhausted. The sun had set; it was beginning to grow dark. He couldn't hold on any longer. Maybe he should jump after all.

Back in the little town of Millen, Carlos's friends tried to keep him out of trouble for playing on the train. Thinking he was on his way back from the crossing, they said nothing. When they finally told everything they knew, and it was discovered that Carlos was missing, the police began to search for him.

By Monday morning, all four adjoining counties began searching by air, by rail and on foot. Family, friends, neighbors and strangers alike searched for Carlos. On Tuesday, Carlos was found along a desolate stretch of rail forty miles down the track. He had died from a broken neck. Everyone in the community of Millen shared the grief and sorrow of his death.

A lady in Savannah read of the tragic accident. The news account stated that the children in Millen had no playground. It went on to say that perhaps if there had been a playground for them, Carlos might have been on a playground and not playing on the train tracks. As a wife and mother of three children, she was concerned that while her city of Savannah had so many playgrounds, Millen did not. A former Girl Scout troop leader, she was accustomed to leadership. She determined she would get a playground built for the children of Millen.

With the dedication of family, neighbors, friends, merchants and contractors, along with a donation of land, a new playground was completed for the town of Millen. People who had been brought together as strangers ended up as friends. In the process, some healing also took place in the community. By their joining together, their grief and sorrow was lessened.

On a sunny spring afternoon, Millen's new playground was officially dedicated as the Carlos Wilson Memorial Playground.

The ceremony was followed by playtime for the children. It was as if they could hear Carlos saying, "Come on, buddy; let's play. Let's go play on my playground!"

Audilee Boyd Taylor

Dreams of the Children

Everyone is good enough
Everyone is right
Everyone deserves a home
And a warm bed at night

Everybody needs a friend
Everyone needs their space
All people are created equal
So why is it the human *race?*

Perhaps our only problem
Is that some refuse to see
Not everyone else is the trouble
The trouble is you and me

So if we work together
As a team, me and you
Maybe we can rebuild our world
And make our dreams come true.

Jody Suzanne Waitzman, age 13

Batgirl

Today, no one questions whether women are equal to men in ability and intelligence.

Julie Nixon Eisenhower

"So what, Ray? So what if I'm not a boy? I can hit better than everybody, except maybe Tommy—and maybe you on a good day. And I'm faster than all of you put together."

"You can still play with the girls at recess," he said.

I stared him down, eye to eye, both of us sitting cross-legged on the sidewalk in front of my house. The cement felt warm. Crabgrass poked through and scratched my thigh.

I won the stare-down.

Ray looked down at the Big Chief tablet on my lap.

"And you sure can't win that contest, Dandi," he mumbled. "I don't know why you're even entering."

A blue-lined page from his tablet stuck to his knobby knee. He pushed a shock of brown hair, straight as harvest wheat, out of his eyes. Ray's mom cut both of our hair. I shoved mine out of my face. Then I pulled out the coupon I'd torn from the *Kansas City Star* sports page.

"I'm entering," I said, "and I'm winning."

Ray jerked the coupon out of my hand and pointed his finger at the print.

"See!" he said triumphantly. "It says right here: 1959 *batboy contest*. Write in seventy-five words or less why you want to be batboy for the KC Athletics pro baseball team. Not bat*girl*." He cackled as if a batgirl was the funniest thing he'd ever heard.

"Well, it's not fair!" I said, half to Ray, half to myself.

I was tired of not getting to do stuff just because I was a girl. Ray played Little League. I could knock him down with a line drive, hitting from my Stan Musiel batting stance. But our small Missouri town didn't have a girls' baseball team.

I was ten, the age when boys stopped caring that you were the only one who could hit an inside-the-park homer or the only one who knew the infield fly rule. They simply wouldn't let you play because you were a girl.

My sister, Maureen, slammed the screen door.

"What's going on out here?" she asked.

Maureen, who was my older sister, couldn't tell a baseball from a football if it hit her in the face.

"Nothing," I answered. I tucked the coupon in my tablet.

"We're . . . umm . . . drawing," I lied.

Ray looked confused. "Drawing? I thought we were . . . "

I nudged him into silence.

Maureen tried giving me one of our mother's suspicious looks. The attempt made her look more like Bruno, our hound dog, when he had to go outside.

Ray and I sat in the sun and set our pencils scratching. At the end of an hour, I had fourteen paper wads to show.

"I'm done," Ray announced.

"Read it," I demanded.

I crossed my fingers and hoped it would be awful.

Ray swatted at a horsefly, then held up his paper and read aloud. "I want to be a batboy for the Kansas City A's because I really, really, really like baseball and I really, really, really like Kansas City and the Athletics."

He looked wide-eyed at me. "What do you think, Dandi?"

I hadn't hoped it would be *that* awful.

"Why so many *reallys*?" I asked.

He looked wounded. "I need the words! What do you know, anyway? You can't even enter the contest."

Ray left me standing alone on the sidewalk. I took in the sweet scent of the cornfields across the road and thought about what I might write.

The words began to flow as I put pen to paper:

> *My whole life people have told me that I can't. My sister has said that I can't sing. My teacher has said that I can't spell. Mom has said that I can't be a professional baseball player. My best friend has said that I can't win this contest. I'm entering this contest to prove them wrong. I want to be your next Kansas City A's batboy.*

I signed it "Dan Daley." My dad always called me "Dan," short for Dandi. I addressed the envelope and mailed my entry.

As the months passed, filled with sandlot baseball, I played whenever I could force my way into a game. Then late one autumn afternoon, there was a knock at our door. When I opened the door, I was surprised to find two men in suits, carrying briefcases. Surely they were from out of town.

"Hello, little girl," the shorter man said. "We'd like to speak to your brother."

"Don't have a brother," I said.

The taller man wrinkled his forehead and popped open his briefcase. He took out a handful of papers. Both men studied them while I stood in the doorway, guarding my brotherless home.

"Is this 508 Samuel Street?" asked the shorter one.

"I guess," I answered.

Nobody used house numbers in our neighborhood. There were only two houses on our road.

"Isn't this the home of Dan Daley?"

A light went on in my head. Then I got it.

"Mom!" I screamed, without taking my eyes off the strangers. "Come here! Hurry!" Sure enough, I had won the batboy contest. My words had done the trick!

I let Mom explain about my not having a brother. I confessed I'd entered as "Dan." Maureen and Bruno started to congratulate me—but not the strangers.

"What's wrong?" I asked, a familiar feeling of dread creeping up my spine.

"Well," said the taller one, "you're not a boy."

"Well, duh," I answered.

"Contest rules clearly state 'a boy aged eight to twelve,'" said the shorter one.

"But I won!" I protested.

"Little girl," he said, "this was not a batgirl contest."

The men left, taking with them my dream of being a Kansas City A's batboy. Hoping to make up for it, they sent us season tickets, team jackets, autographed base-balls, hats and a hardwood bat. I never did wear that hat. I became a St. Louis Cardinals fan instead. But I did grab that bat the day it came. I marched to our school play-ground where Ray, Tommy and the guys were in the middle of a pickup game.

"I'm batting," I said, one-arming Ray away from the plate.

The guys groaned, but Ray seemed to know something more was at stake. He nodded to the pitcher. I took the first pitch, high and outside, just the way I liked it. Before the crack of the bat, I knew I'd send that ball over the fence for a home run. I turned my back before the ball hit the street, finally bouncing into a ditch.

Gently, I released my Kansas City Athletics bat and heard it bounce in the dirt. I proudly walked the bases to home plate, leaving that bat where it had fallen.

"Let the batboy get it."

Dandi Dailey Mackall

G-o-o-o-a-a-a-a-l-l-l-l!

Laugh and learn, because we all make mistakes.

Weston Dunlap, age 8

Running as fast as my small legs could carry me, I concentrated on the black-and-white object spinning ahead,
and realized that this was my chance. This was my
dream come true. I had a jump on the others, and it was
all up to me! I looked behind me and saw the yellow jer-
seys and green shorts of my teammates, the National
Auto Glass Dinosaurs. They looked like a swarm of bees,
all headed toward the soccer ball. I saw the faces of my
opponents and could tell that some of them were running really hard. They wanted the ball, but it was mine,
all mine!

I ran up to the ball and gave it a tremendous, four-year-
old kick. It scooted farther down the field, and again I
sprinted after it. The other players gained on me, but I
was nearing the goal. The confused look on the goalie's
face told me that he wasn't ready to make a save. The
rooting section on the sideline was chanting, "Kick it! Kick

it! Kick the ball!"

I wound up and toed the ball as hard as a four-year-old ever could. It bounced into the net, past the scrambling goalie. I went wild! I had just scored my first real goal!

I ran back to my teammates. Some were cheering and celebrating with me, but most of them had their arms crossed, with scowls on their faces and annoyed looks in their eyes. *They* wanted to score that goal, but *I* had! Ha! Ha!! I looked to my mom and dad on the sideline. They were laughing with some other parents. This is just too cool! I'd scored my first ever goal—*for the other team!*

Heather Thomsen, age 13

With Every Footstep

*You have made known to me the path of life;
you will fill me with joy in your presence. . . .*

Ps. 16:11

I was not only a little surprised, but worried to find myself in the Vault Finals at the 1996 Olympic Games when Kerri Strug was forced to pull out as a result of an ankle injury. I had done well during the team competition, but had just missed qualifying for the Vault Finals competition. When my coach, Steve, and I were notified that I'd become eligible to compete in this event, I wasn't feeling prepared to be Kerri's replacement.

My first reaction was, *How can I?* Due to an extremely sore wrist, I had not been able to work a second vault. Vault Finals require that the gymnast compete on two vaults from two different vault families. This was a moment when all of my gymnastics experience had to be there to support me. Steve encouraged me to give it a try.

Once I recovered from the initial shock, I knew that I didn't want to give up the opportunity to compete in another event of the 1996 Olympics. I fully intended to give it my best shot from that moment forward. With a positive attitude, and with support from Steve and my parents, I gave it everything I had during my workouts, and they went great. I didn't miss a single vault—even while warming up for the actual competition. I focused on how great an opportunity it was to be given the chance to compete.

However, my positive attitude and joy quickly turned to tears of embarrassment and discouragement. When the time came to compete, I sprinted hard down the runway, but as I approached the springboard, I knew that my steps were off. I was not coming onto the vault horse at the right place! In an instant, it was all over. I had missed placing one of my hands down on the horse, which resulted in my performing an outrageous flip in the air and landing on my seat right in front of literally hundreds of thousands of people! I felt the hot flush of embarrassment swimming from my stomach straight up to my bright red face.

As soon as the event was over, I headed up to the USA gymnastics suite, where I knew my parents would be waiting for me. My tears were flowing pretty freely, so my parents took me aside so that we could have a little privacy. I try always to place my trust in God to direct my path. I never pray to win, but I always ask God to help me do my best. I had been so full of joy and confidence going into the competition. What had happened?

Mom asked me if I remembered the poem *Footprints* that hung on the wall of my room. She reminded me that God had always been walking with me. Never had he abandoned me. Maybe it was time for me to allow God to *carry* me. Rather than be worried about once again failing, I could remember that I didn't have to do this all by myself. All I needed to remember was that God is always by my side. Instead of dreading Beam Finals the next day, I needed to be grateful for the opportunity to express the talent that God had given me, and not to be concerned about winning or losing.

The next evening, I was calm and at peace while I waited for my turn to compete. When I mounted the beam, I heard a man yell at someone in the crowd, "Turn your [camera] flash off!" I consciously thought, *How sweet of him to be concerned about my welfare.* A camera flash can cause an accident that could potentially end a career, or worse. It struck me that I had never before heard what was going on around me when I was competing. I was usually so tremendously focused, I had blocked out everything else. But that night's competition was different from any other. I felt an emotional connection with the audience whose love of gymnastics, and the athletes who represented the sport, seemed to completely surround me. At that moment, I was able to let in all the joy of the evening, of being in the Olympic Games, and of the sport of gymnastics.

I took a few calming breaths and thanked God for being with me, and for the talent that he has given me. And then, I *went for it!*

I aced my routine! I felt so great when my feet hit the mat. I honestly had no idea as to whether or not I would win a medal. But at that moment, medals truly did not matter. I had accomplished something far greater than a world record in gymnastics. I had felt the comfort and strength of God's presence with every footstep of the routine.

I took home an Olympic Gold Medal to remind me of that night. But the night was golden in more ways than one. I will always treasure in my heart what it is like to experience God's presence.

Shannon Miller

The Rock Club

*If you don't like the way the world is, you
change it. You have an obligation to change it.
You just do it one step at a time.*

Marian Wright Edelman

One night when I was in second grade, I saw something on the news that really bothered me. It was about a
group of homeless people sleeping outside in the cold,
with nowhere to go for warmth and comfort. I felt sorry
for them, and I wanted to help.

So I decided to start a club. The goal was to raise money
to help the homeless. I called it the Rock Club. When I first
started, we only had about five members, but that quickly
grew to about twenty. It wasn't hard to get people to join
the club. I hardly had to ask anybody if they wanted to be
a member. In fact, they came up to me and just asked me
if they could join!

We spent all of our free time at recess painting rocks. We
painted animals, flowers and shapes—even names of
sports teams. We all just worked on whatever we felt like
painting.

We'd go around the school in search of teachers who would buy our rocks and use them as paperweights. We sold the rocks for five cents, ten cents and even up to twenty cents each. We painted one huge rock with polka dots that sold for five bucks! By Christmas, we had raised thirty-three dollars. We decided to give the money to a local homeless shelter.

My mom offered to take my friend and me to the shelter to deliver the money. When we pulled up, we noticed that there were whole families sitting on the snowy sidewalk. As we went into the building, I could not get the picture of what I had just seen out of my mind. I kept thinking about the little children, and all of the men and women with nowhere to sleep.

When we got inside, we met the lady at the front desk and gave her the money that the club had earned. She seemed really grateful for our donation. She invited us to take a tour of the shelter. I had never seen a real homeless shelter before, so I wanted to see the inside. As we toured the building, what really got to me were the rows and rows of tables set up to help feed the hungry. There must have been over one hundred tables in there. In the kitchen, the helpers were making what seemed like endless rows of gingerbread men. It was amazing to me that for every gingerbread man, the shelter was expecting a person in need for dinner and shelter that night.

As we were leaving the homeless shelter, I saw a man sitting on the snow-covered pavement. He was wearing a dirty, dark green coat and black pants that were covered in mud. He was clutching to his side a Christmas tree covered with red ornaments. I felt so sorry for him because he had nowhere else to put a tree except the streets where he lived. It made me realize that even someone with no home, or money for presents, still wanted to have a Christmas.

The next day, there was a picture of that same man in the newspaper. I knew his image would stay with me forever. I hoped that his picture also reminded others about how much help the homeless people need, and that we should remember them all year—not only at Christmas.

A few days later, a newspaper reporter and a photographer came to our school and took a picture of our Rock Club members. The photo and article came out in the paper the next day. We all felt proud that we had done something that gave more attention to the needs of the homeless in our town.

Our school decided that what we did was really great, so they started a program just for kids. Now kids at our school are helping the homeless shelter and other organizations that help people in need.

Something as simple as some rocks, some paint and a few caring kids made me realize that you're never too young—and you don't need much—to make a difference.

Vanessa Clayton, age 14

Socks for Kerry

"Mom, Kerry just crawled through the plans for my invention, and her leg brace ripped it up!" shouted Jessica.

"You know you can't spread out your work on the floor when she's around," said her mother. "Just be thankful she can crawl at all."

I'm so tired of hearing about poor little Kerry. What about me? thought Jessica.

Then, sighing, she said, "Yeah, right."

Yesterday, Jessica had brought home an announcement for the Invention Convention at her school. The kids in her fourth-grade class were asked to invent a useful item, make a prototype, and show how it worked. "This convention is really going to be cool," she told her mother. "The only trouble is, I want to help someone solve a real problem, but I can't think of anything good."

"I'm sure you'll do fine," said her mom.

"Kerry, stop!" yelled Jessica as Kerry kicked Jessica's homework around. "Mom!" she implored, but her mother just shrugged, sighed, and went back to the dishes.

Kerry, Jessica's sister had heart trouble. Just after she was born, Kerry's heart rate had raced out of control. The doctors were able to slow down her heart with medication, but not before it caused her to lose some of the use of the left side of her body. Still, she learned to crawl almost as soon as any baby would, and her weak leg didn't stop her from being a normal pesky little sister. To Jessica it felt like Kerry, and her other little sister Katie, spent all day thinking up ways to bug her when she got home from school.

Suddenly, Kerry plopped herself down on the floor and started crying. She pulled at the brace on her leg. "Boo-boo," she whimpered. Her sock had fallen down again and the brace had rubbed a large raw patch on her calf.

"I don't know what we're going to do," said Mom, scooping up the baby in her arms. "Look at her leg. I hate to keep her in tights when it's so warm."

"That's it!" Jessica exclaimed. "I know what I'm doing for the Invention Convention!"

"What?"

"Let me work on it for a while and I'll show you." She rushed upstairs, collected a few things from her mother's room and something from her sisters' room, and then locked herself in her own room to work undisturbed.

When she finally emerged two hours later, she was clutching what seemed like a jumble of socks. "Hey, Mom, look at this. I made a special sock for Kerry." Jessica held it up and pointed. "See, it has these Velcro straps on the top that hook around the top of her leg brace and then reattach to her sock. That way the socks can't fall down and Kerry's leg is protected."

"What a wonderful idea! Let's try them on her," said Mom. "Look, Kerry, Jessica made some new socks for you." Katie clapped as she jumped up and down. Kerry smiled, and thumped her hand against the floor as her mother put the new sock on under her brace.

The next day, Jessica brought her invention to school.

When she got home, Kerry and Katie greeted her at the front door, chattering noisily. They hugged her legs and pulled at her. Jessica lost her balance and they all fell to the floor in a heap, laughing and tickling each other.

"How was the Invention Convention Jessica?" asked her mother. "Were the kids and your teacher impressed with your socks?"

"It was okay, I guess. My invention wasn't as cool as Jane's thing that organized her video games, or Nicole's contraption that opened a soda without breaking a nail, or Sandy's Band-Aid dispenser."

"Those things are really interesting, but I like your idea better—it's more helpful," her mom replied.

"Yeah. I wanted to do something for a real person who needed help." Jessica said as she tweaked Kerry on the nose. "Well, almost a real person." They all laughed.

Jessica's socks won first prize in her fourth-grade class. After winning a district-wide competition, she represented her town in the state-level convention at the Garden State Arts Center.

"What an honor! What an accomplishment!" everyone said to her.

Yes, Jessica won the contest, and she was proud; but what really made her feel warm inside was when Kerry looked up at her with a smile that said it all. That's when she knew she'd won something truly important—a special place in her little sister's heart.

Barbara McCutcheon Crawford

Just Ask

*Perseverance is a great element of success. If
you only knock long enough and loud enough
at the gate, you are sure to wake up somebody.*

Henry Wadsworth Longfellow

Not many people have been seated next to Miss America
at a dinner, run with the Olympic torch, received an award
from First Lady Hillary Clinton or had an article published
about them in *People* magazine. But that's exactly what has
happened to me, just a regular kid. Once I read the article
about Stan, I became a "take action" kind of kid.

I probably ought to begin with proper introductions
and credits. One day, while reading the paper, my mom
came across an article about a man named Stan Curtis.
Stan had come up with an idea to feed the hungry at no
cost. His plan was to give leftover food from places like
restaurants, hospitals and fund-raising dinners to places
like soup kitchens and homeless shelters. He started an
organization called Harvest to help him with the idea.
Mom thought I'd find the article interesting and passed it
along to me.

After reading it, I thought about what a good idea it was to do something useful with leftover food. It made sense and was such a simple, logical idea. At the time, I had been thinking about how to fulfill my bar mitzvah project, which, as part of my Jewish religion, required that I show responsibility to my community. Bingo! *This might be just what I've been looking for,* I thought. I decided to become a volunteer at the local chapter of Harvest.

What I found out when I arrived at Harvest is that the volunteers don't actually feed the hungry. They deliver leftover food to the shelters and kitchens. If I wanted to become a volunteer, I would have to drive. *Uhhh, hello! I'm only in the sixth grade!* I had hit my first big problem, but I quickly came up with a solution. I volunteered my parents!

They were actually very cool about it and agreed to drive. I'd mostly lift boxes and stuff like that. Becoming a volunteer who helped to get food to hungry people made me feel really good about myself. I was thinking of other places that could donate food when the idea hit me. *I bet I could get my school to donate the leftover food from the cafeteria.*

The next day, I saw my school principal on campus. I decided it wouldn't hurt to just ask him if our cafeteria could donate leftover food to the Harvest organization. The principal said that he liked the idea but that there were all kinds of legal problems and complications involved with a project like that. "Besides," he said, "I don't have the authority to start such a program." *Fine,* I thought. *I'll go to your boss and ask him.*

Mom explained that the principal's boss was actually a group of people who made up the school board. "It would be best to start by writing letters," she advised me. So I wrote to them and asked if they would allow the cafeteria at my school to give their leftover food (like milk in containers and other untouched food) to the Harvest organization. I included a packet of information about Harvest with each letter. I gave the board members a week to think about it, and then I called and talked to them about what I wanted to do. I had no idea how important these people were. I just knew that I wanted them to say yes, and that meant getting them to listen to me.

Most of them told me that they liked the idea, but that I would need to come before the board at their next meeting and propose the idea in person. So, to prepare for my big presentation, I went ahead of time to check out the room. I was blown away! There were TV cameras, big lights, microphones—totally high-tech looking stuff. It looked like a courtroom that I'd seen on TV. I was impressed. Totally psyched, I rushed home to practice my speech. I was kind of nervous, but I knew that if I really put my heart into it, they wouldn't be able to turn me down.

At last, the big meeting came. I had practiced so much that I was relaxed. I spoke to the board the way I would talk to my parents. My closing line was, "Today is my twelfth birthday, and saying yes would be the best present that you could give me." The audience in the room stood up and clapped for a long time. It seemed like forever as the board quietly discussed my proposal. Finally, the chairman announced that the board would approve my request. Since the board represented all the schools in the district, their approval was for 92 of the 155 schools that they represented (some didn't have their own cafeteria). *Ninety-two schools!*

After the meeting, it was explained to me that even though the board approved the plan, it could take up to a year to see the program actually begin. They would most likely need to take care of a lot of details and "red tape." I had no idea what "red tape" meant, but I soon learned that it was when things got sort of tied up or tangled up in the process of getting something done.

The health department wanted the schools to pack food in airtight containers, and neither the school district nor Harvest had any money to pay for them. I thought, *No problem. I'll get people to donate them.* So I wrote letters to supermarkets and companies that make containers and plastic bags, and all but one made a donation. It turned out that that wasn't enough. I was about to try something else when I received a letter from Glad-Lock. The letter was two sentences long: "We appreciate your letter. Your shipment will be arriving in the next couple of days."

"Shipment?" my mom questioned, her eyebrows raised to their limit. "What do they mean by *shipment?*"

Her question was answered only a few hours later when a UPS truck pulled up in front of our house and the driver delivered not one, not two, but eight cases of containers.

Now that we had containers, I thought that things would finally begin to happen. I contacted the school board again, and was surprised to find out that they thought the program had already started. *Wrong!* I realized then that if you want something done, even though people say that they're handling it, you have to stay involved and on top of things until it really does happen.

Finally, the first donation of leftover food from my school was delivered to a shelter, and my mom and I were asked to make the delivery. What I thought would take about three weeks ended up taking almost a year to accomplish. But the program was finally up and running—two days before my thirteenth birthday!

A few weeks later, my bar mitzvah took place. Instead of gifts, I asked that people make donations to the Harvest Organization. Over five hundred pounds of food were donated in my name. A family friend, who had just started college and was not able to afford a gift, volunteered time at a shelter in my honor. It was a really original gift that helped a lot of people in need.

Through my work with Harvest, I had the opportunity to sit next to Miss America one night at a fund-raising dinner. I decided that inviting Miss America to my bar mitzvah would be a fun thing to do. Even though she wasn't able to come to the party, she actually sent a gift and left a message for me on our answering machine. I popped that tape right out of the machine and played it for all my friends when they came over. I'd tease them by asking, "Did Miss America ever call you? I don't think so!"

After the success of the school program, I received a call from a local disk jockey who suggested, as he interviewed me, that I take my idea all around the state. I thought, *Why not?* So far, all I really had to do was make phone calls, write some letters and give a speech or two, and I had seen some amazing results. So I got in touch with one of our local politicians and went to work once again. I had to write a bill for the House of Representatives to vote on, because the law needed to be changed in order for the program to be started statewide. My sister had taken government classes in school, so she helped me. I wanted the bill to encourage restaurants, schools and other places that serve food to donate their leftovers to organizations like Harvest. Too much food was ending up in Dumpsters.

Although the House of Representatives passed the bill, we are still waiting for it to be voted on by the state senate. We're halfway there. It's just a matter of time.

I think back on the day when my principal told me that he couldn't make the project happen. If I had let it go at that, I would have never come this far. I taught myself that you don't have to be an adult to make a difference. Actually, I think that being a kid can be an advantage. I think that I was more likely to believe that this could work because I hadn't experienced very many failures in life. I just expected that things would happen if I stayed focused. I learned to just start at the bottom and work my way up until the answer was yes.

I believe so strongly that you should *just ask* that while receiving an award at the White House, I took the opportunity to ask First Lady Hillary Clinton what she does with her leftovers. I can only imagine what I'd have to do to get the White House on the list of donors. Talk about red tape!

David Levitt, age 16

[EDITORS' NOTE: *If you would like more information on how to start a program at your school, call 1-800-USA 4 FOOD.*]

7

OVERCOMING OBSTACLES

Don't be a coward, fearful and weak
  Be the last one to quit, and the first one to
    speak
  Don't hide your face from the light of day
  Be courageous in life and stay that way
  No need to run from your trials, troubles
    and problems
  Have confidence in your step as you reflect
    how to solve them
  Yet, if you happen to fall, don't lie there and die
  Get up without a thought, and hold your
    head up high
  Be wise, courageous, bold and brave
  And life will be worth living, from your
    birth to your grave.

Jereme Durkin

Grandfather Learns to Read

Anyone who stops learning is old, whether at twenty or eighty. Anyone who keeps learning stays young. The greatest thing in life is to keep your mind young.

Henry Ford

Joey sat at the kitchen table, reading the sports page of the morning paper. He heard his grandfather coming down the stairs. When his grandfather came into the kitchen, Joey could see he wasn't his usual happy self.

"Morning, Grandfather," he said. His grandfather sat across the table, looking glum. He didn't pick up the paper to read. Instead, he asked, "Joey, is anything happening in town today?"

"There's a ball game between Doraville Middle School and my school tonight," Joey told him. "It'll be a close race, but I think we'll win. Would you like to go?"

Joey felt bad for his grandfather. He knew he couldn't read. His grandfather had told him often, "I didn't have the chance to go to school regularly. Looking after the animals and tending to the crops on the farm were much more important in those days than learning to read."

Joey always listened carefully when his grandfather told him how proud he was to have lived on a farm. He told him about caring for the animals. He described trips to the market to sell produce from the farm. Joey could see how rough and callused his grandfather's hands were. He spoke proudly to Joey about working from sunrise to sunset. Joey noticed how sad his grandfather's face looked when he remarked, "I would have liked to have gone to school more often, but there wasn't much time."

One day Grandfather asked Joey, "Joey, would you go with me to the grocery store? I need several things." In the store, Joey's grandfather walked up and down the aisles, looking at all the pictures on the cans. He saw a can without a picture on it. "What's in that can?" he asked.

Joey, reading the label, said, "It's a can of chicken soup." His grandfather walked to the meat counter, but he couldn't read the prices or the labels.

Finally Grandfather gave Joey the grocery list and stomped out of the store. "I'll meet you at the car," he said. Joey watched him go through the door, and he thought, *I wish I could help him out, but I wouldn't even know where to begin. I wouldn't have any idea how to start.*

The next day was Sunday. Joey and his grandfather always took a walk into town on that day to attend church. Joey stopped at the library to look through some books while his grandfather went down the street to talk with old friends. He was unhappy because he knew his grandfather couldn't even read the street signs.

Going into the library, Joey saw a sign on the library wall. It read: "Do you know somebody who doesn't read? We can help. Just call this number."

When his grandfather returned to the library, Joey showed the sign to him. "Somebody can teach you how to read. It says so right here," Joey explained. Joey jotted the number down, and they hurried home.

Several days later, Grandfather put on his best suit of clothes for his first day of school. He arrived at the library an hour early and met with his teacher. During that first class, he was so worried and nervous that he couldn't concentrate. He couldn't remember anything the teacher said.

A few weeks later, Grandfather was studying when he looked up at Joey and said, "I'm too old to learn all of this." He closed the book in frustration.

"Oh, Grandfather, don't get discouraged," Joey said.

Grandfather was stubborn. "I can't do it," he said.

"How about letting me help you?" Joey asked. Grandfather didn't want to seem ungrateful, so he said, "Thanks, Joey. I'm sure that would be a big help."

They studied together and worked hard on Grandfather's lessons every day. Joey took over all the chores to give his grandfather more time to study. He told his grandfather he could study in his room, where it would be quieter and the phone wouldn't interrupt him.

Months later, his grandfather called Joey into his room. "Joey," he said, "I just got a letter from Aunt Helen. Let me read it to you." As Grandfather read, he pronounced each word very slowly, and tears came to his eyes.

When Joey's grandfather had finished reading the letter, Joey was crying, too. He was so proud of his grandfather for overcoming a lifelong obstacle that his chest felt as though it was about to burst with joy.

Grandfather looked up from the page and locked his tear-filled eyes with Joey's. "Grandfather," said Joey, smiling, "great job! I'm so proud of you." Grandfather smiled back, and then he broke into a grin—a grin so big, so wide, that Joey knew Grandfather was proud of himself, too.

Karen Beth Luckett

"I would have gotten a hundred if I hadn't missed those six problems."

Reprinted by permission of Bil Keane.

School—Moving Up

Teach me to walk and I shall run
Teach me to look and I shall see
Teach me to hear and I shall listen
Teach me to sing and I shall rejoice
For your instructions are imprinted in my mind
And your shared experiences I shall keep
What I have learned, I shall treasure
And by learning to fly
I shall soar!

Donna L. Clovis

"You look tired," I said one evening when Mother trudged into our narrow apartment. It was already dark, and she had put in a long day working two jobs.

"Guess I am," she said, as she collapsed into the over-stuffed chair and kicked off her shoes. With a smile she asked, "What did you learn in school today?"

No matter how tired she was, if we were still up when she got home, Mother asked about school. I got the idea pretty early in life that school was important to her.

She was satisfied with my schoolwork in Boston. I got

good grades at the small, private church school Curtis and I attended. Mother thought that place would give us a better education than the public schools.

But when we moved back to Detroit in 1961, I found out that we had been mistaken. The fifth-graders at Higgins Elementary School knew so much more than I that they left me in the dust in every subject. There was no doubt in anyone's mind that I was the dumbest kid in the whole class. I felt stupid from the top of my head to the bottom of my sneakers.

I thought I was too stupid to even read the letters in an eye test that we took halfway through the year. The boy in front of me rattled off every single letter on the examination chart. I squinted, tried to focus and just barely made out the first line.

But there the problem was not with my brain; it was my eyes. I had no idea that my eyesight was so bad. The school provided me with free glasses, and when I wore them to school, I was amazed. I could actually see the writing on the chalkboard from the back of the classroom! Getting glasses started me on my climb upward from the bottom of the class.

When my next report card came out, I was thrilled to see that I had gained a D in math. "Benjamin, on the whole you're doing so much better," Mrs. Williamson said to me. *I'm improving,* I thought. *There's hope for me. I'm not the dumbest kid in the school.*

Despite my excitement and sense of hope, though, my mother was not happy. "Oh, it's an improvement all right," she said. "And I'm proud of you for getting a better grade. But you can't settle for just barely passing. You're too smart to do that. You can make the top math grade in the class."

"But Mother, I didn't fail," I moaned. "I'm doing the best I can."

"But you can still do better, and I'm going to help you." Her eyes sparkled. I should have known from that look that she had already started hatching a plan.

Mother was a goalsetter by nature. That was why we had moved back to Detroit in the first place. Mother had her heart set on getting back into our old house, which she was still renting out. For the time being, we lived in a top-floor apartment in a smoggy industrial area while she worked two and three jobs at a time. But as the weeks and months passed, she said, "Boys, just wait. We're going back to our house on Deacon Street. We may not be able to afford living in it now, but we'll make it."

Mother set the same kind of high goals for Curtis and me, and she wouldn't take no for an answer. I remember when Curtis came home with a note from his junior high counselor. Curtis had to read some of the words to her, but she understood exactly what the counselor had done. He had placed Curtis in the less challenging classes for those kids who would not be going to college.

Curtis was one of the few black kids in the school. Mother had no doubt that the counselor thought blacks were not capable of doing college work.

"They're not going to treat my boy that way," she declared, staring at the paper Curtis had given her.

"What are you going to do?" I asked in surprise. I never imagined that anyone could argue with a decision made by school authorities.

"I'm going right over there in the morning and get this straightened out," she said. The tone of her voice showed she meant business. That evening, Mother told us what had happened. "I said to that counselor, 'My son Curtis is going to college. I don't want him in any vocational courses.'" Then she put her hand on my brother's head. "Curtis, you are now in college prep courses."

Mother refused to lower her sights for her boys. At the

same time, she would not settle for anything less than the best we could give. She certainly was not going to let me be content with a D. "I've got two smart boys," she insisted. "Two mighty smart boys. Now, since you've started getting better in math, Bennie, you're going to go on. And here's how you'll do it. First thing you're going to do is memorize your times tables."

"My times tables?" I cried. "Do you know how many there are? Why, that could take a year!"

She stood up a little taller. "I only went through third grade, and I know them all the way through my twelves."

"But Mother, I can't. . . ."

"You can do it, Bennie. You just have to set your mind to it. You work on them. Tomorrow when I get home from work, we'll review them."

I argued a little more, but I should have known better.

"Besides"—here came her final shot—"you're not to go outside and play after school until you've learned those tables."

I was almost in tears. "Look at all these things!" I cried, pointing to the columns in my math book. "How can any-one learn all of them?" But talking to Mother was like talk-ing to a stone.

I learned the times tables. I just kept repeating them until they fixed themselves in my brain. Mother kept prodding me and went over them with me at night. Within days after learning my times tables, math became so much easier. I'll never forget how I practically shouted my score to Mrs. Williamson after another math quiz. "Twenty-four! I got twenty-four right!" School became much more enjoyable. Nobody laughed or called me dummy anymore.

I thought I was on top of the world, but Mother was far from satisfied. She had proved to me that I could succeed in one thing. The next part of her plan was to keep setting higher goals. I can't say I cared much for this plan.

"I've decided you boys are watching too much television," she said one evening, snapping off the set in the middle of a program.

"We don't watch that much," I protested. I tried to argue that some of the programs were educational and that the smartest kids in the class watched television.

As if she did not hear a word, she said, "From now on, you boys can watch no more than three programs a week." She had also decided what we were going to do with all those hours we had spent on television. "You boys are going to go to the library and check out books. You're going to read at least two books every week. At the end of each week, you'll give me a report on what you've read."

I couldn't believe it. Two books? I had never read a book in my life except those they made us read at school. But a day or two later, Curtis and I dragged our feet the seven blocks from home to the public library. We obeyed Mother because we loved her and because we could tell when she meant business. But that did not stop us from grumbling the whole way.

Several of Mother's friends criticized her strictness. I heard one woman ask, "What are you doing to those boys, making them study all the time? They're going to hate you."

"They can hate me," she answered, "but they're going to get a good education just the same."

Of course, I never hated her. I did not like the constant pressure, but she made me realize the hard work was for my own good. Almost every day, she would say, "Bennie, you can do anything you set yourself to do."

Since I have always loved animals, nature and science, I chose library books on those subjects. My fifth-grade science teacher, Mr. Jaeck, discovered my interest and gave me special projects to do, such as identifying fish or rocks.

By the end of the year, I could pick up just about any rock along the railroad tracks and tell what it was. After reading fish and water-life books, I started checking streams for insects. Mr. Jaeck let me look at water samples under his microscope.

Slowly, I began looking forward to my trips to the library. The staff there got to know Curtis and me. They began offering suggestions on what we might like to read. Soon my interests widened to include books on adventure and scientific discoveries.

As I continued reading, my vocabulary and spelling improved. Up until the last few weeks of fifth grade, our weekly spelling bees were one of the worst parts of school for me. I usually dropped out on the first word. Mrs. Williamson gave us one final spelling bee that covered every word we were supposed to have learned that year. As everyone expected, Bobby Farmer won the spelling bee. He was clearly the smartest boy in the fifth grade. But to my surprise, the final word he spelled correctly to win the contest was *agriculture*.

I can spell that word, I thought with excitement. I had learned it just the day before from my library book. As Bobby sat down, a thrill swept through me. *I'll bet I can spell any other word in the world. I'll bet I could learn to spell better than Bobby.*

Learning to spell better than Bobby Farmer challenged me. I kept reading all through the summer. By the time I began sixth grade, I had learned to spell a lot of words. In the sixth grade, Bobby was still the smartest boy in the class, but I was gaining ground on him. I kept improving until, by the time I entered seventh grade at Wilson Junior High, I was at the top of the class.

The very kids who once teased me about being dumb started coming up to me and asking, "Bennie, how do you solve this problem?" I beamed when I gave them the answer. It was fun to get good grades, to earn people's respect. But by then, making it to the top of the class was not good enough for me. Mother's influence had started to sink in. I did not work hard just to be better than the other kids. I did it because I wanted to be the very best I could be—for me.

Ben Carson, M.D.

[EDITORS' NOTE: *Ben Carson, M.D., is a graduate of Yale University and the University of Michigan Medical School. He is currently the Director of Pediatric Neurosurgery at Johns Hopkins University in Baltimore, Maryland. In 1987, Dr. Carson gained worldwide recognition for his part in the first successful separation of Siamese twins joined at the back of the head, which took five months of planning and twenty-two hours of surgery.*]

In Control

I was six years old when it all started—I was diagnosed with A.D.D./L.D. That means I have attention deficit disorder and a learning disability. That's a big problem to grasp for someone so young. People were not sure how I would function, and I did terribly. I didn't want to sit down in class. I remember that the teachers were always on my case. During lessons, I had trouble understanding what the teachers were saying. I worked on my homework from dinnertime to almost bedtime with my parents. It was very hard for me to do homework because I didn't understand it. I would get frustrated, and then my parents would get upset.

At school, I was in the principal's office more than I was in the classroom. The teacher would ask me *why* I didn't understand something, and I would just shout, "It's none of your business!" at her because I was embarrassed that I couldn't understand the work. Then the teacher would send me to the principal's office. I finally started to improve a little, but I still had problems throughout elementary school.

By the time I got to middle school, my behavior was

really bad. My worst memories were the rides home on the bus. I remember getting off the bus one day, saying good-bye to the driver, and as the bus left, two guys beat me up. I tried to defend myself, and at the same time, I was trying to flag the bus down. I remember feeling all alone. I walked home with a black eye and a swollen face.

I also remember running my mouth one day to a kid who was bigger than I was. I was defending my brother. I talked trash about the kid's family. He punched me and accused me of calling him a bad name. I got in-school suspension (ISS) for two days.

The kids where I lived were very mean and hateful, and they called me names like "fatty" and "loser." This hurt me because I felt inside that I *was* a fatty and a loser.

I felt I was a failure—but I was raised to believe that you are only a failure if you truly believe you are. I didn't want to be a failure.

When I finally reached seventh grade, I was making D's and F's, and pulling ISS all the time. I was always getting the whole class in an uproar by flinging rubber bands and throwing spit wads at the board. I remember punching a boy for calling me a "fat boy." I got ISS for three days. During those three days, I got the ISS students in an uproar by making fun of what the teacher did and imitating him. For my actions, I got more and more ISS.

My parents started to look for other schools that might help me to learn to function better. That's when they found Knollwood, a school for special students. I was enrolled last year. It's great! I know now that there will always be people who care, whether they're parents or teachers. They will always help, but you have to want to get better to be successful, or it won't matter how much they do to help you. I finally realized that I could change. I can prove that John Troxler can be a success.

I am no longer getting D's and F's. I am making A's, B's

and C's. I am now completing the eighth grade, and I am in a tenth-grade social studies book. In other subjects, I am also above average. Though I still have some trouble, I feel deep down inside that my return to a regular school is just around the corner. With the help of my teachers, I will be ready for high school. It has taken me seven years to finally realize that A.D.D. and L.D. are handicaps that I will always have, but I can, and will be, successful and in control. It's up to me!

John D. Troxler, age 14

The Sandbox

*I expect to pass through life but once. If there-
fore, there can be any kindness I can show, or
any good thing I can do to a fellow being, let me
do it now, and do not defer or neglect it, as I
shall not pass this way again.*

William Penn

One day, when I was five, I went to a local park with my
mom. While I was playing in the sandbox, I noticed a boy
about my age in a wheelchair. I went over to him and
asked if he could play. Since I was only five, I couldn't
understand why he couldn't just get in the sandbox and
play with me. He told me he couldn't. I talked to him for
a while longer, then I took my large bucket, scooped up as
much sand as I could and dumped it into his lap. Then I
grabbed some toys and put them in his lap, too.

My mom rushed over and said, "Lucas, why did you do
that?"

I looked at her and replied, "He couldn't play in the
sandbox with me, so I brought the sand to him. Now we
can play in the sand together."

Lucas Parker, age 11

What a Year

Applaud us when we run,
Console us when we fall,
Cheer us when we recover. . . .

Edmund Burke

"Why do you wear such big pants?" kids on the bus would tease. At the after-school YMCA program, kids were equally cruel. I was so hurt by their comments, I didn't know how to answer back. At the age of nine, I weighed 115 pounds, more than most other kids at school!

I thought of myself as a regular kid. But according to many of the children in my school, I was a nobody. I had friends here and there, but that year, friends began to fade away. My interests were in reading a good book, writing and schoolwork in general. I pulled some of the highest grades in my fourth-grade class. But I didn't fit in and wasn't socially accepted because I wasn't interested in athletics like most of the other boys, and I was overweight.

My one friend, Conner, would stand up for me sometimes with things like, "How can you judge someone you don't even know?" Conner had a lot of challenges when it came to the other kids making fun of him, too. He had a stuttering problem that became the target of the same kinds of put-downs.

The teasing got so bad that every day after school, I came home either crying or totally destroyed mentally. I was very much a perfectionist in my schoolwork and other interests, achieving goals that I set for myself. I couldn't stand that I was losing friends and just couldn't take the joking any longer.

I decided to starve myself. I figured that if I could control my eating habits, I could change my physical appearance and end the teasing. I started checking the calories on the labels of everything I ate. If I could get away with it, I skipped meals altogether. A salad was usually the most I ate in a day. My mom and dad were totally unaware of my plan as long as my lunch box was empty and my cereal was partially eaten.

At dinner, I made excuses about having had a big lunch so I'd only have to eat a few bites, or nothing at all. Whenever possible, I came up with ways to get rid of my food. I'd wipe most of the food into the trash or hide it in extra paper towels. Often, I tried to get my parents to allow me to do my homework while eating so that I could ditch the food without their knowing about it. I was caught up in a contest with myself, and I was determined to win.

Then the sickness and headaches began. I suffered week after week of horrible headaches and endless colds. My clothes no longer fit, and it wasn't long before I was too thin to wear the new clothes Mom replaced them with.

At that point, my parents realized that I had an eating disorder and rushed me to the doctor. I weighed in at only eighty-three and a half pounds. The doctor told me how dangerous this disorder is to a person's health. I realized that I was slowly starving my body of the nutrients that it needs in order to function normally. If I kept up this behavior, I could become seriously sick and maybe even die.

The doctor and my parents helped me to set up new, healthy goals for myself. I went to see a counselor, started a weight-lifting program and decided to try playing sports.

My mom heard about a winter-session lacrosse clinic that would help me learn about the sport before I would be expected to compete in it. Lacrosse is big in our area, but I had never given it a try. After the first few clinics, I didn't want to go back. I hadn't mastered the game in the first few tries, so the perfectionist in me couldn't stand not being able to be in control. But I kept going, and finally, I started feeling better and better after each time out on the field. I was getting the hang of the game, and I liked it. Lacrosse gave me then, and still gives me now, confidence in myself. It's also great exercise, so it helps me stay healthy.

The year after the clinic, I was playing so well that I was chosen to be on a travel team of kids more experienced than I. I began to make new friends with kids on my team, and they don't tease me. They respect me for working so hard at the game that I can play at their level.

It's been three years since the beginning of fourth grade, when my life had started to fall apart. What a year! I have learned to find self-esteem in the things that make me special and not in what others say or don't say about me. I am still the same perfectionist that I was born to be, but I know when I need to stop pushing myself so hard. I concentrate on perfection where it really matters. I still get high grades and love to read and write, and I have also discovered interests like playing the drums, football and tennis. I plan to play basketball during the next season.

Trying to totally change my physical appearance didn't lead to happiness. I learned that "beauty is only skin deep," and it's what's inside that counts. Getting involved with things that I enjoy has helped my self-confidence, and I have made the kind of friends who like me for who I am—not for what I look like.

Robert Diehl, age 12

Dear God, This Is Charles

A man, as a general rule, owes very little to what he is born with—a man is what he makes of himself.

Alexander Graham Bell

Dear God,

This is Charles. I turned twelve the other day. If you noticed, I'm typing this letter. Sometimes it's hard for me to write, you know. It's this thing called dysgraphia. I also have Attention Deficit Disorder—oftentimes learning disabilities accompany A.D.D. My IQ was tested at 140, but if you graded my cursive, you'd think I was dumb.

I never could hold a pencil the right way. I never could color in the lines. Every time I would try, my hand would cramp up and the letters would come out sloppy, the lines too dark, and the marker would get all over my hands. Nobody wanted to switch papers with me to grade them because they couldn't read them. Keith could, but he moved away.

My brain doesn't sense what my hand is doing. I can

feel the pencil, but the message doesn't get through right. I have to grip the pencil tighter so my brain knows that I have it in my hand.

It's much easier for me to explain things by talking than it is to write. I'm really good at dictating, but my teachers don't always let me. If I am asked to write an essay on my trip to Washington and Philadelphia, it's like a punishment. But if I can dictate it, or just get up and talk about it, I can tell everyone about the awesomeness of seeing *the* Declaration of Independence in the National Archives or the feeling of true patriotism that rushed through me when I stood in the room where our founding fathers debated the issues of freedom.

If I got graded on art, I'd fail for sure. There are so many things that I can picture in my mind, but my hands just don't draw it the way I see it.

It's okay. I'm not complaining. I'm really doing fine. You see, you gave me a wonderful mind and a great sense of humor. I'm great at figuring things out, and I love to debate. We have some great Bible discussions in class, and that's where I really shine.

I want to be a lawyer when I grow up, a trial lawyer in fact. I know I'd be good at that. I would be responsible for researching the crime, examining the evidence and truthfully presenting the case.

You have told me that you made me special when you said that I am fearfully and wonderfully made. You have assured me that you will see me through, and that you have plans for me to give me a future and hope.

My parents want to help me, so they bought me a laptop to take to school. My teacher is the best this year! I am allowed to do a lot of my work on the computer. We have a character trait book due every Friday, and guess what? She lets me use Print Shop Deluxe for the artwork. For the first time, I'll be able to show everyone some of the things

I have in my mind.

Lord, this is a thank-you letter, just to let you know I'm doing fine. Life's hard sometimes, but you know what? I accept the challenge. I have the faith to see myself through anything. Thanks for making me *me*. Thanks for loving me *unconditionally*. Thanks for everything.

In your service,
Charles

Charles Inglehart, age 12

Missy and Me

I sold my bike to a friend in my sixth-grade class when we moved from Oklahoma. I planned to buy a new one in California when we got settled, but that never happened. The house we bought in San Diego was near a busy highway, outside of town, and I wasn't allowed to ride there, even if I had wanted to.

Instead I spent my bike money on Missy, a cuddly, brown-eyed cocker spaniel puppy. It was love at first sight. The other puppies at the kennel hopped all over each other, but Missy walked straight up to me and gently licked my hand with her pink tongue. When I picked her up, she looked at me with those big, sad eyes, and I was hooked.

I missed my friends in Oklahoma. I wrote to all of them every week. The kids in my new school made fun of my Southern accent. One red-haired girl named Melissa mimicked me every time I spoke. She showed off by arguing with the school bus driver and using swear words. When I heard him call her "missy," I felt like changing my puppy's name.

In those days, my only friend was my dog. Every day, I

spent hours training her and brushing her blond, wavy coat. Within a few weeks, she was house trained. At night, she slept curled up in my bed. In the morning, she licked my face to let me know she was awake and wanted to go outside.

One morning when she was six months old, I was dressing for school when I heard screeching brakes and a yelp. I ran down our driveway to see a huge truck pulled over to the side of the highway and the limp body of Missy lying in the ditch. "You hit my dog!" I screamed at the driver. I jumped into the ditch and picked up Missy's lifeless body. "Wake up, wake up!" I yelled at her.

My parents thanked the man for stopping. "The dog ran out right in front of me," he said. "I tried to stop." I knew he meant it, but all I could do was cry.

I carried Missy into the house and wrapped her in her favorite blanket. I rocked her and cried, hoping she would wake up, but she never did.

Before my dad went to work, we dug a little grave and buried her. The three of us held hands, and my dad thanked God for giving us Missy. Then he prayed to God, asking for him to send me new friends here in California. My dad ended his prayer by thanking God for the joy Missy had brought to my life. But I didn't feel thankful. The thoughts just went around and around in my head. *Why hadn't God protected her? Why hadn't he kept her from running out on the highway? He knew how lonely I was. Why had he taken my only friend away?*

For weeks, I cried myself to sleep. I woke up every morning to the bad dream that was my reality—Missy was gone. Classes, teachers, homework and weekends all blurred together through my tears. I tried to concentrate on my schoolwork, but all I could think about was Missy. My parents offered to buy me another dog, but I didn't want just any dog. I wanted Missy. Nothing else mattered anymore.

One day, my gym teacher gave me a hall pass and told me to go to see the vice principal. *I must be in trouble if I'm being sent to Mrs. Stevens's office,* I thought.

Mrs. Stevens asked me to sit down. In a gentle voice, she said, "You must be wondering why I called you in. Your teachers are concerned about you. They have seen you crying in class. Do you want to talk about it?"

I began sobbing so violently that I couldn't speak. She handed me a box of tissues. Finally I choked out, "My dog got run over." We talked for the whole gym period. When the bell rang, Mrs. Stevens gave me a little notebook.

"Sometimes it helps when you write down your feelings," she said. "Be honest. You don't have to ever show it to anyone—it's just for you. It may help you decide what you are learning about life and death." She smiled and led me to the door with her arm around my shoulder.

For the next week, I did what she said, spilling out all my sadness and anger. I wrote to God about letting Missy die. I wrote about my parents moving to this awful place. I wrote about Melissa and the kids who hurt my feelings. I even wrote to Missy: "I loved you so much. Why were you so stupid? I taught you not to go near the highway! Now you are gone forever. Forever. Things will never be the same. Never."

When I couldn't write any more, I finally closed my notebook and wept. I cried and cried. I cried because things never would be the same, because Missy wasn't coming back and because I knew we weren't going to move back to Oklahoma. When I was finished crying, there was nothing else to do. I decided I would just have to make the best of it.

As difficult as it was, Missy and her death helped me to grow up that year. God answered my dad's prayer and gave me new friends to fill my loneliness. I finally stopped missing all my old friends. My time was filled with school and activities instead of just memories. I was surprised that these friends became just as special as the ones that I had left behind in Oklahoma. My heart was starting to heal.

Even though I still believe that no other dog could ever take Missy's place in my heart, maybe one of these days I'll let my parents buy me another dog. Maybe.

Glenda Palmer

The Miracle of Life

Courageous risks are life-giving; they help you grow, make you brave and better than you think you are.

Joan L. Curcio

I never knew how valuable life was until I almost lost my little brother. It all started when my brother got sick. I was nine, and he was just nine months. My mother thought it was an ear infection because he kept grabbing his ear. The first doctor she took him to told her that it was an ear infection. After a week, he was still grabbing his ear. My mother took him to a different doctor for a second opinion. They immediately started running blood tests on him. The doctor knew that he needed to be in the hospital as quickly as possible. My mother, father and brother all rode to the hospital in a speeding ambulance.

At first the doctors did not know what was wrong with him. Then a couple days later, they found out he had a type of bone marrow cancer. My mother and father stayed with my brother the first few weeks. Then my mother would stay with my brother while my father would come home and see my sisters and me. It was hard not seeing my mother all the time, but I did go to the hospital about once a week.

The doctors tried one round of chemotherapy. It helped, but my brother lost his hair. Then he needed a bone marrow transplant. They needed to find a donor, so the doctors tested my family first. I was so scared to get a shot. My sisters and I were all crying. We got it over with quickly, and it did not hurt as much as I thought it would.

A couple of weeks later, we found out that one of my sisters and I were both matches. My parents had to choose which one of us should be the donor. After thinking about it for a long time, they chose me because I was the oldest. I was excited and scared at the same time, but I knew that I might save his life.

My brother was moved to Duke Hospital. It was a unit of about ten kids who all had a disease. About two weeks later, I went to Duke to do the transplant. The doctors showed me what it was going to be like. I was not scared until the next day, when I had to wake up at 5:00 A.M. I had to be at the hospital at 6:00 A.M. When I got there, I had to put on a gown. Then my mother and I went into the operating room with the doctors. They put a mask over my face, and in about ten seconds I fell asleep.

When I woke up, there was a tube stuck into the back of my hand, putting fluid into my body to keep me from getting dehydrated. I immediately wanted to know how my brother was. My mother told me that he was getting my bone marrow right then.

About two hours after I woke up, I went to see him. He was asleep, and my father was holding him. All of the bone marrow that I had donated had gone into him. Everybody hoped and prayed that it would work.

About a month and a half later, my mother came home. My brother was doing fine. We still had to be careful to not let him get sick with a cold or the flu. He could not be in the sun, either. Also, we had to wear surgical masks when we held him.

Now, two years later, he is doing great! He is full of life and is very energetic. He is always doing something. We have to watch him and make sure he does not get too curious!

This experience has shown me that all you have to do is believe. You have to believe that the best will happen. Also, you need to be strong no matter what happens. That makes a true hero!

Lacy Richardson, age 12

8

ON CHOICES

I can overcome my fears
I can buy for the hungry
I can help stop pollution
I can give to the poor
I can be what I want
I can use my head
I can give advice
I can receive
I can behave
I can listen
I can think
I can teach
I can know
I can give
I can feel
I can see
I can.

Kendra Batch, age 12

Goodwill

I cannot and will not cut my conscience to fit this year's fashions.

Lillian Hellman

Annie leaned against her locker and sighed. What a day! What a disaster! This school year wasn't starting out the way she had planned it at all.

Of course, Annie hadn't planned on that new girl, Kristen. And she definitely hadn't planned on the new girl wearing the exact skirt Annie was supposed to be wearing.

It wasn't just any skirt. Annie had baby-sat three active brothers all summer to buy that skirt and its designer accent top. When she saw them in her *Teen* magazine, Annie knew they were meant for her. She had gone right to the phone and called the 800 number for the "outlet nearest" her.

With price and picture in hand, she had set off to convince her mother.

"It's great, hon," her mother agreed. "I just can't see spending as much on one outfit as I do for all your clothes." Annie wasn't surprised, but she was disappointed.

"Well, if it's that important, we could put it on layaway," her mom said. "You'd have to pay for it, though."

So she did. Every Friday, Annie took all her baby-sitting money and paid down the balance.

She had made her final payment just last week and hurried home to try on the skirt and top. The moment of truth had arrived and she was afraid to look! She stood in front of the mirror with her eyes squeezed shut. She counted to three and forced herself to open them.

It was perfect. From the side, from the back and even from the front, it was perfect. She walked, she sat and she turned. She practiced humbly taking compliments so her friends wouldn't think she was stuck up.

The next day, Annie and her mother gave her bedroom the end of summer "good going over." They washed and ironed the bedspread and curtains, and vacuumed behind and under everything.

Then they sorted through the closets and drawers for clothes to give away. Annie dreaded all the tugging on and pulling off, the laundering and the folding into boxes. They dropped the boxes off at Goodwill, then headed to her grandmother's for the weekend.

When they got home Sunday night, Annie ran straight to her bedroom. Everything had to be just right for her grand entrance at school the next day.

She flung open her closet and pulled out her top and her . . . and her . . . skirt? It wasn't there. *It must be here!* But it wasn't.

"Dad! Mom!" Annie's search became frantic. Her parents rushed in. Hangers and clothes were flying everywhere.

"My skirt! It isn't here!" Annie stood with her top in one hand and an empty hanger in the other.

"Now, Annie," her dad said, trying to calm her, "it didn't just get up and walk away. We'll find it." But they didn't. For two hours they searched through closets, drawers, the laundry room, under the bed and even in the bed. It just wasn't there.

Annie sank into bed that night, trying to figure out the puzzle.

When she woke up the next morning, she felt tired and dull. She picked out something—anything—to wear. Nothing measured up to her summer daydreams.

It was at her school locker that the puzzle became, well, more puzzling.

"You're Annie, right?" a voice said from behind her.

Annie turned. Shock waves hit her. *That's my skirt. That's* my *skirt! That's my* skirt?

"I'm Kristen. The principal gave me the locker next to yours. She thought since we lived on the same block and I'm new here, you could show me around." Her voice trailed off, unsure. Annie just stared. *How . . . ? Where . . . ? Is that my . . . ?*

Kristen seemed uneasy. "You don't have to. I told her we didn't really know each other. We've only passed each other on the sidewalk."

That was true. Annie and Kristen had passed each other, Annie to and from her baby-sitting job and Kristen in her fast-food uniform that smelled of onions and grease at the end of the day. Annie pulled her thoughts back to Kristen's words.

"Sure. I'll be happy to show you around," Annie said, not happy at all. The entire day, friends gushed over Kristen and *the skirt* while Annie stood by with a stiff smile.

And now Annie was waiting to walk Kristen home, hoping to sort this out. They chatted all the way to Annie's house before she worked up the nerve to ask the big question. "Where did you get your skirt, Kristen?"

"Isn't it beautiful? My mom and I saw it in a magazine while we were waiting for my grandma at the doctor's office."

"Oh, your mom bought it for you."

"Well, no." Kristen lowered her voice. "We've had kind of a hard time lately. Dad lost his job, and my grandma was sick. We moved here to take care of her while my dad looked for work."

All that went right over Annie's head. "You must have saved most of your paycheck then."

Kristen blushed. "I saved all my money and gave it to my mom to buy school clothes for my brother and sister."

Annie couldn't stand it. "Where did you get your skirt?"

Kristen stammered, "My mother found it at Goodwill in a box that was dropped off just as she got there. Mom opened it, and there was the skirt from the magazine, brand new, with the tags still on it!" Kristen looked up.

Goodwill? Brand new? The puzzle pieces finally fell into place.

Kristen smiled, and her face glowed. "My mother knew it was meant for me. She knew it was a blessing."

"Kristen, I . . . " Annie stopped. This wasn't going to be easy. "Kristen," Annie tried again, "can I tell you something?"

"Sure. Anything."

"Kristen." Annie took a deep breath. She hesitated for a moment. Then she smiled and said, "Do you have a minute to come up to my room? I think I have a top that would go great with your skirt."

Cynthia M. Hamond

Putting My Best Foot Forward

Destiny is not a matter of chance; it is a matter of choice. It is not a thing to be waited for; it is a thing to be achieved.

William Jennings Bryan

I could feel the sweat start to trickle down my back, right between my shoulder blades. There I was, standing in the hot sun, while the team captains chose who they wanted on their team for a baseball game during fourth grade recess.

There were only four of us left.

"I'll take Sandy," said one of the team captains.

"David," said the other. The palms of my hands started to sweat.

"Rachel." My heart sank.

"Alright . . . I'll take Kathy." I was sure everyone was looking at me . . . skinny Kathy, with the skinny legs and arms—Kathy, that no one wanted on their team. I wanted to crawl under a rock and hide. I was humiliated . . . once again.

I was a geek to most of the kids in school. I was shy, quiet, scrawny . . . and afraid to make friends.

At home with my parents, I always felt okay with myself. My folks were hard-working people who loved and supported me, and believed in my capabilities. They taught me to go for what I wanted no matter what it was.

In kindergarten, I had been invited to a birthday party. I wanted to get a really nice present for the girl who invited me, and my parents encouraged me to work for the money to buy the present. My dad said to me, "You have two arms and two legs and a brain, Kathy. If you want extra money, you can simply earn it."

Because my parents believed in me so much, I believed in myself, too. To earn the money, I painted pictures on rocks and sold them door to door in my neighborhood, sold fruit and vegetables from our garden, and did yard work for our neighbors. Although I was just a small child, buying a gift for my friend with the money I earned myself gave me a tremendous sense of empowerment.

By the time I was in fourth grade, I was making enough money to buy my own clothes and toys, and whatever candy and treats I wanted from the ice cream man.

However, that was at home. When I got to school, I felt gawky and awkward. To the kids at school, I was just a skinny, dumb kid who couldn't play baseball. More than anything, I wanted to feel just as successful and capable at school as I did at home. And I wanted friends . . . but no one would play with me.

One afternoon near the end of my fourth grade year, my teacher, Mrs. Sween, asked me if I would stay after school for a few minutes.

When I sat down in front of her desk, she started right in.

"I've noticed that you don't hang around with any of the kids during recess, Kathy."

"They don't want to play with me, Mrs. Sween," I answered.

"Do you think that is their fault?" she asked. "If you do, I have news for you. It's not. It's your fault. If you think it is someone else's responsibility to make friends with you first, you are mistaken. They aren't going to come to you, you have to go to them."

I dropped my eyes from her face, and felt tears start to sting the corners of my eyelids.

"Look at me, Kathy." I looked back at Mrs. Sween.

"I know you are a wonderful girl. But how are they going to know you if you don't give them the opportunity? You have to be the one to make the effort, to be friendly, and to talk to other people. Don't get caught up in your shyness. Take a risk! Be a friend, and you'll make a friend."

I don't remember exactly how I made it out of the classroom that day. But I do remember lying on my bed that night, thinking about Mrs. Sween and the things that she had said to me. She had talked to me like my parents had always talked to me: like an equal, not like just a kid. Something sank in that night, and it changed my life. I made a decision. I decided to be happy, and to have a happy life. No one else could do it for me; I had to do it for myself.

Over the summer, I started watching baseball. I mean really watching. I watched baseball on television; I watched baseball on the street where I lived. I studied how the best players played—how they held the bat, and what they did to improve their game. I copied everything the best players did. And I got good at baseball.

When school started the following year, it was amazing that I was not picked last—I was picked first! I had worked to become a good player, and the teams wanted me. Not only that, but it was easier to make friends because I felt more confident about myself. Sure, I was still skinny tomboy Kathy, but now I had friends to laugh with and to share my stories with. I learned to have faith in myself and to know that God doesn't make mistakes. I became more of what I wanted to be because I had made a conscious decision to step out and put my best foot forward.

Later in my life, when I began my modeling career, I realized that not all adults were like my parents and Mrs. Sween. It made me sad to see how some older people took advantage of young girls. My parents and Mrs. Sween wanted the best for me, but there were people out there in the world of modeling that only wanted the best for themselves—it didn't matter who got hurt in the process of them getting what they wanted.

But I never let myself be in a compromising position—I never had to take my top off to become a popular model; I could say no and mean it. No one was ever going to tell me how to run my life; if it wasn't something I knew was the right thing for me to do, I didn't do it.

I have been lucky to have my faith and the love of my family to support me throughout my life. Other girls around me in the modeling profession didn't have what I have had: people like my parents and Mrs. Sween to encourage me. They have done self-destructive things and have been vulnerable to bad people. I have walked off modeling jobs when I didn't like what was going on. My self-esteem gave me the freedom to do that. I always knew if a modeling job didn't work out, there were lots of other interesting jobs out there for me. I could do anything if I set my mind to it, and made a conscious decision to excel.

All I've ever had to do was to step out . . . and put my best foot forward.

Kathy Ireland

Understanding

I discovered I always have choices and some-
times it's only a choice of attitude.

Judith M. Knowlton

My friend Jervais was fading away. He was a boy in my science class who had had a brain tumor removed. No one else really paid much attention to him, or seemed to care, but I always wondered what he felt like and what he'd been through.

I was going through a stage of deep depression. I was having a lot of family problems and feelings of very low self-esteem. I just hated myself—I have no idea why. I would joke about death to my friends, and a few times I would even talk about trying to kill myself. All I wanted to do was to go somewhere where I would feel no pain and no sadness.

One day I noticed that Jervais hadn't been coming to school lately. About two days later, my adviser, Mrs. Baar, announced that Jervais had developed another brain tumor. I was so shocked that I started to cry. I felt as though I had a connection with Jervais. I spent the rest of the day thinking about how devastating it would be to know that at any hour, minute or even second you were going to die. His life was being ripped away from him, and he didn't have a choice. I did. I had been thinking about taking my own life away.

One of my other friends told me that Jervais loved lizards. I remembered that my brother had recently taught me how to make toy lizards out of big plastic beads. Right then, I decided to make Jervais one for luck and hope. When I walked through my bedroom door that afternoon, I went right for my beads. I picked out the colors—yellow, green and clear. I took my time to make it special.

The next day at school, I made Jervais a card on the computer and wrote a little poem that told him he would always have a place in my heart. After the card was printed, I signed my name and gave it to my teacher. She was going to see him at the hospital the next day.

The next week I was walking to lunch, and as I passed the computer lab, I saw a lot of people sitting down inside. Being the nosy person that I am, I took a closer look. It was almost all of my teachers, Jervais and a woman I had never seen before. Then one of the teachers invited me to go in, and told me that the other woman was Jervais's mom and she was asking about me. I started to cry, and then the teacher hugged me and said I didn't have to go in if I didn't want to. But I did want to—so I wiped my tears and walked into the room. I was introduced to Jervais's mom. I looked at her and was amazed! She wasn't crying or showing any sorrow at all. I admired her for being so strong.

I said, "Hi, I'm Jessica." She smiled at me and told me that she had hung the lizard on the hospital bed so that Jervais was always able to reach it. I looked over at Jervais. He didn't look like himself. He had a bandage over his eyes. Our teacher was kneeling down, talking to him, and

I didn't want to interrupt so I left for lunch. I never saw Jervais again.

That night I finally realized that I would have made a big mistake by killing myself. I felt so guilty. I thought of all the people I would have hurt if I had—all the people who care about me, whom I had overlooked. At that moment, I promised myself that I wouldn't ever even think about doing something harmful to myself again.

As the rest of the school year passed, I became more clear about my life, and I have been much happier. I think of Jervais less often, but I never will forget what he did for me and my whole life. My life was just beginning, while his life was ending. He gave me the gift of understanding myself, and that is truly a gift from God.

Jessica Stroup, age 14

Nine Gold Medals

The athletes had come from all over the country
To run for the gold, for the silver and bronze
Many weeks and months of training
All coming down to these games

The spectators gathered around the old field
To cheer on all the young women and men
The final event of the day was approaching
Excitement grew high to begin

The blocks were all lined up for those who would use
    them
The hundred-yard dash was the race to be run
There were nine resolved athletes in back of the starting
    line
Poised for the sound of the gun

The signal was given, the pistol exploded
And so did the runners all charging ahead
But the smallest among them, he stumbled and staggered
And fell to the asphalt instead

He gave out a cry in frustration and anguish
His dreams and his efforts all dashed in the dirt
But as sure as I'm standing here telling this story
The same goes for what next occurred

The eight other runners pulled up on their heels
The ones who had trained for so long to compete
One by one they all turned around and went back to help
  him
And brought the young boy to his feet

Then all the nine runners joined hands and continued
The hundred-yard dash now reduced to a walk
And a banner above that said "Special Olympics"
Could not have been more on the mark

That's how the race ended, with nine gold medals
They came to the finish line holding hands still
And a standing ovation and nine beaming faces
Said more than these words ever will

David Roth

Without a Nightlight

Whatever failures I have known, whatever errors I have committed . . . have been the consequence of action without thought.

Bernard M. Baruch

The moon shone down on the lake like a spotlight. It was a warm summer evening, and I found the night sky, with its glistening stars, relaxing to watch. Five of us were sitting on the dock, wishing we could go for a swim. Paul asked Chelsea and me if we wanted to get on a big yellow tube and go across the cove. It sounded like fun.

We were on the tube, paddling across the lake, when Chelsea said that she was having doubts. Was it safe crossing the lake in this tube? Paul said that he had done this before and that there was nothing to worry about. The boat speed limit was five miles an hour and all boats needed to have at least two lights on.

We were cruising along when, suddenly, Kari started yelling from the dock, saying she heard a boat coming. We didn't think anything about it, figuring we were on the opposite side from where the boat would be. Then suddenly, the noise became loud enough for us to hear over our splashing feet. We all began to panic.

We yelled back to the dock, asking them if they could see a boat, but no one could. So we kept going until the roar was louder than our voices. Then, all of a sudden, Kari started screaming, "Come back!" Her voice sounded scared, so we desperately started looking for a boat. Out of nowhere, over the roar of the engine and the kicking of our feet, Kari yelled, "Oh my God, there's a boat!" The way she said it terrified me and I started to cry. None of us knew what to do.

We stayed as still as we could. Chelsea and I were on the tube. She was on my left and Paul was on my right, floating in the water. Once we were still, all I could hear was my heart pounding, the yelling all around me, and the roar of a boat coming closer and closer every second. Then suddenly, right in front of me, was my worst nightmare. There, just a few feet away, was the boat. It was coming right at us!

Chelsea froze right in her spot, screaming. I pushed her into the water and jumped in after her, just in time to save my own life. As I went under water, I felt the boat skidding over my shoulder like a jet.

I looked up through the water, but at first I could not find the surface. Finally, I got to the top and took the biggest breath I've ever taken. But the terrifying situation was not over. The boat came back, looking for what it had struck, and almost hit us again.

Chelsea was above the water by the time I came up, and I could hear her yelling for Paul and me. I answered her, but Paul did not. It seemed as though we were calling for Paul forever, but thinking back, it was only about twenty seconds. At last, Paul came to the surface, and we made it back to the dock. Kari had to pull me in with the life rope because I felt like I could not move. Once we all got onto the dock, one of the men who was in the boat brought our tube in for us.

Paul kept saying that it was his fault and that he was to blame for us almost being killed. We assured him that we had made the decision to go and that he was not to blame. We sat on the dock telling our own versions of what had happened. The only way that our stories differed was the way the boat hit all of us. The boat hit me on the shoulder while I was trying to push off the bottom of the boat. Chelsea pushed off the boat with her hands; Paul got hit on the head. Everyone agreed that I had saved Chelsea by pushing her off the tube.

The next afternoon, which was Father's Day, my parents and I went over to Paul's house to have a cookout. When we were all sitting on the dock, we told them our story. I spent a lot of the day thinking about how lucky we were just to be alive. That moment gave me nightmares for almost a year. To this day, I can still see the color of the waves and feel the way my heart was beating when I finally came up for air. That was one experience that I will never forget.

Without a doubt, the next time we go out on the lake at night, we'll bring along a light!

Jessica Harper, age 14

Nobody Knows the Difference

The man who knows right from wrong and has good judgment and common sense is happier than the man who is immensely rich! For such wisdom is far more valuable than precious jewels.

Prov. 3:13-15

School volunteers don't get paid money, but sometimes we receive special gifts. One morning, just before Christmas vacation, I was selling tickets to our grade school's last evening performance of *The Nutcracker*. The evening before had been a sellout. People had lined the walls of the auditorium. Some had even peeked in from outside to watch the show.

One of my customers that day was a parent. "I think it's awful that I have to pay to see my own child perform," she announced, yanking a wallet from her purse.

"The school asks for a voluntary donation to help pay for scenery and costumes," I explained, "but no one has to pay. You're welcome to all the tickets you need."

"Oh, I'll pay," she grumbled. "Two adults and a child."

She plunked down a ten-dollar bill. I gave her the change and her tickets. She stepped aside, fumbling with her purse. That's when the boy waiting behind her emptied a pocketful of change onto the table.

"How many tickets?" I asked.

"I don't need tickets," he said. "I'm paying." He pushed the coins across the table.

"But you'll need tickets to see the show tonight."

He shook his head. "I've already seen the show."

I pushed the pile of nickels, dimes and quarters back. "You don't have to pay to see the show with your class," I told him. "That's free."

"No," the boy insisted. "I saw it last night. My brother and I arrived late. We couldn't find anyone to buy tickets from, so we just walked in."

Lots of people in that crowd had probably "just walked in." The few volunteers present couldn't check everyone for a ticket. Who would argue, anyway? As I'd told the parent ahead of this boy, the donation was voluntary.

He pushed his money back to me. "I'm paying now, for last night," he said.

I knew this boy and his brother must have squeezed into the back of that crowd. And being late to boot, they couldn't possibly have seen the whole show. I hated to take his money. A pile of coins in a kid's hand is usually carefully saved allowance money.

"If the ticket table was closed when you got there, you couldn't pay," I reasoned.

"That's what my brother said."

"Nobody knows the difference," I assured him. "Don't worry about it."

Thinking the matter was settled, I started to push the coins back. He put his hand on mine.

"I know the difference."

For one silent moment our hands bridged the money.

Then I spoke. "Two tickets cost two dollars."

The pile of coins added up to the correct amount. "Thank you," I said.

The boy smiled, turned away and was gone.

"Excuse me."

I looked up, surprised to see the woman who had bought her own tickets moments earlier. She was still there, purse open, change and tickets in hand.

"Why don't you keep this change," she said quietly. "The scenery is beautiful, and those costumes couldn't have been cheap." She handed me a few dollar bills, closed her purse and left.

Little did that boy know that he had given us both our first gift of the Christmas season.

Deborah J. Rasmussen

The New House and the Snake

There was a time when my favorite thing to do in the entire world was to play in the woods near our house in Pennsylvania. A river ran through them, so not only could I climb branches and hide beneath piles of dried leaves, but I could turn over rocks on the riverbank and find baby eels that squirmed around in the small pool of water where the rocks had been. I loved the smell of the leaves and would drag my feet through them to stir up the scent.

My favorite book was called *Guide to Reptiles and Amphibians*. My father had given it to me for my birthday, and I read every page over and over, looking at the pictures of colorful animals. Some of the snakes were the most beautiful creatures I had ever seen.

Little did I know that my book would end up saving a life.

My family moved to Virginia, into a new house in a new subdivision. The houses were so new that no one had lived in them before. In fact, woods had been there first, and almost all the trees had been cut down to make room for houses and asphalt driveways. Inside our new house, everything smelled like fresh paint. Outside, no lawns had been planted, but my father tossed out grass seed using a machine that spun as he pushed, and baby seedlings grew. My brother, Patrick, and I could not walk on them. We had to play in the driveway.

All the same, I liked our new house. One of the best things, and at the same time one of the worst, about living near the woods were the animals that would come into our yard. Rabbits and toads hopped across the back patio almost every night, and once, we found a box turtle walking underneath the barbecue. Even though I loved to watch the rabbits and toads and I played with the turtle, I felt sorry for the animals. It seemed as if they were only trying to go home, and instead, what they had found was a big new subdivision where their old burrows and tunnels used to be.

Besides playing in the driveway as we waited for the new grass to grow, we spent time in a sandbox, which my father built right next to the driveway. The cat sometimes used the sandbox for a litter box, so my father had to put a plastic cover over it. When I wanted to build sand castles or dig a tunnel, I had to pull the cover off.

One day before dinner, I ran to the sandbox to build a miniature city, and then to find some ants to occupy it. I pulled off the plastic cover, and there in the sandbox was a snake.

It was lying very still, all coiled up, and it was beautiful. The snake had rings of color around it—red, then white, then yellow, then black. I had seen a picture just like it in my reptile book, and I remembered that it was one of the prettiest snakes in it. It said in the book that the poisonous coral snake looked very much like the king snake; the only difference was in the sequence of the colors. I ran inside to get the reptile guidebook.

"Mom! Mom! There's a snake in the sandbox!" I yelled. "I have to find out what kind it is!"

Mom came running. "Don't touch it, Chris! It might be poisonous!"

Dad was at work, so my mother went to get our neighbor, Mr. Cook.

"Mr. Cook!" my mother yelled across the fence, "We have a snake in the sandbox, and it might be a poisonous king snake!"

Mr. Cook was retired and lived with his wife in the house on the other side of our back fence. He came running toward the gate with a shovel.

"Wait!" I said, waving the guidebook in my hand. "I have to see what kind of snake it is!"

Mom and Mr. Cook stood over the snake. It was coiled, lying still, while Mr. Cook held the shovel over its head. "It's better to be safe than sorry," Mr. Cook said, taking aim. I felt so bad for the snake. Even if it were poisonous, all it was doing was trying to hide there in the dark, under the plastic tarp. It wasn't hurting anybody.

I tried to turn the pages of the book to the coral and king snake section. It's funny, but whenever you're trying to do something too fast, it seems like it takes all that much longer to do it. Finally, I found it. Red, white, yellow, black: that meant a poisonous coral snake. A king snake was yellow, white, red and black. I checked the colors. This definitely was a king snake, and the book said that it was rare and should be protected.

"Don't kill the snake!" I yelled. I was crying by now, feeling the snake was doomed. I showed my mother and Mr. Cook the picture. "See? It says it's a rare snake that should be protected!"

I ran to get a pillowcase. I had seen a show on TV that recommended pillowcases for catching snakes. I buried one side of the material beneath the sand and held it up like a tunnel. Mr. Cook nudged the snake with the shovel. The snake uncoiled and glided right into the pillowcase. I picked up the pillowcase and clenched the top of it shut with my fingers. My mother called the zoo and told them I had just captured a king snake.

"Wow!" said the man from the zoo. They had rushed right over when my mother described the snake's colors. "You sure are right. You've captured a king snake! We'll put it on display at the zoo where it will have a nice home. You should come to visit it!"

I felt good that the king snake had been saved. I also felt sorry for the snake because after all, like the rabbits and the toads and the box turtle, it was only looking for its old home. I knew that feeling. Sometimes I liked to hide, too.

I hoped that the snake would like its cage. I hoped they would give it a branch to climb on, some water and lots of sand. Maybe they would even put in dry leaves for the snake to hide under. No matter how the zookeepers fixed up the cage, or whether or not it was like the outdoors where the snake was used to living, I was sure that it was better than having Mr. Cook chop its head off with his shovel.

Eventually, the new paint smell would go away, the grass would grow and the new home would become much like the old one. And maybe, if the snake was lucky, there would be someone around to build a sandbox. In a way, I thought, that snake was a lot like me.

Christine Lavin

PEANUTS. Reprinted by permission of United Feature Syndicate.

I Found a Tiny Starfish

An effort made for the happiness of others lifts us above ourselves.

Lydia M. Child

I found a tiny starfish
In a tidepool by the sand.
I found a tiny starfish
And put him in my hand.

An itty-bitty starfish
No bigger than my thumb,
A wet and golden starfish
Belonging to no one.

I thought that I would take him
From the tidepool by the sea,
And bring him home to give to you
A loving gift from me.

But as I held my starfish,
His skin began to dry.

Without his special seaside home,
My gift to you would die.

I found a tiny starfish
In a tidepool by the sea.
I hope whoever finds him next
Will leave him there, like me!

And the gift I've saved for you?
The best that I can give:
I found a tiny starfish,
And for you, I let him live.

Dayle Ann Dodds

$\overline{9}$

TOUGH STUFF

We cannot tell what may happen to us in the strange medley of life. But we can decide what happens in us—how we can take it, what we do with it—and that is what really counts in the end. How to take the raw stuff of life and make it a thing of worth and beauty—that is the test of living.

Joseph Fort Newton

Get Help Now!

If I can stop one heart from breaking,
I shall not live in vain.
If I can ease one life the aching,
Or cool one pain,
Or help one fainting robin unto his nest again,
I shall not live in vain.

Emily Dickinson

"Now's your chance to ruin my life," my father said. How did I, a twelve-year-old girl, wind up in a situation like this? How did my early happy life get to this point? As far as I can remember, things really started to change when I was six.

I was the youngest child and the only girl in my family. One night, I got to stay up late and sleep in the living room—which was rare—and watch the Jerry Lewis telethon with my brother, who was eight. My oldest brother was away on a fishing trip, and my mom, who then worked all night, was on the job.

What I remember about that night was falling asleep and waking up in my parents' room. I pretended to be

asleep while my father did things that I didn't understand and touched me in places that made me feel really
uncomfortable. I wish I could have fallen asleep and forgotten the whole thing, but it isn't like that. I didn't know
if this was normal or not; I was only six.

The next day he acted totally normal, and it stopped—
for a while. I guess maybe *he* was scared. Then the abuse
started up again, and it went on for six horrible years. I
would try to lock my bedroom door to keep him out, but
he'd make excuses.

He'd say, "Keep your door unlocked in case there's a
fire." He would even ground me if I didn't keep it
unlocked. And since my mom had no idea of what was
going on, she agreed with him.

I didn't say anything to anyone because I was so
scared of what could happen if I did. My father threatened to kill my family, himself and me if I told anyone.
But my biggest fear during all this was what would happen if my mom found out. Would she believe me? Would
my dad really do the things that he had threatened?
What would happen?

When I was twelve, our town had a Christian concert. I
went to the concert and accepted God into my life that
night. It was a friend's birthday, so I left early to go to his
house and give him a birthday present. I ended up at a
coffee shop, a place where my dad had told me he did not
want me to go. After I had been there for ten minutes, my
dad walked in and commanded, "Let's go!"

I was so embarrassed and so scared of what he would
do. We got into the car, and the whole way home he was
yelling at me. I cried so much.

When we got home, my dad, my mom and I sat down
at the kitchen table. They were going to plan my punishment for going to the coffee shop without telling them
and for being there with older guys. My mom got up and

went to their bedroom to do something, leaving just my dad and me.

He was yelling at me and telling me I wasn't going to be able to do anything until I was sixteen. "I'm going to ruin your life," he said angrily.

"If you're going to ruin my life, then I'll ruin yours," I answered.

"Don't threaten me!" he warned. Since he had his back to the kitchen, he did not see my mom walk in right when he said it.

"Threaten you with what?" she screamed over and over.

"Now's your chance to ruin my life," he challenged me.

"Has he been touching you?" Mom asked me. I just started to cry. My mom started hitting my dad, cursing and yelling at him.

"Get out! Get out!" she demanded loudly. I ran into the bathroom, and she came in, held me and apologized for not knowing what had been happening. She told me to go to my room. I ran down to my room and cried and cried.

"He's leaving, Tia. He's gone," Mom said.

"Mom, we can't stay here. We have to leave!" I pleaded. "Dad said if I ever told, he would kill me, our whole family and himself!" I was so scared. My dad could easily follow through with his threat since our house had a lot of windows. I didn't want to die or have my family die, either.

"Pack up," she directed. "We're leaving."

I quickly threw some clothes into a bag. She helped my fourteen-year-old brother get ready to leave with us. He was in another part of the house and had no idea what had been going on.

We just drove and drove, and cried and cried. Since that big concert was happening, all the hotels in our town were full. We had to drive over a hundred miles to a motel where we could stay and feel safe. Then we had to find a new house to rent in a different town.

That was two years ago. My dad was sentenced to at least six years in prison. I haven't spoken to him since that night when we left our house.

I am so happy that my mom stood by me 100 percent. She left my dad and turned him in to the police without thinking twice. She filed for divorce, and now she's happier than I've ever seen her. She's remarried to the "perfect man" for her.

If you are being molested or mistreated by anyone and they are threatening you, it's probably just a bluff. Don't allow terrible threats to control you. No one should get away with that. *Turn them in. Don't wait for it to get worse.* I suffered for six years!

No matter if you're a boy or girl, if someone touches you and it makes you feel uncomfortable, it's wrong. It's a sin. *Please listen to me.* Tell an adult—a parent, a friend's parent, a teacher, a pastor or the police. Keep telling, until someone will help. But get help *now!*

Tia Thompson, age 14

[EDITORS' NOTE: *To get help with child abuse issues of any kind call Childhelp USA at: 800-4-A-CHILD.*]

The Big Director

*In everything you do, put God first, and he will
direct you and crown your efforts with success.*

Prov. 3:6

"You wanna help us get back at the guys who beat up
our friends?" a kid asked me during recess. "Meet us after
school."

I had never been to a gang meeting before. But the kids
at school made it sound like if I didn't go, I wasn't being
loyal to my friends who had been roughed up by a gang
from another neighborhood. So I decided to check it out.

When I got there, everyone joined hands and said what
sounded to me like a prayer. Then they named all these
gang members that they looked up to. After that, the
leader said, "This is your family. I am your father, I am
your mother, I am your brother." He was repeating what
he had seen done in some of the gang meetings with older
kids in his neighborhood.

I was in the seventh grade at a Christian academy in
Chicago when I was asked to be a part of that gang. For a
lot of kids who didn't get much attention at home, the

gang gave them something to belong to. It was more than just a club to them—for some kids it was their only family.

During the meeting, I looked around at the other kids. I thought to myself, *No, no this isn't right. I don't need this gang to be everything to me. I've got a good family, and I know the great "I Am." That's God—not this dude.* My mom and dad had always told me that the Lord is my friend, and that if I put him first in all that I do, he would continue to bless me.

I walked away from the gang that day, but it still took me a long time to finally realize that my parents had been trying to steer me in the right direction by telling me about God.

Even though I listened to my parents, I still wasn't, by any stretch of the imagination, a perfect child. There were times when I was bad to the bone. Once in a while, people will say to me, "How do you know what I'm going through? You've never been in trouble." But I *do* know. I used to get into trouble a lot.

In the neighborhood where I grew up, my friends and I didn't have any place to play, so we hung out near the railroad tracks and an old factory that was in back of my house. My friends and I would do things we had no business doing, like yelling things at the neighborhood gang members that made them mad enough to shoot at us. We literally had to run for our lives.

You had to be able to run fast where I came from. It seems as though we were always running away from some kind of trouble, or being chased by the police for trespassing at the train yards, "expressing our artistic talents" with spray paint, or breaking windows at the factory.

A lot of my friends from school became gang members. I've lost many of them over the years. They either ended up in prison, or they're dead from gang warfare.

I had a friend who lived in the neighborhood across the

train tracks from mine, near our church. We became friends through the Boy Scout troop that met there. One day, kids from my neighborhood went over to that neighborhood with baseball bats and beat up some of the kids. Later, when I was hanging out with the kids from my neighborhood, some guys drove by in a van. They slowed down as they passed us.

My friend from the other neighborhood was in the van with some of the guys who had been attacked. Just before they were about to shoot into the group of guys I was standing with, my friend recognized me and stopped his friends from shooting us. Had my back been turned and my friend not recognized me, we would have been killed. After he saved my life, we became really good friends.

At school, I was a troublemaker and spent a lot of time in detention. I pulled pranks like putting Crazy Glue on my friend's chair. The janitor had to be called finally to pry him loose, leaving wooden chips stuck to the seat of my friend's pants.

One teacher decided that for every pink slip a kid got for bad behavior, he would give them a spanking with a paddle. While other kids would have about six by the time he got around to giving spankings, I'd have more like twenty. One time, when the day came to trade in my pink slips for a paddling, I put on every pair of shorts I could find in the house before I put on my pants. Then, right before the time came for the paddling, I slipped into the school bathroom and packed tissue into my pants.

"Bend over, Mitchell," commanded the teacher with a grin of satisfaction. Down came the paddle with enough force to really hurt, but instead of producing a loud smack, the paddle landed with a POOF!

"Mitchell, are you packing? Huh? Are you packing?" he screamed. His face was red with fury and humiliation. Kids began to crowd around me to see what was happening. He marched me into the bathroom and made me take off every pair of shorts, until the only shorts left on me were the first pair I had found that morning—my sister's pink bike shorts!

Things just got worse until my mom found a way to help me stop acting up so much in school. As she tells it, the Lord sent her a message in a dream. He told her to take me to the local theater to join a summer acting class. I got on stage and acted out like I did in school, only this time the teachers loved it! I had found my God-given talent. From then on, I spent most of my time after school and on the weekends learning about acting, and performing in television and film as well as in live theater.

I later moved out to Los Angeles to pursue my acting career. One day, I got a call about my friend who had saved my life from gang warfare. He had been killed when a gang cornered him in an alley and shot him. That's how I might have ended up too, if I didn't have the Lord directing my life. I realize that God is "The Big Director" of it all, and he has blessed me and made my life better than I ever imagined it could be.

Someday, when I have children of my own, I plan to pass my faith in him on to them. I am going to tell them about the blessings he has given me, and the troubles that he has helped me out of. I hope they will continue to keep the faith in him, so if the neighborhood they live in is dark and going wrong, or if it seems that civilization has lost its mind, they will have a friend to lean on. They can ask "The Big Director" to help them find their way, just like he did for me.

Kel Mitchell

A Personal Message from Kel Mitchell

I know from my own experience that kids often get into gangs or drugs or other destructive situations because they are bored or lonely, or they feel rejected and angry. They don't know where to go, or how to develop their God-given talents. And they don't know that there are other choices available.

There *are* other choices. Get involved in a youth group at a local church, encourage your school to start an after-school program, or find a Boys & Girls Club you can join. Get involved in sports or a play. We're all good at something—it's just a matter of realizing what that is and going after it.

If you're having problems, or if you see friends going the wrong way, ask someone for help. If you don't know who to go to, or feel afraid to share the situation with someone that you know, there is always someone out there to help. In the front of the Yellow Pages in your phone book (or in some areas, the Blue Pages) there are 800 numbers to call for advice or help. You can often find a list of issues and problems that will likely include what you're going through.

You can also pray and ask the Lord to guide you, as I have. You can talk to him any time of the day or night. I pray about things that are big or small, and I truly believe that God will make it happen for me. Although it might not come when I think I need it, or exactly how I expect it, it's always right for me. He has changed my life, and that's enough evidence for me that he is real.

[EDITORS' NOTE: *To find a Boys & Girls Club nearest you, call: 800-854-CLUB.*]

I Love Her More Than Ever

In my short life, I have learned a lot about drugs and what they can do to a family.

When I was really young, I lived with my mom, my brother, Christopher, and his father, Michael. I didn't know it then, but there was a lot of drug use happening. Michael used drugs, and I think he was a dealer. He also used to beat my mom sometimes.

All I remember of my natural father when I was growing up is a time when my mom and I were staying in an apartment and he showed up there. He started drinking beer and throwing the bottles everywhere in the apartment. My mom made me stay outside. She finally ran outside to get me, and we drove away. I saw him last year before he moved to Colorado. I think he's getting into drugs again. Sometimes he lies, and sometimes he doesn't. You just never know.

When I was in the first and second grades, my mom wouldn't send me to school all the time. She didn't have a job, and she just stayed around the house all day. I missed a lot of school. Sometimes, she'd tell me to just stay home. She was too busy doing her drugs. I didn't really mind staying home because I didn't like the people at that school. It wasn't a good school because there were gangs hanging around. I missed so much school that I got held back. I am supposed to be in the sixth grade right now, but I'm only in fifth.

During those years, I didn't live with my mother all the time. Sometimes I lived with a lady named Deann and her family because my mom would be out partying all the time. Sometimes I lived with my grandparents when I couldn't stay with Deann.

One of the times I remember most clearly was when I was about seven years old. I was in the car with my mom and my grandma. We were going to an apartment where we would drop my mom off. I was going to live with my grandmother again because she believed that my mom was using drugs, and she wanted to take care of me. I was really mad at my grandmother because I didn't believe what she was saying about my mother.

Later, when I went to visit my mom, I walked in from playing outside and saw her and some of her friends doing drugs. That's when I finally believed what my grandmother had been trying to tell me, and I ran out the door, crying. I was afraid that my mother was going to hurt herself with the drugs.

For a long time, I lived partly with my grandmother or Deann or my mom. One day, when I was living with my mom, I came home from school to find that our house was totally trashed. The police had raided it because they were looking for drugs. I didn't know what a raid was then, but my mom told me. Then, a few months later, I found out for myself what it meant.

I had been sleeping in the living room, but that night I got up and went to the bedroom where my mom was sleeping. I was lying on the bed with my mom, when all of a sudden the door burst open and the police came in pointing guns. They told everybody to put their hands up. I was scared. My mom had a needle in her purse, and she was arrested. She told me it was a friend's, but it had really been her needle. She used to lie to me.

I finally called my grandmother one night when my mom was doing drugs. I didn't want to see her using drugs anymore. My grandmother came to pick me up, and I lived with her for a long time. I felt like my grandmother was the one person who was there for me. She took care of me and got me all the things that I needed. If I needed shoes, she got them for me. She'd do anything for me. Still, every night I used to cry myself to sleep because I missed my mom so much, and I was afraid for her. I would lie in the living room with my grandma, and she would just sit there by my side.

After some time, my mom moved in with us at my grandma's house. She got a job at a restaurant, but she was still using drugs. One night she borrowed my grandma's car to go to work. She brought back the car and left a note saying that she'd be back later. That was at one o'clock in the morning. She didn't come back when she said she would. I was worried about her, so we called Deann to ask if she had seen her, but she didn't know where my mom was, either. No one could find her.

We didn't hear from my mom for six months. We didn't know it then, but she had been accepted by a recovery house and was getting off drugs.

Then one day my mom called. She sounded different— happy. She was off the drugs. She told me that she had felt that God would make her die after all the bad things she had done, and she had become very afraid. She decided to get clean and that she wanted to have a better life.

Then, on my birthday, my mom came and surprised me. She said that in a couple months, I might be able to live with her again. She continued to get better, and we finally moved near the beach, where my mom always said that she wanted to live.

Going to the beach is our favorite thing to do together. We go in-line skating there all the time now. We go out to dinner sometimes, and to movies, too. My brother lives with his grandparents, but sometimes he comes to visit us. We go everywhere when he visits and we buy him toys.

My mom has a job now with a company that makes hardware. We go to church, and sometimes we just read the Bible together. We pray every night for my grandmother now because she has cancer and just went through chemotherapy.

My mom and I have a better relationship now that she is clean and sober. We get to spend more time together, and we have more fun. But most of all, we are both happier. Now we're telling the truth. There are no more lies. We share everything, no matter what. My mom is my best friend, more than anyone else is. I am proud of her, and I love her more than ever.

Amber Foy, age 11

Dear Momma

Who ran to help me when I fell,
And would some pretty story tell,
Or kiss the place to make it well?
My Mother.

Anne Taylor

Dear Momma,

I miss you. I miss all the good things that we used to do. I miss how you would laugh and tuck me into bed. I miss your kisses and hugs. I miss the way you would talk about how you loved your kids and your family. You said if you were God, you wouldn't leave us.

Every night I think I see you and hear your voice, but I guess I really don't. Momma, I know you hear and see everything I say and do. Sometimes I want to cry, but I try to hold it in. Momma, I love you from the bottom of my heart. Your love is deep in my heart. I wish I could see you just one more time. I wish you didn't have to die. I'll love you always.

"

Your Son

My mother died when I was nine years old, and I was in the third grade. I just wrote to her because I miss her.

Darnell Hill, age 13

My Dad

When my dad left, I started to cry.
I was very sad because I thought he would die.
My mom said not to worry, and to pray.
I think about him every day.

I remember the fun we had together.
We would play forever and ever.
Together we would go to the park and walk.
Then we would have lunch and start to talk.

He always helped me with my homework.
That's why I'm so good at my schoolwork.
In the morning he fixed my hair.
If it was messy, I did not care.

Now that he is gone, I hope he's all right.
I cry so much, every day and night.
Now that he is gone, I hope he misses me, too.
If my dad is reading this, I just want to say
That I really love you!

Aljon B. Farin, age 7

Smoking Is Cool. . . . Not!

There's right, and there's wrong. You get to do one or the other. You do one, and you're living. You do the other, and you may be walking around, but you're as dead as a beaver hat.

John Wayne

Last summer, I went to Los Angeles to visit my cousin, Victoria. My dad had been outside smoking a cigarette when my aunt called him into the house. He left his cigarette on the front porch steps so he could continue smoking it when he came back out.

My cousin was curious to see what smoking was really like, so she picked up the cigarette to check it out. She asked me if I had ever smoked before. "No way," I sneered. I couldn't believe what she did next. Victoria put the cigarette in her mouth and sucked in smoke. The next thing you know, she's coughing her head off. She looked like she was about to throw up, but she still stretched her hand out toward me to offer me the cigarette. "Come on, try it," she said. "It won't hurt you."

I just grabbed the stupid thing out of her hand. Then I

threw it on the ground and smashed it with the heel of my shoe. I did it so fast I didn't think about what Dad would do when he came back out. Just then, my dad came back outside and looked at the place where he'd left his cigarette.

"Where'd my cigarette go?" he asked. I just stood there, not wanting to admit what I had done, or what my cousin had done before that. But I knew that this was the moment of truth. I took a deep breath and began to explain.

I told my dad that I couldn't really believe that he would choose to smoke. I was sure he knew how bad it was, so why did he do it? He said that he started a long time ago, when he was just a teenager. They didn't know how bad it was for you back then. Now he was so addicted that he couldn't stop. It was just too hard to quit.

Here was a grown man, my own dad, admitting there was something that he couldn't control that was probably slowly killing him. I stood there in disbelief. I had always thought of my dad as the strongest man I knew. Then I remembered this commercial that I had seen on TV. There was this lady who was so addicted to cigarettes that she'd gotten really sick. But she still couldn't stop smoking. They had to cut a hole in her throat for her to breathe, and she was still smoking through the hole! It was the most disgusting thing I've ever seen. Standing in front of my dad, I began to cry. What if that happened to him?

Ever since that day, I think my dad has tried to cut back on cigarettes. I'm still telling him how much I love him and don't want to lose him because of smoking. I know one thing: I want to live a long time. And I don't want to be sick or out of control of my life, the way that lady was. I'll never smoke. I'll take fresh air, thank you.

Valeria Soto, age 12

[EDITORS' NOTE: *To learn more about the effects of smoking, contact the Campaign for Tobacco-Free Kids at their Web site: www.tobaccofreekids.org or call 800-284-KIDS to get involved in their campaign against the tobacco industry.*]

DARE Rap

When you SMOKE
It's no JOKE

Smoking turns lungs BLACK
And causes you to HACK

If you go ahead and SMOKE
You are going to CROAK

If you smoke POT
Your brain will ROT

When you drink BEER
You can't think CLEAR

When you drink BOOZE
Your brain will SNOOZE

If you take a DRUG
You turn into a SLUG

When you get HIGH
You might try to FLY
And you will DIE

So if you go to a PARTY
Be a SMARTY!

Listen to my VOICE
Make the right CHOICE

If you never drink and DRIVE
You have a good chance of staying ALIVE.

Shelly Merkes, age 12

I'm Not Dana

I am the force; I can clear any obstacle before me, or I can be lost in the maze. My choice; my responsibility; win or lose, only I hold the key to my destiny.

Elaine Maxwell

My mother raised all three of us kids right, and that's a fact. But for some reason two of us turned out right—and my older sister, Dana, didn't.

When she went to the same elementary school where I go now, she was perfectly fine. She started having problems after she went into seventh grade. Dana dropped her old friends and began hanging with new people that our family didn't know. No matter what my mom and dad said to her, she still did what she wanted. Everyone in the family was feeling terrible, especially me. I had always looked up to my sister and had wanted to be just like her. Now I just couldn't figure out what was happening. Dana didn't act as if she liked any of us anymore, and she never talked to me at all.

It kept getting worse and worse. By the time she was in high school, she had started drinking alcohol and staying out late at night. She only came home to take a shower, make a mess and then leave again. I couldn't believe that this person was my sister Dana. My sister, who took D.A.R.E. and who had gone to church with us, had turned into a stranger.

One day when I was in sixth grade, I came home from school and heard screaming. I ran into the kitchen, and there was my dad, my mom, my grandma and Dana. They had Dana tied up on the floor, and my mom and grandma were holding her. Tears were running down Dana's cheeks, and her face was all red from screaming. My dad was sitting on the floor next to her, and he was crying. The only other time I had seen my father cry was when his father died. I couldn't stand to look anymore at what was going on, so I ran into my room and slammed the door.

Some people came and took Dana away. My mom and dad sent her to Utah, to a home for kids who have problems. We all miss her so much. She came home for a short visit this summer, but she can't come home to stay yet. Sometimes my mom cries when we talk about her.

After Dana went away, I found this note in her room:

> To Sabrina,
>
> When Death knocks, you hide in the corner, while I run and greet it.
>
> Dana

I think she felt so bad about herself that she wanted to die. I think she felt like she had no control over the bad things she did to herself. I can't imagine what happened to her to have her do the things that she did. But I do know this. I'm not going to drink, and I won't do bad things to myself. I don't want to ruin my future or regret my past. I hope that it's not too late for Dana. She's my sister and I still love her. Maybe someday she will find the person deep inside that she used to be—I know she's still in there somewhere.

Sabrina Anne Tyler, age 11

No Home

America is an enormous frosted cupcake in the middle of millions of starving people.

Gloria Steinem

My mama lost her job. She has no money, so we have to move out of our house. We have nowhere to live because Mama has no money. While we look for a place to sleep, I help take care of my sister. I tell her not to cry and dry her tears with my mitten.

We find a church basement to live in at night. Because it's late, all the cots are taken. The basement is cold, and the cement floor hurts my head. I wonder what will happen if Mama never finds a job. We might have to live in a basement forever.

During the day, I watch my sister on the street corners while Mama looks for a job. Mama talks to lots of people. We stand on lots of street corners. All day, people rush by us. I think about why they hurry. Maybe they're going to their jobs, or maybe to their homes. I guess only people without homes stand still on street corners.

Mama finishes talking to people for today. I decide not

to ask her if she got a job. Her face, all tight with worry, tells me the answer. As we walk, I think about school. Mama says I can't go to school for a while. I wonder if I'll like it when I go back. Maybe the work will be too hard for me. Maybe the kids will tease me because we lost our home. What will happen to my sister if I go back to school before Mama finds a job? Mama tells me not to be afraid, drying my tears with her glove. She says she will find a job soon.

At night, we eat at the soup kitchen. A woman wearing plastic gloves and a baseball cap puts food on my tray. I'm real hungry, but I look in my stew for anything mushy. I see lots of peas. Picking out each one, I hide them under the rim of my bowl. Mama is reading want ads in the newspaper and doesn't notice. But a man with dirty hair sitting across from me does. When he smiles, I see he has lost both his front teeth. He hisses when he tells me his name is Joe. As I eat my stew, I wonder if I missed a pea. I chew slowly, just to be sure. After supper, Mama takes my tray to the trash can. She sees the peas but says nothing. When we had a home, she used to make me eat my peas. Things are different now.

Later on, we find three cots to sleep on. Each has a pillow, a blanket and a small towel. Picking up my towel, I follow Mama to the bathroom. She shows me how to take a bath at the sink. I use grainy soap that hurts my skin. I wonder if someone will come in while I'm taking my bath. I wash fast. I'm cold. Even with my clothes on, I'm cold. Mama says my hair will have to wait. I think about Joe's hair. Living in a church basement for a long time must have made his hair look that way. I think about my hair. Maybe I'll wash it in the sink sometime.

Joe's hair is a mess, but he has money. I see the shiny coins in his guitar case. At night, he plays his guitar. I listen real hard to the music, and then I'm not so cold. When the music stops, I see my sister shiver. Mama puts her coat over us. I wonder if Mama sleeps.

My mama lost her job, and it takes a long time to find another. But I'm not afraid because I know my mama is smart. She keeps me warm at night. She dries my tears with her glove. I know she will find a job. I know my mama will carry us home.

Elizabeth A. Gilbert-Bono

10

ECLECTIC WISDOM

I am me.
There will not ever be anyone like me.
I am special because I am unique.
I am stardust and dreams.
I am light.
I am love and hope.
I am hugs, and sometimes tears.
I am the words "I love you."
I am swirls of blue, green, red, yellow, purple,
orange, and colors no one can name.
I am the sky, the sea, the earth.
I trust, yet I fear.
I hide, yet I don't hold anything back.
I am free.
I am a child becoming an adult.
I am me, and me is just right.

Beth Schaffer, age 15

Baby's Ears

How many a man has thrown up his hands at a time when a little more effort, a little more patience, would have achieved success?

Elbert Hubbard

Mom poured herself a glass of orange juice. "I'm worried about Grandma," she said. I was pouring syrup on my French toast, hot and sweet, just the way I liked it.

"Why?" I asked as I licked a drop of syrup from my fork.

"Well, remember before she moved to Florida, how early Grandma would get up?"

"Before the sun," I said, "to make pancakes and bacon."

My mom nodded. "But now Grandma sleeps most of the day or watches television. I can't get her out of the house, and she won't try to make friends." Mom frowned and lowered her voice. "Grandma's even talking about going back to New York."

"Back to New York? But you said that she couldn't live alone anymore. That's why she came to live here." I like Florida. Of course, I have a lot of girlfriends to play with in my sixth-grade class.

"If Grandma went back to New York, she would have to live in a nursing home," my mother told me. "That's a place where old people live and nurses take care of them."

"It sounds like a hospital to me," I said. I thought for a minute. "I'll find a way to make Grandma like Florida."

Mom smiled and said, "I wish you could."

After school, I saw Grandma watching television and figured she hadn't moved all day. In my room, I sat on my bed and took out my seashell collection. I had found Striped Whelks, Purple Sea Snails and even a Queen Conch Shell. You can hold a conch shell up to your ear and actually hear the ocean waves. My very favorite shell was called a Baby's Ear. It's a beautiful white shell shaped just like the ear of a baby, all swirly and delicate.

Looking at my seashells gave me an idea. I went into the living room and sat on the couch. "Did you ever go to the beach when you were little, Grandma?" I asked.

"Once my mother took me, but I didn't enjoy it at all," she said, frowning.

"Really?" I took an oatmeal cookie from the plate on the coffee table. "Why not?"

"I'm afraid of the water, and I can't swim." Grandma pursed her lips as though she'd tasted a lemon. I wished Grandma could feel the way I did about the beach. I loved to see pelicans flying over the water, and once I even saw a huge green iguana.

"Well, I was wondering if you could take me to the beach, Grandma. I need some new shells for my collection."

Grandma didn't even look up from the TV. "I'm watching my show, Val. Can't you go by yourself?"

"No. I'm not allowed to go to the beach by myself. Please!" I begged, imagining Grandma in a nursing home.

"Oh, all right," Grandma sighed. She took my hand as we left the house, and we walked to the beach. The sun felt hot enough to melt metal. I handed Grandma a plastic bag. "Here. This is for the seashells you find."

"Oh, I'll leave that to you," she said. A soft ocean breeze blew her gray curls across her eyes.

I shook my head. "No, Grandma. I need all the help I can get."

"Oh, all right," she said. We walked side by side up the beach, our heads down, looking for only the most beautiful shells.

"Doesn't look like there's much to choose from," Grandma said, shading her eyes with her hand. "Maybe we should go home."

"Not yet, Grandma! I'll go ahead like a scout and see if I find anything good." I looked back at her as I walked ahead. Grandma stood watching the ocean waves and the seagulls that flew over the water searching for fish. She took off her shoes and carried them.

I ran on ahead and slipped a Pink Triton shell from my pocket, dropping it in the sand. Farther up the beach, I did the same with my Blue Starfish and my Green Serpent Star. Finally, I dropped my favorite shell, the Baby's Ear.

Just then, I heard Grandma shout, "Val! Look what I found!" Grandma stood in the sand, holding up the pink Triton.

"That's beautiful, Grandma!" I cried. "It will look great in my collection."

Grandma nodded and smiled. "Let's keep looking!" she said, suddenly excited. I pretended to pass right by the Blue Starfish, but Grandma bent down slowly and picked it up. "Val! Look at this starfish. It's blue!"

"You're really good at this, Grandma!"

She carried her plastic bag proudly. At last, Grandma came to my favorite shell.

"Val, look at this strange thing." She handed it to me.

I cradled the shell in my hand. "It's called a Baby's Ear because that's what it looks like."

"You're pretty good at this yourself, Val," Grandma said, giving me a hug. On the way home we waded in the ocean. Grandma seemed to have forgotten her fear of water.

We met my mom on the front porch. "We've been to the beach," Grandma told her. "And you know, I think I'll start a shell collection of my own. You can help me, Val."

"Okay, Grandma," I said.

My mom and I shared a secret smile.

Valerie Allen

Kindness Is Contagious

The place to improve the world is first in one's own heart and head and hands. . . .

Robert M. Pirsig

When I was through with my doctor's appointment, I made my way down to the lobby. My mom was going to pick me up, but knowing how she was always late, I realized I had some time to spare. I took a seat in the lobby and smiled politely at the three elderly people sitting near me. There were two women and one old man. Then I dug into my backpack for my library book.

Just as I started to read, one of the women struck up a loud conversation with anyone who would listen. She relayed her adventures purchasing her new eyeglasses. I smiled and listened to her tale; she had a lot to say. When her husband pulled up in front of the big glass doors, her story ended abruptly. She was gone.

The old man's ride arrived just as quickly. His daughter pulled up in a station wagon filled with kids. She burst through the doors, saying, "Pop, are you ready?" That left just me and a beautiful gray-haired woman in the lobby.

I looked directly at her. She appeared dignified, serious and stern. I thought she might be a former English teacher because she impressed me as a person with knowledge and confidence. She intentionally avoided my direct glance, but as I lifted my book to read, I could feel her eyes carefully gazing in my direction.

Concentrating on reading was impossible. My thoughts kept shifting from the beautiful gray-haired woman to thoughts of school.

Everyone was talking about graduation. The other kids had been discussing what presents to buy for each other. My face turned red at the thought. It had never occurred to me that kids bought presents for graduation. In our home, relatives bought the graduate presents, not friends. I had no money. And I couldn't ask my parents; they hadn't any money either. Yet I longed to be able to share with my best friends something that would help them remember our friendships, even if it was just something little.

I prayed, *Oh God, help. What am I going to do?*

My mind was still deep in thought when suddenly I heard a commotion at the entrance doors. There was an elderly woman in a wheelchair and another older woman trying to push her along. They were struggling with the heavy glass door. A bustling crowd too busy to help side-stepped them to get by, leaving them to struggle alone.

I jumped up to help them. It was only then that I realized the woman pushing the wheelchair could barely walk. I eased them through both sets of doors and helped them to the elevator. They thanked me, but I could see that they still had a monumental struggle ahead. They still needed to get on and off of the elevator, and into their doctor's office safely.

I decided to ride with them on the elevator. I asked them which floor they needed, and then I made sure they found the correct office. They thanked me again. I told them it was my pleasure, and I really meant it. I was truly happy to help them.

I was on my way down in the elevator when I realized that I had left my backpack on the lobby chair. My backpack had nothing of value in it, just a wallet with fifty-nine cents in change, a small mirror, a comb and some tissues. But then I remembered that my precious library book was also on the chair.

The elevator could not go fast enough. As the doors opened, I held my breath, hoping against all hope that my backpack and library book were still there. I rushed into the lobby.

They were both safely on the chair, just as I had left them.

As I sat down, I could feel the beautiful gray-haired woman's smiling eyes on me. She seemed proud for some reason. Then her taxi arrived, and, without a word, she was gone.

I decided to pick through my pennies to see if I had enough money to buy a package of peanuts at the little pharmacy. I opened my backpack. To my surprise, tucked neatly inside my wallet was a fifty-dollar bill!

My mind flashed to the beautiful woman with the proud look in her eye. I had been kind to a stranger, and in turn, a stranger had been kind to me. I knew that God had answered my prayer.

Kristin Seuntjens

Do You Have Your Wallet?

The experience gathered from books, though often valuable, is but the nature of learning: whereas the experience gained from actual life is of the nature of wisdom.

Samuel Smiles

This is a story about a learning experience that had a big effect on the way that I live my life. The teacher in the story did not scream, assign homework, give me tests or even grade me on my work. I was taught by one of the most effective methods of teaching, one that only people with lots of love can do.

"My wallet! Where is it?" were my first words when I found out my wallet was missing. I searched my memory for a few good seconds, then realized that I had left my precious wallet at the library. Not only did I leave it at the library, but I had left it in the library's public restroom! I distinctly remembered seeing it on the shelf as I went to the bathroom.

Because the library was now closed, I had to wait until the next morning to begin my search. When I got there the next day, all I found was a sparkling clean restroom, its counters clean and its floors shiny white. This was the first time I could remember ever hating to see a clean bathroom. As I walked out, I looked at myself in the mirror and shook my head at the forgetful fool in front of me.

Now all I could hope for was that the person who cleaned the restroom had found my wallet. So I politely approached an old lady reading her book at the front desk. I asked her if a wallet had been found in the bathroom yesterday. She didn't answer me until she found a good place to pull herself away from her book. Then she peered at me from behind the thick black glasses parked on her nose. Letting out a quiet sigh, she slowly struggled out of her comfortable sitting position. She walked through a door and vanished for a moment. Then she came back to the desk.

"No."

That was that. I quickly thanked her and walked off.

I wondered what *I* would do if I had found a wallet containing sixty dollars, a phone card and many other irreplaceable personal items. Finally, I painfully accepted the fact that my wallet was gone.

A week later, after I had canceled my bank card and reported my license missing, I received a mysterious package in the mail. Sure enough, it was my wallet! And most amazingly, nothing was missing! But something *was* different about it. There was a little yellow sheet of paper folded up in one of the wallet pockets that had not been there before. I slowly unfolded the paper. Into my hand fell a little copper medallion of Christ. The letter read something like this:

> *Always keep this medallion with you, no matter what your religion is, so that the angel that was watching over you last week will always be close.*

This person didn't even leave a return address, so I couldn't thank whoever it was. I felt that this was an act of pure kindness that was extremely rare.

From that day on, I promised myself that whenever I am in a situation where I can help others the way that this person helped me, I will follow this example and make them as happy as I was when I opened that package!

Laksman Frank, age 16

Small Talk

I will speak to youth which can accomplish everything, precisely because it accepts no past, obeys no present and fears no future.

Rudyard Kipling

Coffee Soldiers

My mom is a first-grade teacher. It was around Christmas, and all the kids were really hyper. A little boy came into her room and put a coffee mug filled with toy soldiers on her desk. She asked what it was for, and he said, "The best part of waking up is soldiers in your cup."

Vanessa Breeden, age 12

Belated Birthday

One day after work, I was driving my two sons home

from school when Christopher asked if we could stop at a store so he could buy a birthday gift to take to school the next day. I said, "Sure, but why?" He proceeded to tell me that tomorrow would be George Washington's birthday, and he wanted to take him a gift.

His older brother, Richard, looked at Christopher and said, "He's dead, stupid!"

Christopher's quick reply was, "Darn, I *knew* we should have bought it sooner!"

Lois Wooster Gopin

Turkey Day

As a teacher, I know that kindergarten has always been a place to learn important lessons. So, one day when I was visiting the school where my husband was the principal, I went to discover the place of wonder—the kindergarten class.

There, I noticed a little girl busily slapping paint on an easel. To my eye, her creation seemed to be nothing more than a big red blob. "Tell me about your painting," I said.

The young artist stopped painting. She backed away from the easel and gave her work a careful look. Then she heaved a heavy sigh and exclaimed, "It's a turkey!"

After what seemed an eternity, she added, "And tomorrow, I'm going to put the skin on it!"

Meg Conner

Being Tall

I wish I was tall. Taller than the basketball players, so that I could dunk the ball *so bad*. My friends tell me that I am not going to grow any more—but that's not true. I don't believe them. I *am* going to be taller. I just have to wait.

Bader Alshammeri, age 14

Yes, Sir!

My three-year-old brother had been told several times to get ready for bed. The last time that my mom told him, she was very insistent. His response was, "Yes, Sir!" Since he was talking to our mother (and she is a woman), we didn't expect him to call her "Sir."

"You would say, 'Yes, Sir,' to a man. I am a lady, and you would say 'Yes, Ma'am,' to a lady," Mom said. To quiz him on his lesson, she then asked him, "What would you say to Daddy?"

"Yes, Sir!" came the reply.

"Then what would you say to Mama?"

"Yes, Ma'am!" he proudly answered.

"Good boy! Now what would you say to Grandma?"

He lit up and said, "Can I have a cookie?"

Elizabeth Cornish, age 12

Just a Slight Misunderstanding

In my class, when a person has a birthday, instead of being given a present, the birthday person brings a book to our class for the in-room library. On my birthday, I chose my favorite book: *There's a Boy in the Girls' Bathroom.*

I went to the bookstore and asked the lady behind the counter, "Do you carry *There's a Boy in the Girls' Bathroom?*" Instead of looking it up on the computer as I thought she would, she said, "Just a minute," and she disappeared. My mom and I waited and waited.

Finally she came back, and she said to me, "There's no one there now—he must have gone home with his mother."

I started laughing, and so did my mom. The lady was embarrassed—I guess she hadn't heard me say the words, "Do you carry . . . ?" She had been gone that entire time, looking for a boy in the girls' bathroom.

Melanie Hansen, age 10

A French Accent

Last summer my family and I went to the beach for a camping trip. When we arrived at the campground, all my cousins, aunts, uncles, and even my grandparents were there. After we got the tent set up, the adults started to make dinner. All of the kids went down to the river.

When we arrived, there were some older kids throwing rocks in the river, so we decided to go downriver a little. As we turned around to leave, my little ten-year-old cousin was already having a blast. He was yelling and throwing rocks in the river. My cousin has a speech problem, so he speaks in kind of a funny way.

As we were walking away, the older kids started laughing at my cousin. They were teasing him and making fun of how he talks. At first he started to get really upset, but then he turned around and asked them why they were laughing. They told him that he talked stupidly. Then he asked them, "What, haven't you ever heard a French accent before?"

They just stood there for a minute with dumb looks on their faces and finally just walked away.

Erin Althauser, age 13

The Science Snack

In my class, we were doing an experiment on mold and how it grows. We were studying the effects that light and dark would have on the mold. For our concluding science project, we placed pieces of moist bread in various places in the room. Some were placed in the back corner, where it was darker, and others were placed in the front part of the room. We also put some pieces out on our back porch, in the sunlight.

Several hours later, we checked on our specimens to see how they were doing. The ones left on the back porch were nowhere to be found. We searched high and low, but the pieces of bread had simply disappeared.

We later found out that the kindergartners, out at recess, had seen this "feast" laid out before their very eyes. They decided that this was a snack made just for them, so they ate our science experiment—soggy bread, mold and all.

Dr. Sherry L. Meinberg

Eyelids

When I was five years old, my dad told me that I could watch a movie all night called *Eyelids*. I got excited when bedtime came. "Can I watch *Eyelids* now?" I asked. But Dad said, "Time to go to bed, son." I reminded him of how he had told me that I could watch the movie *Eyelids*. He said, "You have to go to sleep, with your eyes closed, to be able to see your eyelids." So ever since then, I *think* before I ask questions like that. I don't want to be tricked again.

Joshua Cantrell, age 12

The Great Pumpkin

By the time I entered the eighth grade, I had already grown to six feet two inches tall. I was at least a foot taller than any of the other kids at my school, and I was so self-conscious that I didn't even want to talk to anyone. I walked around sort of bent over to hide my height.

All the kids at school listened to a disk jockey on WLS called the Great Pumpkin. He had a popular program where he answered letters on the air from the kids who wrote to him. I figured that if anyone could solve my problem, it would be the Great Pumpkin. So I wrote:

> *Dear Great Pumpkin:*
>
> *My name is Mark Victor Hansen, and I am in the eighth grade at Jack Benny Junior High. I am six feet two inches tall and taller than anyone else in school. What should I do?*
>
> *Yours truly,*
> *Mark Victor Hansen*

A week after mailing my letter to the Great Pumpkin, I was getting ready for school while I listened to his show. Then I heard, "To Mark Victor Hansen at Jack Benny Junior High: Cut off your head and carry it to school in a paper bag!"

The rest of the week everyone at school kept asking me, "Hey, Markie, where's your paper bag?"

Just because someone is popular like the Great Pumpkin doesn't mean they know all the answers.

Mark Victor Hansen

The Day I Figured Out That No One Is Perfect

Once there was a girl in my class that I thought was beautiful and smart. I believed that she was perfect. When it came time for my birthday, I invited her to my party, and she came.

A few months later, it was her birthday. I got a special necklace for her. Thinking about how happy she would be to receive my gift made me so excited.

I asked her when her birthday party was going to be. She replied, "Why do you want to know? You're not invited. You're just a dork with glasses!"

I felt really bad when she said that. I just stood there looking at her. Everyone standing by her came to stand next to me. Then we all left.

That day, I figured out that even if someone looks perfect, there is a very good possibility that they aren't. When it comes to perfection, it's how someone treats you that is more important than how they look.

Ellie Logan, age 9

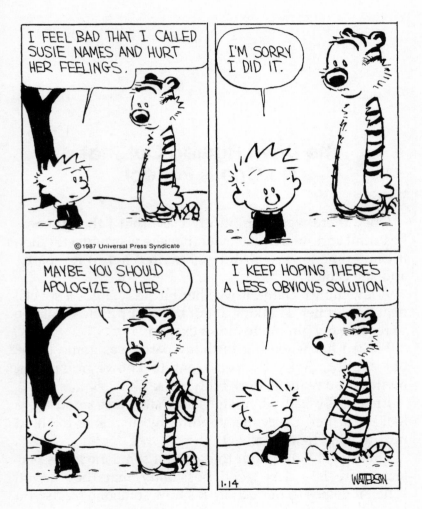

The Little Notice

Honesty's the best policy.

Benjamin Franklin

Once upon a time, when I was in the sixth grade, I got a disciplinary, "Child-Has-Done-Bad" notice, "Child-Has-Been-Cutting-Up-In-Class" type notice, which was actually known as a "Yellow Slip." I brought it home, but I was really bad about dealing with this kind of thing. My plan was to always get my disciplinary slips signed in the morning before school, right before I had to get out of the car. I would say, "Well, Dad, there's one more thing. I got this little notice, and I need you to sign it so I can go to class." That way, I could avoid a punishment. I was thinkin' that I was really smart!

But this particular morning, I was kind of chicken, and I just got out of the car. My father got out, too, to tell me something. I walked around to his side and showed him the little notice. He was in the middle of the street with the car still running.

I was like, "Sign it real quick," you know. Then I began

to joke around with him by saying stuff like, "Actually, it isn't a *real* disciplinary notice; it's a fake one. It's just a test. See, see, you're getting mad! You're passing the test! You're *supposed* to get mad—it's a test for the parents. I'm supposed to report to my teacher, 'cause they're looking to see if we're having family problems and stuff like that. . . . "

He didn't laugh at my joking about it. He signed the little notice, but he told me that this time I wasn't gettin' off easy and that I was really gonna get it when I got home.

That was the longest day I'd ever gone through. The day just dragged on and on. I was thinking about all the ways that Dad could decide to punish me, like grounding me from hangin' around with my friends, or even worse, no TV for a month. *That* would have *killed* me, 'cause I'm such a big TV head!

When my father picked me up, I tried to be a little angel, you know, hoping that he'd forget about the punishment. We got home and went in the house, and everything was cool, right? But then he says, "Alright, get upstairs and wait for me." I was thinkin', "OOOHHH maaan!"

Well, I didn't lose a month of TV, but I got a spankin' that I never forgot. It got the message across real clear, and I learned my lesson. Don't hold out on your parents! Just go ahead and tell the truth, 'cause it shall *set you free!*

Kenan Thompson

Teenagers

They wear clothes too tight.
They wear clothes too big.
They have funky hair styles,
I think they need a wig.

They're allowed to stay out.
They're allowed to make out.
They're allowed to wear clothes
That let it all hang out.

They're allowed to have boyfriends.
They're allowed to have girlfriends.
They can't mind their business.
They're way far into trends.

They're snotty and conceited.
They think they're all that,
They make me want to puke.
Next year . . .
Will I be like that?

Melissa Mercedes, age 12

"I sure hope Billy's guardian angel
doesn't go on strike."

My Guardian Angel

We all take for granted the great gift of life. You don't really notice how special it is until death looks you in the eyes.

When I was about two years old, I had a near-death experience. I don't really remember much about it except for what my mom told me.

It was a hot summer day, and everybody had gone outside to enjoy the weather. My sister and her friend jumped into our backyard pool to cool off. I did not know how to swim yet. My mom would always watch all of us very closely, but just for a minute, she had walked over to the side of the yard to talk to my dad. She told my sister to watch out for me, but my sister was busy laughing and having fun with her friend.

Before anyone knew it, I fell into the pool. No one heard me because I was so little; there was hardly a splash.

What happened next was amazing. My mom says it felt as though someone tapped her on the shoulder, but when she turned around no one was there. It was then that she noticed I wasn't in sight. She ran over to the pool, looking for me. She saw me in the pool, kicking and waving my arms in the air, trying to keep my head above the water. She jumped in and pulled me out. Luckily I was okay. She held me in her arms and thanked God that I was all right.

All of this happened within less than a minute. It shows how very precious life really is and how it can be lost in the blink of an eye.

No one really knows why my mom turned around. To this day, she thinks that it was my guardian angel tapping her on the shoulder.

Travis Ebel, age 14

Grandpa's Bees

I *have known it for a long time but now I have* *experienced it. Now I know it not only with my* *intellect, but with my eyes, with my heart, with* *my stomach.*

Hermann Hesse

A long time before I was born, my grandma and grandpa moved into the house on Beechwood Avenue. They had a young family of four little girls. The little girls slept in the attic in a big feather bed. It was cold there on winter nights. Grandma put hot bricks under the covers at the foot of the bed to keep the girls warm.

During the Great Depression work was hard to find, so Grandpa did whatever jobs he could. He dug ditches during the week, and on weekends he and Grandma dug a garden to grow some of their own food.

The house on Beechwood Avenue had a big front yard with shade trees and fruit trees. In the middle of the yard was a water pump where the four little girls pumped water for cooking, cleaning and watering the garden. On one side of the yard Grandma and Grandpa planted

tomatoes, beans, squash, cucumbers, peppers and straw-
berries to feed their growing family. They planted roses,
geraniums, lilacs and irises on the other side of the yard,
around the statue of the Blessed Mother.

Everybody worked to keep the garden growing. All
summer long the family ate food from the garden and
enjoyed the beautiful flowers. Grandma put up strawberry
jam, tomatoes, beans, peppers, pears and peaches in can-
ning jars. They were good to eat through the long winter.

The family grew up, and before too many years had
passed, grandchildren came to visit. Grandma and
Grandpa still planted their garden every spring. Everyone
still enjoyed the good food from the garden and always
took some home.

Grandchildren grow up, and grandparents grow older.
It became harder for Grandma and Grandpa to keep up
the garden, so they made it a little smaller. There was still
plenty to eat from the garden and lovely flowers to enjoy.

Then one summer when Grandpa was eighty-nine
years old, all he could do was watch from his lawn chair
as the vegetables grew and the roses bloomed. Summer
slowly faded, and Grandpa died before it was time to
bring in the harvest.

It was a lonely winter for Grandma. She sat near the
window, looking out at the yard and wondering if she
should plant a garden in the spring. It would be hard to
care for it by herself. When spring came, she planted only
a little garden.

One sunny day in early summer, Grandma heard a
commotion in the front yard and looked out the window
to see a frightening sight. A gigantic swarm of bees filled
the air between two tall trees. There were thousands of
bees in the air, so many that the swarm reached the tree-
tops! The buzzing sound was tremendous.

Grandma watched as the bees made their way into a

hole high up in one of the trees. Before long, every one of those bees had disappeared into its new home.

Grandma wondered what in the world she could do. Should she hire someone to get rid of the bees? That would cost more than she could afford. She decided to wait and think it over.

During the next few days, the bees were busy minding their own business. Grandma could always see a few bees buzzing in and out and around the opening high in the tree. Before long, she decided the bees weren't bothering anyone, so she went about her business and didn't give them another thought.

That summer, Grandma's little garden grew and grew. The neighbors would stop to admire her huge crop of vegetables and puzzle over why their own gardens weren't doing as well. No matter, because Grandma had enough to give some away. Of course, everyone who came to visit was treated to a meal of good things from the garden.

One day, Grandma's brother Frank visited from Arizona. As Grandma made Frank a delicious lunch of squash pancakes and homemade applesauce, she told him the story about the swarm of bees.

Frank said, "In Arizona, the farmers often hire bee-keepers to set up beehives near their fields. The bees pollinate the crops and help them to grow."

That was when Grandma realized that her bees had helped with the garden all summer.

"So that's why my little garden had such a big crop!" she exclaimed.

From that time on, Grandma always believed that since Grandpa couldn't be there with her to help that summer, he had sent the bees to take his place and make Grandma's little garden grow and grow.

Barbara Allman

"If the bees make honey, do butterflies make butter?"

The Flying Fish

Your big opportunity might be right where you are now.

Napoleon Hill

One summer my family and I went on a vacation to Sunriver, Oregon. We rented a cabin and a small power-boat at Big Lava Lake and were ready for a week of serious fishing. Our first morning, we packed a big picnic lunch, fishing poles and Mom's camera. She loves to take a picture of the proud person with his or her catch, a rare thing in our family of unlucky anglers. We went down to the lake with high hopes of catching "the big one." Little did we know just *how* big our catch that day would be.

It was a really bright, sunny morning. The sky was pale blue and full of big, fluffy white clouds. The blue-green lake sat in the middle of the surrounding mountains like a spoonful of gravy in the middle of your mashed potatoes. The entire area, including the lakeshore, was covered with huge, dark green pine trees, which filled the air with their beautiful smell. You could see their giant reflections on the quiet surface of the lake.

We motored as far away from the other boats on the lake as possible. After anchoring the boat, we set up our fishing lines in five different directions. Then we opened up our picnic lunch, passed out sandwiches and started to relax.

"There's nothing like a peaceful day on the lake," Dad said, enjoying his peanut butter and jelly sandwich. "Your Uncle Pat would say, 'The family that fishes together, stays together.' What a beautiful day."

After a while, we realized that the reason our end of the lake was so uncrowded was because our end had no fish.

"Hey, how come we always seem to pick the side of the lake where we're never gonna catch anything?" my brother Ethan asked.

"Just be patient. You guys will catch something. You always do," Mom said, trying to encourage us.

"Something big enough for a family of five would be nice," grinned my brother Colin. "I think I'll just relax while I wait for those *big* fish down there, just lining up for my bait . . ."

The loud buzz of a small plane overhead interrupted him. Above the engine noise, Mom cried out, "Look, everybody. This will be so exciting. It's a pontoon plane that's about to land on the water!"

"No, it's not, Trish. That pilot's in trouble!" Dad shouted.

Dad was right. The plane that Mom thought was able to float on the water was actually a plane that needed to make an emergency landing, and the pilot had chosen our lake to land on! Within seconds, the plane crashed on its belly, as though it were doing a giant cannonball. *Splash!!!* Huge waves filled the lake. The nose of the plane was pointing downward—the plane was sinking fast!

Dad, who knew right from the beginning that the pilot was in trouble, immediately tried to start the motor of our boat. The boat jerked forward, throwing our bits of sandwiches on the deck and tangling up all of our fishing lines. Food and fishhooks were flying everywhere! We were hurrying and scurrying as our parents called out commands and our family charged into action. At first, it was like a comedy movie. But my parents were great. They kept their cool. "Everybody stay calm! Don't stand up! Pull in your lines! You guys sit down! Grab the extra life jacket! Let's go! Let's hustle! This is an emergency!"

Dad gave the engine full throttle, and its ten horsepower puttered as fast as it could. We only had to go a few hundred feet, but it seemed to take forever. We could see the pilot—a gray-haired man wearing a checkered shirt, blue jeans and cowboy boots. He had climbed onto the plane's wing while the nose was sinking and the tail was pointing straight up. He was standing on the wing, holding an old brown suitcase, waiting for us to come to his rescue. He seemed so calm, just standing there, like he was waiting outside at a bus stop.

When we finally reached the pilot, Mom grabbed a life jacket and threw it out onto the water for him. By that time, the plane had sunk. The pilot was clinging for dear life to his suitcase, which he seemed to be using as a life preserver. He seemed to have difficulty swimming and couldn't get to the life jacket that was only five feet away from him. After several tries, Mom and Dad hoisted the pilot by the belt loops of his jeans onto our boat. He was safely on board.

"Oh my gosh. . . . Thank you, thank you!" The pilot's face was frozen with fear. "My goodness, thank you. . . . My name's Wave, Wave Young. . . . I've been flying for over forty years . . . " he stammered. He seemed out of breath and really shaken up.

"Hi, I'm Mike; this is my wife, Trish; our children, Megan, Ethan and Colin," Dad said, trying to put the pilot at ease.

"I knew I had engine trouble and knew I was coming down, so I tried to land on the lake. A couple years back, another pilot landed in those beautiful pines and started a big forest fire. I didn't want to do the same!" Wave's voice was shaking.

"Did you say your name is Wave? I can see why. . . . "

"Colin!" I whispered under my breath. We all laughed a little nervously, even Wave.

"Well, thank God you people were here. I don't know what I'd have done without you. I was in such shock I couldn't even swim! Thank God you were here to rescue me."

Once he was comfortably seated on the boat, we rushed the pilot ashore to let the waiting paramedics and other emergency crews take care of him. Even though we still had rental time left on the boat, we turned it in early because, as Dad said, "I think we're done fishing for the day." We said our good-byes, and as a crowd formed, we decided to sneak out of the way, get into our car and head back for the day.

"I'm really proud of you kids. You were terrific. You handled that emergency really well," Dad told us, his face beaming with pride.

"What do you think you guys learned from all this today?" Mom asked as she turned back toward us in the car.

"We were on the wrong side of the lake again for fishing, but this time it turned out good," Ethan answered shyly.

"We learned how important it is to be ready for emergencies," Colin added.

"And you never know when God will use you to help someone," I said to my family. "We were there for a reason. We were the only people on that side of the lake. The pilot was so scared that he couldn't swim. If we had gone to the other side of the lake, we couldn't have reached him in time to save him."

That night we saw video coverage of Wave's plane crash on the evening news. Amazingly, Mom had also snapped an awesome picture of Wave standing on the wing of his plane, right before we reached him. She gave the photo to the local paper, which printed it the next morning on the front page.

We still need to frame that photo of "the big one." We could hang it somewhere in our home to keep our memory of that day alive. And maybe we wouldn't have a picture of a fish, but we would have a picture of a pilot we fished out—and that would sure be the biggest "flying fish" anyone had ever seen!

Megan Niedermeyer, age 12
with Killeen Anderson

Mother Says . . .

Throughout the centuries, mothers have given their children plenty of good advice and notable quotes. Here's just a small sampling:

PAUL REVERE'S MOTHER: "I don't care where you think you have to go, young man. Midnight is past your curfew!"

MARY, MARY, QUITE CONTRARY'S MOTHER: "I don't mind your having a garden, Mary, but does it have to be growing under your bed?"

MONA LISA'S MOTHER: "After all the money your father and I spent on braces, Mona, that's the biggest smile you can give us?"

HUMPTY DUMPTY'S MOTHER: "Humpty, if I've told you once, I've told you a hundred times not to sit on that wall. But would you listen to me? Noooo!"

COLUMBUS'S MOTHER: "I don't care what you discovered, Christopher. You still could have written!"

BABE RUTH'S MOTHER: "Babe, how many times have I told you—quit playing ball in the house! That's the third broken window this week!"

MICHELANGELO'S MOTHER: "Mike, can't you paint

on walls like other children? Do you have any idea how hard it is to get that stuff off the ceiling?"

NAPOLEON'S MOTHER: "All right, Napoleon. If you aren't hiding your report card inside your jacket, then take your hand out of there and prove it!"

CUSTER'S MOTHER: "Now, George, remember what I told you—don't go biting off more than you can chew!"

ABRAHAM LINCOLN'S MOTHER: "Again with the stovepipe hat, Abe? Can't you just wear a baseball cap like all the other kids?"

BARNEY'S MOTHER: "I realize strained plums are your favorite, Barney, but you're starting to look a little purple."

MARY'S MOTHER: "I'm not upset that your lamb followed you to school, Mary, but I would like to know how he got a better grade than you."

BATMAN'S MOTHER: "It's a nice car, Bruce, but do you realize how much the insurance is going to be?"

GOLDILOCKS'S MOTHER: "I've got a bill here for a busted chair from the Bear family. You know anything about this, Goldie?"

LITTLE MISS MUFFET'S MOTHER: "Well, all I've got to say is if you don't get off your tuffet and start cleaning your room, there'll be a lot more spiders around here!"

ALBERT EINSTEIN'S MOTHER: "But Albert, it's your senior picture. Can't you do something about your hair? Styling gel, mousse, something . . . ?"

GEORGE WASHINGTON'S MOTHER: "George, the next time I catch you throwing money across the Potomac, you can kiss your allowance good-bye!"

JONAH'S MOTHER: "That's a nice story, Jonah, but now tell me where you've *really* been for the last three days."

SUPERMAN'S MOTHER: "Clark, your father and I have discussed it, and we've decided you can have your own telephone line. Now will you quit spending so much time in all those phone booths?"

And finally . . . THOMAS EDISON'S MOTHER: "Of course, I'm proud that you invented the electric light bulb, Thomas. Now turn off that light and get to bed!"

Martha Bolton

What I've Learned So Far

When you're confused, sit down and think it through.
Ignore people who put you down.
Never, ever, ever give up on yourself.

Andrea Gwyn, age 12

If nothing is in the refrigerator, don't eat dog food.
Never cheat because it's not worth it.

Samantha Jean Fritz, age 9

When your dad or mom slams the door when they come home from work, it is best to stay out of their way.

If you don't care what grades you get and do badly in school, the main words in your vocabulary will be, "Do you want fries with that?"

Michelle Nicole Rodgers, age 10

Never ask your dad to help you with a math problem. It will turn out to be a three-hour lesson.

If you have a problem or secret, share it with your mom.

Katie Adnoff, age 13

Check if there is toilet paper *before* you sit down.

Don't make a bad impression on your neighbors when you first move in.

Laugh at your parents' jokes.

Natalie Citro, age 12

When my parents are talking, not to interrupt but wait until later. Unless someone is bleeding or something.

Alle Vitrano, age 8

Read the book before you have to go in front of the class to give a report.

Never leave your little sister alone with your stuff.

Amanda Smith, age 12

If you wear a child's extra large in clothes, an adult small is too big.

If someone dies, think about the good, not the bad. The bad will make you feel worse.

Don't judge people by their looks. Someone could be the ugliest person in the world and still be nice.

Ashlee Gray, age 9

When your mom is mad, hide the stuff that you don't want thrown away.

Katie Fata, age 10

When you tell a lie, you have to keep telling a lie.

When your parents get divorced, you have to move on.

Ronnie Evans, age 10

When you take off your sweatshirt, your shirt comes up.

Ben Hall, age 10

You only have one life. So be careful.

When your friends do something stupid, you don't have to follow.

If you think something will taste bad, it will. If you think something will taste good, it might.

Maria McLane, age 9

If you write somebody's name wrong, it makes them feel bad.

Benjamin Mitchell, age 10

A promise is a promise.

Ask before you touch something that isn't yours.

If you make someone cry, say that you're sorry.

You're never too big to ask for help.

Being nice can get you somewhere.

People who do mean things to you are not your friends.

Cats are not water-resistant.

Don't ride your bike on ice.

Never tell stuff to other friends that another friend said.

Never, ever say "I hate you."

Take turns using stuff.

Don't use the front brake on your bike first.

If you slow down and take your time, your work is better.

Don't smart off to the teacher.

You will get there just as fast if you don't push and shove, and no one will be mad at you.

Don't tease a girl if she is wearing boots.

Wear comfortable shoes on field days.

Don't bother Chad.

Mrs. Pat Wheeler's fourth-grade class

Don't get hit in the stomach right after you eat.

Don't ever unplug the computer.

You do have a dream. . . .

Never run with your shoelaces untied.

Never throw overhand when playing egg toss.

Miss Tracey Alvey's fourth-grade class

Never sleep with gum in your mouth.

Ashley Parole, age 12

Don't go in somebody's backyard that you don't know, especially if it says "Beware of Dog."

Nedim Pajevic, age 13

You don't have to win a race to feel good about yourself; all you have to do is finish. Never, ever give up.

Becky Rymer, age 12

Don't cough or sneeze in other people's faces, especially if you don't know them.

Karen Perdue, age 12

Pain is not good.

Girls are more important than you think.

Philip Maupin, age 13

Don't bug your mom when she's going to have a baby.

Elvis Hernandez, age 12

Life is like a "choose your own ending" book—you can take whatever adventures you want.

Erika Towles, age 12

Keep your room dirty so your mom will be afraid to come in, and then she won't take your stuff.

Geoff Rill, age 12

When your mom's on a diet, don't eat chocolate in front of her.

Corey Schiller, age 12

Don't mess with a kid bigger than you are.

David Neira, age 12

When my teacher gets mad, she *really* gets mad.
The funnier you are, the better life is.

Lauren Aitch, age 10

Moving was the hardest thing I have ever done in my life.
I can't hide my lima beans in my sister's milk cup.

Evan de Armond, age 12

Attitudes are contagious.
Don't make fun of someone doing their best.

Mikie Montmorency, age 12

Don't tell a teacher your dog ate your homework, especially if you don't have a dog.

Raelyn Ritchie, age 12

Afterword

It is our hope that these stories have brought you hope, joy, courage and inspiration, and that they will live on through you. You are now the storyteller. May they continue to touch you and empower you.

Reading Stories: An Act of Co-Creation

A story is a magical, mysterious
Instrument.
Told
——— through words, not pictures ———
A written story
allows readers or listeners,
in creative collaboration with the author,
to be co-creators of the story
and thus fully and uniquely
to live
the story's
rhythms, lessons and meanings.

James Elwood Conner

Who Is Jack Canfield?

Jack Canfield is a bestselling author and one of America's leading experts in the development of human potential. He is both a dynamic and entertaining speaker and a highly sought-after trainer.

Jack spent his childhood years growing up in Martins Ferry, Ohio, and Wheeling, West Virginia. Jack admits to being shy and lacking in self-confidence as a kid, but through a lot of hard work, he managed to earn letters in three sports and graduate third in his high school class.

After graduating from college, Jack taught school in Chicago's inner city and in Iowa. Most of his professional career after that has been spent teaching teachers how to empower kids to believe in themselves and to go for their dreams.

He is the author and narrator of several bestselling audio- and videocassette programs, including *Self-Esteem and Peak Performance, How to Build High Self-Esteem* and *The GOALS Program*. He is a regularly consulted expert for radio and television broadcasts and has published fourteen books—all bestsellers within their categories.

Jack addresses over a hundred groups each year. His clients have included schools and school districts; over one hundred education associations, and corporate clients such as AT&T, Campbell Soup, Clairol, Domino's Pizza, GE, Re/Max, Sunkist, Supercuts and Virgin Records.

Jack conducts an annual seven-day Training of Trainers program in the areas of building self-esteem and achieving peak performance. It attracts educators, counselors, parenting trainers, corporate trainers, professional speakers and ministers.

For further information about Jack's books, tapes and training programs, or to schedule him for a presentation, please contact:

The Canfield Training Group
P.O. Box 30880 • Santa Barbara, CA 93130
phone: 805-563-2935 • fax: 805-563-2945
To e-mail or visit our Website:
www.chickensoup.com

Who Is Mark Victor Hansen?

Mark Victor Hansen was born to Danish immigrants, Una and Paul Hansen, in Waukegan, Illinois. He began working at nine. He also had his own newspaper route, and by age sixteen was an assistant supervisor at that newspaper.

When Mark was a sophomore in high school, he watched the Beatles premiere on TV. He called his best friend, Gary Youngberg, and said, "Let's start a rock 'n' roll band!" Within two weeks, they had a five-member group called The Messengers. Because of the band, Mark made enough money to pay his own way through college.

Mark went on to become a professional speaker who, in the last twenty-four years, has made over four thousand presentations to more than 2 million people. His presentations cover sales excellence and strategies, and personal empowerment.

His mission to make a profound and positive difference in people's lives continues to be his main focus. Throughout his career, Mark has inspired hundreds of thousands of people to create a more powerful and purposeful future for themselves.

A prolific writer, Mark authored *Future Diary, How to Achieve Total Prosperity* and *The Miracle of Tithing*. He is co-author of the *Chicken Soup for the Soul* series, *Dare to Win* and *The Aladdin Factor* (all with Jack Canfield) and *The Master Motivator* (with Joe Batten).

Mark has also produced a complete library of personal empowerment audio- and videocassette programs that have enabled his listeners to recognize and use their innate abilities in their business and personal lives. He has appeared on ABC, NBC, CBS, HBO, PBS and CNN.

Mark lives in Costa Mesa, California.

For further information about Mark contact:

Mark Victor Hansen & Associates
P.O. Box 7665
Newport Beach, CA 92658
phone: 949-759-9304 or 800-433-2314
fax: 949-722-6912
Website: *www.chickensoup.com*

Who Is Patty Hansen?

Patty Hansen has contributed many of the most loved stories in the *Chicken Soup for the Soul* series. She is the coauthor and editor of *Condensed Chicken Soup for the Soul,* and coauthor of (with Mark Victor Hansen and Barbara Nichols) *Out of the Blue: Delight Comes into Our Lives.*

Patty was committed to making *Chicken Soup for the Kid's Soul* relevant to the issues that kids face today, and to make sure that it would be a book that kids, ages nine through thirteen, would not only love to read but could also use as a guide for everyday life.

A third-generation California native, Patty was raised in Pleasant Hill, where her mother, Shirley, still lives. Her sister, Jackie, lives in Oregon.

Prior to her career as an author, Patty worked for United Airlines for thirteen years as a flight attendant. During that time, she received two commendations for bravery. She received the first one when, as the only fight attendant on board, she prepared forty-four passengers for a successful emergency landing. The second was for extinguishing a fire on board a mid-Pacific flight, thus averting an emergency situation and saving hundreds of lives.

After "hanging up her wings," Patty became the chief financial officer and troubleshooter for M. V. H. & Associates, Inc., in Newport Beach, California.

In 1998, Mom's House, Inc., a nonprofit organization that provides free childcare for young mothers, nominated Patty as Celebrity Mother of the Year.

Patty has two children Elisabeth and Melanie. With the help of their housekeeper, Eva, they share their lives with one rabbit, one duck, two horses, three dogs, four cats, four birds, five fish, and twenty-one chickens.

If you would like to contact Patty:

Patty Hansen
LifeWriters
P.O. Box 10879 • Costa Mesa, CA 92627
phone: 949-645-5240 • fax: 949-645-3203
To send e-mail or to visit our Website:
www.chickensoup.com or
www.PreteenPlanet.com

Who Is Irene Dunlap?

Irene Dunlap began her writing career in elementary school when she discovered her love for creating poetry, a passion she believes to have inherited from her paternal grandmother. She expressed her love of words through writing fictional short stories and song lyrics, as a participant in speech competitions and eventually as a vocalist.

During her college years, Irene traveled around the world as a student of the Semester-at-Sea program aboard a ship that served as a classroom, as well as home base, for over 500 college students. After earning a bachelor of arts degree in communications, she became the media director of Irvine Meadows Amphitheatre in Irvine, California. She went on to co-own an advertising and public relations agency that specialized in entertainment and health care clients.

While working on the book, Irene managed to stay involved with her children's sports and after-school activities, to be the busy president of the Parent-Faculty Organization at Kaiser Elementary School, to carry on a successful jazz singing career, and to continue to be an active member of her church's music team.

Irene lives in Newport Beach, California, with her husband, Kent, daughter, Marleigh, son Weston, and Australian shepherd, Gracie. Her mother, Angela, who has been her lifelong source of tremendous support and unconditional love, lives in nearby Irvine. Irene's sisters, Kathi, Pattie and Pam, who are also three of her best friends, live in California with their families.

In her spare time, Irene enjoys singing, horseback riding, painting, gardening and cooking. If you are wondering how she does it all, she will refer you to her favorite biblical passage for her answer, Ephesians 3:20.

If you would like to contact Irene, write to her at:

Irene Dunlap
LifeWriters
P.O. Box 10879 • Costa Mesa, CA 92627
phone: 949-645-5240 • fax: 949-645-3203
To send e-mail or to visit our Website:
www.chickensoup.com or
www.PreteenPlanet.com

Contributors

Valerie Allen is an editor at a crossword puzzle company, and is the published author of *The Night Thief*, a children's picture book. Valerie can be reached at 930 SW 86th Ave., Pembroke Pines, FL 33025.

Barbara Allman is a children's writer and former editor of *Schooldays Magazine*. Barbara enjoys speaking to school groups and encouraging children to write. School visits can be arranged through her publisher, Carolrhoda Books, Inc., phone: 800-328-4929.

Bader Alshammeri, age fourteen, is an eighth-grader from Rio Bravo Middle School in El Paso, Texas. He plays all sports, especially basketball. He is now six-feet-two-inches tall, and says he still has four more years to grow. His goal is to reach seven feet, and to play professional basketball.

Erin Althauser is a fifteen-year-old freshman at Timberline High School. She is thinking of taking after her dad and becoming a computer professional. She enjoys talking, hanging out with friends, listening to music, and writing short stories and poems.

Killeen Anderson is a sociology major who enjoys her volunteer work with the disabled students on her college campus as well as foreign languages, music, film and a good day of bodysurfing. She resides in California with her husband, Ralph, and their Labrador retriever, Digby.

Nate Barker is a thirteen-year-old from Colombus, Ohio. He likes to draw, write and participate in swimming, track, basketball and snow skiing.

Kendra Batch, age twelve, is an eighth-grader from Indiana. When she is not writing, she likes to ride her bike and go-cart.

Anne (A. F.) Bauman, a professor of English, specializing in writing and children's literature, has had her work published in books, anthologies and magazines. She is now working on a mystery for children.

Martha Bolton has been a staff writer for Bob Hope for fifteen years. She is the author of twenty-four books and has been published by *Reader's Digest, The Christian Herald* and *Breakaway Magazine*. She has received an Emmy nomination for Outstanding Achievement in Music and Lyrics and is the winner of two International Angel Awards.

Vanessa Breeden is a thirteen-year-old who lives in Texas. She enjoys writing, playing the piano, in-line skating, track, canoeing and collecting pictures of Leonardo Di Caprio.

Marcia Byalick is a freelance writer, award-winning columnist, college writing instructor, and author of three young adult novels and three self-help books. One of her novels, *It's a Matter of Trust*, was honored as an International Reading Association Young Adult Choice for 1997. Marcia can be reached through Writer's House Literary Agency.

Joseph Cantrell is a thirteen-year-old from Greenville, South Carolina. He likes surfing the Internet, baseball, fishing and biking. He has two sisters and one brother, with another on the way.

Ben Carson, M.D., was born in Detroit, Michigan, in 1951. Dr. Carson attributes his metamorphosis from an unmotivated ghetto youngster to one of the most respected neurosurgeons in the world, to his mother, Sonya. Dr. Carson is a graduate of Yale University and the University of Michigan Medical School. Presently director of Pediatric Neurosurgery at Johns Hopkins University Hospital in Baltimore, Maryland, Dr. Carson and his wife, Candy, and their three sons reside in West Friendship, Maryland.

Vanessa Clayton is a fourteen-year-old who lives in Salt Lake City, Utah, where she is a dedicated student and avid reader. She enjoys volunteering with children and food drives, playing basketball, tennis, skiing and playing the piano.

Donna L. Clovis, a Columbia University Fellow in New York, is a storyteller, author and associate producer. She is also an ESL teacher at Princeton Schools in New Jersey. *Storybook of Native American Wisdom* is her fifth published book. Contact Donna at P.O. Box 741, Princeton Jct., NJ 08550.

James Elwood Conner, Ed.D., has had numerous careers, including teacher, principal, college professor, college president, curriculum specialist, senior associate for education with the U.S. Chamber of Commerce, and governor's speech writer. He is currently freelancing and ghostwriting.

Meg W. Conner resides in North Carolina with her husband of fifty years. Meg is the author of the popular sourcebook *Career Mentoring at Work*. Meg is the recipient of the United Nations Human Rights Award and has been cited in *World Who's Who of Women*.

Elizabeth Cornish, age twelve, has recently been recognized as the top fifth-grade student in her school, winning awards in her district for writing. She enjoys performing arts in the areas of ballet and piano.

Barbara McCutcheon Crawford, author and seasoned teacher, shares her experience in her current book, *The Common Sense, Early-Childhood Classroom*. She owns Jugtown Mountain School where she is the director and head teacher. For information about books and presentations, she can reached at 454 Mine Rd., Asbury, NJ, or by calling or faxing 908-537-4444.

Jennifer Rhea Cross, age seventeen, plans to study journalism at the University of Southwestern Louisiana in Lafayette. She enjoys spending time with her family, boyfriend, friends and dog. In order to help educate others, she is involved with hemophilia and AIDS organizations.

Jason Damazo is a thirteen-year-old who lives in California. He enjoys playing the cello, reading, writing and playing percussion. Jason loves dogs and would like to see a wolf someday.

Jesse Damazo is a fourteen-year-old who lives in Paradise, California. He is an avid reader and writes for a monthly editorial column in his local newspaper, *The Paradise Post.* Jesse enjoys music and plays the violin, piano and guitar.

Harmony Davis is a fourteen-year-old who lives in California. She has been involved in creative activities since the age of three, including dance, theatrical productions, and writing plays and short stories.

Jennifer Genereux Davis had her first poem published in 1996 and received an Editor's Choice Award from The National Library of Poetry. Since then, she has had four poems published and hopes to continue with children's books and short stories.

Robert Diehl, age twelve, is an eighth-grader whose hobbies include playing lacrosse, football and basketball. He enjoys playing the drums in his school's band, is a member of his church's junior youth group and is an avid New York Giants fan.

Dayle Ann Dodds has published eleven books, newspaper articles, poems and magazine stories for children. Her first picture book, *Wheel Away!* was number one on *The San Francisco Chronicle's* bestsellers list. Dayle just completed another novel and her first full-length screenplay.

Jereme Durkin is a nineteen-year-old student at Orange Coast College in Costa Mesa, California. He plays basketball, bodysurfs and likes to make people laugh. Jereme loves writing poetry and is thankful for the encouragement of his family and friends.

Travis Ebel, age fourteen, is from Battle Creek, Michigan, and maintains a 4.0 grade point average at St. Philip's School and the Battle Creek Area Math and Science Center. Travis likes sports and hopes to become a doctor or an architect.

Adam Edelman, age thirteen, attends Bayside Middle School in Wisconsin. He enjoys reading and social studies and plays football and basketball. He would like to be a music or film critic.

Aljon B. Farin is seven years old and goes to school in San Diego, California. His favorite subject is science. He has two sisters, one-year-old Jasmine Marie and thirteen-year-old Vanessa. After he does his homework, Aljon plays video games and watches sports.

Robert J. Fern lives outside of Phoenix, Arizona, with his wife, Suzanne and their daughter, Jill. He teaches psychology at the local community college and manages a counseling program for children. Robert may be reached at 311 West Straford Dr., Chandler, AZ 85224.

Danielle Fishel discovered her love for acting by performing in community plays, and has been acting professionally since she was ten years old. Her first break in acting came when she landed a recurring role on the hit television show, *Full House.* Danielle joined the *Boy Meets World* cast in 1993 in the role of Topanga. She is excited to be a part of the Celebrity Sightings team, an on-line celebrity fan club which features exclusive photos, chats, give-aways, prizes, games and a fan club merchandise store. The site can be found at: HYPER-LINK http://*www.celebritysightings.com.*

Laksman Frank is a sixteen-year-old honor student at a private school in Sebastian, Florida. He loves sports, especially in-line skating, hockey and surfing. Laksman is a community volunteer for AIDS awareness.

Amber Foy, age twelve, learned to write from her fourth-grade teacher, Ms. Maxner. She has been writing ever since and would like to thank Ms. Maxner for all her support.

Judy Fuerst is a first-time author who usually works with paint rather than words. Her previous productions include newspaper art, murals, posters, textbook illustrations and two well-designed children.

Judy M. Garty currently writes for a local newspaper, *The West Bend Daily News*. Her story in *Chicken Soup for the Kid's Soul* is a tribute to her youngest brother who died in his sleep. Judy can be reached at 210 Oak St., Slinger, WI 53086-9366.

Elizabeth A. Gilbert-Bono earned her master's degrees in both business administration and education from Harvard University. She is now enjoying life with her husband, Mark, and their three children, Alexandra, Bryson and Blake.

Candace Goldapper earned both a bachelor of arts and a master's degree from Queen College in Flushing, New Jersey. She is a former social studies teacher who is now a freelance fiction writer for magazines.

Lois E. Wooster Gopin is a bookkeeper, mother of three grown sons and grandmother of six small grandsons. She loves to paint and write children's books. She also enjoys sailing with her husband.

Louise R. Hamm is a former legal administrator who started writing seriously after retirement. Married for fifty-one years, Louise has three children and two grandchildren. Lou can be reached at 1003 E. Houston St., Garrett, IN 46738-1622.

Cynthia M. Hamond (Cindy) lives in Monticello, Minnesota. She volunteers her time at St. Henry's Church as a teacher, communion minister, lector and visitor to the homebound. She may be reached at 1021 W. River St., Monticello, MN 55362, by calling 612-295-5049, by faxing 612-295-3117, or via e-mail at *candbh@aol.com.*

Candice Hanes is a ten-year-old student from Costa Mesa, California, who enjoys ballet, soccer and spending time with her friends. Candice enjoys writing stories and sometimes composes them on her computer.

Melanie Hansen, age ten, is a fourth-grade student in Costa Mesa, California. She loves to write stories and poetry, and sing. She enjoys riding her horse, Shawnee Dancer, and in-line skating with her father, Mark.

Jessica Harper finds enjoyment working, editing videos and going to church. She is seventeen-years-old and lives in a small town in Illinois with her mom, dad and three brothers.

Patricia (Patty) Hathaway-Breed lives on the northern coast of California where she teaches art at her studio and at The College of Redwoods in Fort Bragg. Her hobbies include camping, playing music and listening to the sea with her husband. She may be reached at 32760 Simpson Ln., Fort Bragg, CA 95437.

Debbie Herman is a special education teacher and author of children's books. She enjoys sitting on the balcony of her fifth-floor apartment where she gets her writing inspiration. She may be reached by e-mail at *dhermnm@netvision.net.il.*

Lillian Belinfante Herzberg developed an interest in writing while at Grossmont College in La Mesa, California, where she was published in their literary magazine. She has received awards in local contests for her short stories. Lillian and her husband are enjoying retirement by keeping busy going to the movies and live theatre.

Darnell Hill is thirteen years old and would like to be an actor when he grows up. His favorite sports are basketball and football. He comes from a family of seven children—three boys and four girls.

Jillian K. Hunt is a twenty-year-old who dreams of someday writing a novel and teaching second grade. For now, she is getting a head start as a pre-school teacher. Writing is Jillian's source of relaxation and therapy.

Charles Inglehart is a freshman at Reynolds High School in Troutdale, Oregon, where he participates in public speaking classes. He also enjoys music, outside activities and "hanging out" with friends.

Kathy Ireland has appeared on countless magazine covers including *Glamour, Cosmopolitan, Mademoiselle, Seventeen* and *Shape.* Her association with *Sports Illustrated* is legendary: thirteen years, three magazine covers, the magazine's twenty-fifth and thirtieth anniversary shows, their 1992 swimsuit edition and the *Sports Illustrated* Class of '95. Kathy has always been involved with humane causes. Two of her most recent are Project Inform in San Francisco, which provides information on treatments for HIV/AIDS worldwide, and Athletes and Entertainers for Kids in Los Angeles, a national nonprofit youth-service organization which provides exposure to alternative life options for disadvantaged youth. Kathy lives in Southern California with her husband Greg, an emergency room physician, and their young son, Erik. Kathy and Greg enjoy a variety of sports, including snow skiing, hiking, mountain biking and especially scuba diving. Visit Kathy's website at *www.kathyireland.com.*

Diana L. James is a professional speaker and writer whose work has appeared in several national magazines. Before becoming a full-time writer/speaker, Diana produced and hosted her own television and radio interview programs.

Lou Kassem was born in the mountains of eastern Tennessee and inherited a natural talent for storytelling. In 1984, she put her talent on paper by publishing the first of eleven novels. With four one-of-a-kind daughters, Lou enjoys writing for young people. She is now working on her twelfth novel.

Christine Lavin has spent twenty years as a reporter and editor for newspapers, including *The Burlington Free Press* in Vermont and *The San Francisco Chronicle*. She may be reached at 701 Cleveland, Oakland, CA 94610, by calling 510-536-4529, or via e-mail: *brooklyn@lanminds.com*.

Stephanie Lee is a twelve-year-old whose goal in life is to be a doctor. She enjoys writing poems and short stories, and finds inspiration at the beach and through her friends and family. Her musical talents include playing the flute and the piano.

David Levitt, age sixteen, is a tenth-grade student at Osceola High School in Seminole, Florida. His interests include drama, music and computer games. As the youngest volunteer for Tampa Bay Harvest (TBH), David delivers food donations and speaks to groups about the program.

Damien Liermann, age fifteen, enjoys writing, especially when an important event occurs, because it gives him the opportunity to express his feelings in a non-physical way. Damien also likes to collect key chains, rocks and dead insects. His favorite hobby is collecting music.

Ellie Logan is ten years old and participates in basketball, soccer, swimming, tennis and horseback riding. Ellie has two dogs, two cats and a bird. She would like to thank her third-grade teacher, Mrs. Arnold, for encouraging her to write a story for *Chicken Soup for the Kid's Soul*.

Karen Beth Luckett is a freelance writer of children's stories and writes primarily for magazines. She is currently working on picture books and collections of short stories.

Dandi Daley Mackall has been writing professionally since 1978. She has published over 150 books for children and 27 books for adults, such as *The Princess and the Pea, Picture Me Goldilocks*, and *Town and Country Mouse*, as well as storybooks on *The Flintstones, Scooby Doo, Yogi Bear* and *The Jetsons*. Her newest eleven-book series, *Puzzle Club Mysteries*, will be animated by Hanna Barbera and aired nationally on television. Dandi writes from rural Ohio, where she lives with her husband, Joe, and her three children, Jenny, Katy and Danny—along with two horses, a dog, a cat and a rabbit.

James Malinchak, is the author of *Teenagers Tips for Success* and a dynamic public speaker. He is a contributing author to *Chicken Soup for the Teenage Soul*. You may contact James at P.O. Box 32, Monessen, PA 15062, by calling 888-793-1196, via e-mail at *JamesMal@aol.com*, or visit his Website at http://*www.Malinchak.com*.

Tyler Vaughn Marsden, age eleven, is a seventh-grader from Southern California. He grew up near the beach where he likes to Boogie Board, bike ride and ski. When he's at home, he loves to cook.

Taylor Martini, age nine, was encouraged by his third-grade teacher, Mrs. Thompson, to submit to *Chicken Soup for the Kid's Soul*. He likes sports and is active in soccer. Taylor is very involved in chess and competes in tournaments. He would like to be a chess teacher and achieve a grandmaster ranking someday.

Page McBrier is the author of over thirty-five books for young readers. She grew up in Indianapolis, Indiana, and St. Louis, Missouri, and credits her wacky family with providing much of the inspiration for her stories. She currently lives in Connecticut with her husband and two sons. Page may be reached through Writer's House, New York City.

Jessica McCain is fourteen years old and has always loved to read and write. She is active in basketball, softball and tennis. She likes to spend time with her friends and family and finds joy in helping others.

Marie P. McDougal is a recently retired English and psychology teacher, former newspaper writer and local history columnist. Currently a freelance writer, she is a member of The Society of Children's Book Writers and Illustrators, Detroit Women Writers, Romance Writers of America and The Bay Area Writers' Guild. Marie can be reached at 41556 Gloca Mora, Harrison Twp., MI 48045.

Dr. Sherry L. Meinberg retired after thirty-four years as a teacher and librarian and is now a university professor. She provides custom-designed speeches, workshops and staff development seminars. Her books include *Into the Hornet's Nest: An Incredible Look at Life in an Inner City School* and *Be the Boss of Your Brain!* Dr. Meinberg can be reached at 5417 Harco St., Long Beach, CA 90808.

Melissa Mercedes is a thirteen-year-old who enjoys writing poetry, listening to R&B music, in-line skating and annoying her little brother, Leonard. She also likes going to the movies with her friends.

Shelly Merkes, age eleven, is a sixth-grader from Oshkosh, Wisconsin. She likes bike riding, in-line skating and swimming. Her musical talents include playing the piano and singing in a chorus.

Shannon Miller has won more Olympic and World Championship Medals than any other male or female American gymnast in history. She earned seven Olympic Medals and nine World Championship Medals in the past four years. During her career, Shannon won an astounding fifty-eight International and forty-nine National Competition Medals; over half of each have been Gold Medals culminating with two Gold Medals at the 1996 Olympic Games in Atlanta. As a member of "The Magnificent Seven" at the 1996 Games, she won Team Gold and—for the first time for any American gymnast—the Gold Medal in the balance beam competition.

Kel Mitchell is a nineteen-year-old Chicago native, who received his training from ETA Creative Arts Foundation in drama, dance and voice. Kel gained much of his acting experience performing in local theatrical productions and made his television debut as a cast member of Nickelodeon's all-kid sketch comedy series, *All That*. Kel recently made his first major feature debut in *Good Burger*.

Lori Moore is a freelance writer and editor, specializing in the children and young adult markets. She is currently writing scripts for the kids' television show *Hall Pass*, and has recently formed her own youth consulting company, YouthScope. Lori can be reached at 1827 W. 246th St., Lomita, CA 90717.

Korina L. Moss grew up in Wappinger Falls, New York, graduated from Texas Tech University, and is currently residing in New England. She enjoys travelling with her husband, David, and spoiling their two cats, Ophelia and Franklin. Her greatest passion is writing; she recently completed a young adult mystery novel.

Tim Myers is a writer, professional storyteller and songwriter who lives in Plattsburgh, New York. He has two stories published in *Cricket Magazine* and a book soon to be published entitled *Let's Call Him Lauwiliwililihumuhumunuku-nukunukunukukuapua'aoioi!* "The Bobsledder's Jacket" is a true story that happened to his friend, Jack Mulholland, who was an Olympic bobsledder.

Tara M. Nickerson has been telling and writing stories ever since she was a child. Now living on Cape Cod, she has a bachelor of arts degree in English literature. Tara recently completed the manuscripts for four young adult novels. She may be contacted at P.O. Box 131, Cotuit, MA 02635.

Megan Niedermeyer, age twelve, is a seventh-grade student who lives in Lafayette, California. She has twin ten-year-old brothers, Ethan and Colin. Her favorite activities are reading, writing short stories and poetry, playing basketball and playing with her dog, Swoops.

Chuck Norris is one of the world's most popular and successful action film stars. As a young man, he joined the Air Force and was sent to Korea where he earned a black belt in karate and a brown belt in judo. When he returned to the United States he became a martial arts instructor. He later started competing, earning endless championship titles including Middleweight Champion of the World. He established The United Fighting Arts Federation and was named "Man of the Year" in 1979. After starring in several martial arts films, Chuck soon became a box office success. With films such as 1983's *Lone Wolf*, followed by *Missing in Action, Invasion USA* and 1986's *Delta Force*, he is now starring in his own television series for CBS, *Walker, Texas Ranger*. Chuck's charity work is extensive. He developed and now serves as chairman for Kick Drugs Out of America Foundation.

Carla O'Brien is a wife, mother and published children's book author. She is also a singer/songwriter for the contemporary Christian group, Heartsong. She is developing a journal to teach children about values. Carla can be reached at 8109 Greenshire Dr., Tampa, FL 33634.

Christa Holder Ocker is a happy grandmother and author of four picture books. When she is not writing, she enjoys sailing, cross-country skiing and playing with her granddaughter, Tiana. Christa can be reached at 55 Royal Park Terr., Hillsdale, NJ, 07642.

Mary Beth Olson is a former human services worker turned freelance writer.

Shaquille O'Neal was the number-one pick in the 1992 NBA Draft and is one of basketball's greatest centers. Known worldwide as the Shaq-Attack, his athletic awards include 1993 Rookie of the Year, Olympic Gold Medalist and Most Valuable Player. Shaq is also a rap artist who released two hit CDs, and an actor with several feature films to his credit, including *Kazaam*. Shaquille also makes time to give of himself and his resources.

Glenda Palmer's sixteenth children's book, *God Must Have Smiled When He Made Animals,* is currently being published. She lives in San Diego with her husband, Richard. They have two grand cats, and a grand iguana, but no grandchildren yet. Glenda can be reached at 1687 Via Elisa Dr., El Cajon, CA 92021.

Diana Parker is a thirteen-year-old living in Birmingham, Michigan, with her parents and her brother, Nate. She has a dog named Abby and a cockatiel named Lori. She enjoys reading, drawing, hiking, playing the flute, and engaging in political debates. Someday she hopes to be a scientist and help the world.

Lucas Parker, age eleven, is a seventh-grader who enjoys baseball, snow skiing, surfing and hiking. He does well in school, and earned a place on the principal's honor roll. He would like to attend UCLA, and perhaps work as a volcanologist.

Judie Paxton, born and raised in West Virginia, has lived in the Atlanta, Georgia area for the past twenty-six years. Wife, mother, and proud owner of a Jack Russell terrier, Judie's interests include reading, walking on the beach and enjoying sunsets. You may contact Judie at 2320 Melrose Trace, Cumming, GA 30041.

Jan Peck loves to write children's books and contribute to children's magazines such as *Highlights for Children* and *Boys' Life*. Dial Books published her most recent picture book, *The Giant Carrot,* for young readers in March of 1998. Jan can be reached at 6217 Loydhill, Fort Worth, TX 76135 or by e-mail at: HYPERLINK mailto: *janpeck@startext.net.*

Joanne Peterson lives on the Olympic Peninsula in the Pacific Northwest. She has produced expository writing for business and civic organizations and is the author of stories for both children and adults. Her poetry has appeared in several publications and received awards at The Northwest Writers' Conference.

Berniece Rabe is the author of sixteen children's books; her first five novels earned nominations for The Newbery Award, and two children's books won The Society of Children's Book Writer's Golden Kite Award. She is a sought-after speaker for schools and educators. She can be reached at 724 Smokerise, Denton, TX 76205.

Deborah J. Rasmussen is a freelance writer/editor with a special interest in children's literature, and was a winner of the Highlights for Children Fiction Contest in 1995. Deborah resides in Florida with her husband and eleven-year-old son. She can be reached at 9149 Arundel Way, Jacksonville, FL 32257-5080.

Lacy Richardson is thirteen years old and lives in a log cabin in Blue Ridge, Virginia. She is the eldest of four children—two sisters and a brother. Her hobbies include reading and playing the flute. Lacy swims on a local swim team and plans to continue in college.

Belladonna Richuitti, age thirteen, loves to sing, write poetry and read mystery books. Her favorite sports are basketball and volleyball. She would like to thank her English teacher, Ms. Moronta, for all her help and support.

Ann McCoole Rigby loves people, nature, healing ideas and words. She combines these loves as a wife, mother, teacher, astrologer and writer. Ann is the author of *Why Moon Goes Round* and other astrological materials for children. She can be reached at 5313 E. McDonald Dr., Paradise Valley, AZ 85253, or by calling 602-952-0127.

Linda Rosenberg is a freelance writer, middle-school English teacher, and a writer for Disney In-School Video Programs. Since 1991, she has been involved with Disney, scripting the in-school versions of *Aladdin, Snow White* and *Pinnochio*. Linda's hobbies are reading and writing and teaching her students to do the same. Her most important editors are her two children, Daniella and Mark. She can be reached at 3353 Caminito Gandara, La Jolla, CA 92037.

David Roth is a musician, songwriter, recording artist, conference presenter, occasional NBA national anthem singer, animal lover, playwright and workshop facilitator. David's work can also be found in other *Chicken Soup for the Soul* books. He can be reached at 18952 40th Place NE, Seattle, WA 98155-2810; phone: 1-800-484-2367 ext. 3283; e-mail: HYPERLINK mail to: *RothDM@aol.com:* Web page: *http://songs.com.dr.*

Donna Russell is a native New Yorker who has earned masters degrees in education and corporate finance. She is currently self-employed and spends her free time writing fiction. Married with one daughter and a grandson, she loves to play tennis.

Mary Ellyn Sandford is a happily married mother of seven children. Her writing has been published in several magazines, including *Venture, Counselor, Reader's Digest* and *Police Magazine*. She enjoys making homemade bread and chicken soup. Mary Ellyn can be reached at 4507 Chelsea Ave., Lisle, IL 60532, or via e-mail at *sand@enteract.com.*

Beth Schaffer, age sixteen, enjoys reading and writing poetry. She would like to dedicate her piece in *Chicken Soup for the Kid's Soul* to her mom, dad, and Ms. Jan who have given her guidance, love and support.

Kristin Seuntjens has pursued a career as an elementary educator, but enjoys being a full-time mom the most. Kristen makes time to read, draw, sing and play the violin. She is currently working on her first chapter book for children. She can be reached at 227 Isanti St., Duluth, MN, 55803.

Matt Sharpe is twelve years old and lives in San Diego, California. He plays on his school's basketball and football teams. He likes skateboarding, bicycling and playing at the beach. Matt would like to dedicate his story to the memory of his father, "the best dad ever," Steve Sharpe.

Katie Short, age twelve, is a seventh-grader at Read Mountain Middle School in Cloverdale, Virginia. She likes to read and listen to music. She is a softball player and an Atlanta Braves fan. She has two older sisters and a dog named Peaches.

Alan D. Shultz resides on an Indiana farm with his wife, Deb, and their three teenage children. He is a lawyer, real-estate broker and award-winning newspaper columnist. Alan can be reached at 5852 W. 1000 North, Delphi, IN 46923.

Bernie Siegel, M.D., lives in a suburb of New Haven, Connecticut, with his wife and coworker, Bobbie. Dr. Seigel (Bernie) has cared for and counseled people whose mortality has been threatened by an illness. In 1986 his first book, *Love, Medicine & Miracles,* was published. *Peace, Love & Healing* and *How To Live Between Office Visits* followed. He is currently working on other books with the goal of humanizing medical education and medical care.

Stacie Christina Smith is a twelve-year-old seventh-grader from Lincoln, Massachusetts, who enjoys singing in church, talent shows and plays. Stacie spends a lot of time with her family and friends. Her hobbies include basketball, swimming and softball.

Valeria Soto is a twelve-year-old student attending Ensign Intermediate School in Newport Beach, California. Her favorite subject is science and she enjoys writing. Her family is the most special part of her life.

Rider Strong, seventeen-year-old star of ABC's hit show *Boy Meets World,* landed his first professional acting job at the tender age of nine when he played the coveted role of the ill-fated Gavroche in *Les Miserables.* Since then, he has made numerous guest star appearances on many hit television shows including *Home Improvement, Empty Nest, Evening Shade, Time Trax,* and most recently a recurring role on FOX Television's *Party of Five.* Rider, a prodigious writer, is currently putting the final touches on his book of poetry entitled *On the Impulse,* which he is showcasing at local clubs in the Los Angeles area. He also attends college in the Los Angeles area.

Jessica Stroup is a freshman in high school who dreams of singing on stage in front of millions of fans. For now, she enjoys being a teenager; shopping, spending time with friends, and writing poems. She lives with her mother, stepfather and two younger brothers.

Audilee Boyd Taylor is the published author of a children's picture storybook entitled *Where Did My Feather Pillow Come From?* Her other children's books in progress are *The Other 99 Sheep, The Mulberry Connection,* and *The Savannah River Pirates.* Audilee can be reached at P.O. Box 60728, Savannah, GA 31420-0728.

Kenan Thompson began his acting career at the age of five, playing a gingerbread man in the school play. From his kindergarten classroom to the silver screen, Thompson's acting career has skyrocketed with roles in the major motion pictures *D-2 The Mighty Ducks, Heavy Weights* with Ben Stiller, and the Nickelodeon release *Good Burger.* A native of Atlanta, Georgia, Thompson's other television credits include reporting for CNN's *Real News For Kids,* co-host of the ABC special *Night Crawlers* and *T-Rex,* which won an Emmy Award.

Tia Thompson is a fifteen-year-old who enjoys writing fiction and non-fiction stories, letters and poems. She loves listening to music and spending time with her friends. She considers herself to be an outgoing, talkative person.

Heather Thomsen, age thirteen, is from Shoreline, Washington, where she likes to play soccer and run track and cross-country. She plays the French horn and sings in the school concert choir. Heather enjoys reading and writing stories about her detective agency called The Four Investigators.

Reverend Mark Tidd is the pastor of Crestview Christian Reformed Church in Boulder, Colorado. He is the father of five children ranging from four to twenty years old. He records and performs with NO I NO, an acoustic rock/funk/Latin/pop (but no rap) group.

John Troxler is fifteen-years-old and lives in Summerfield, North Carolina, with his parents and two brothers. His hobbies include playing soccer, playing video games, reading and crafts.

Sabrina Anne Tyler is a twelve-year-old from Costa Mesa, California. She wants to be a Harvard-educated lawyer or a marine biologist when she grows up. She enjoys biking, doing theatre work and writing short stories.

M. A. Urquhart is a freelance writer and the author of a dozen children's books. She lives in Maine with her husband and three children, all of whom have had enormous influence on her writing.

Julie J. Vaughn, Tyler's mother, is a student earning her certificate in drug and alcohol counseling. She enjoys cycling and is learning to play golf.

Adrian Wagner is a twenty-six-year-old sports writer for *The St. Cloud Times,* a daily newspaper in central Minnesota, who says he is more concerned with the heart of the team than the score of the game. Adrian aspires to be the sports editor of a large daily newspaper. He may be reached at 3200 N. 15th St., Apt. #315, St. Cloud, MN 56303.

Jody Suzanne Waitzman, age thirteen, loves to read, listen to music and write about human rights and racism. She has had the fortune to travel, which she says has made her more open-minded to other cultures and customs.

Joel Walker, age eleven, is a sixth-grader from Costa Mesa, California, who has enjoyed playing soccer and baseball since he was five years old. He is a member of "THE UNDERGROUND" at Calvary Church Newport Mesa and thanks God for the blessings he receives daily.

Kerri Warren, age thirty, wrote her story for *Chicken Soup for the Kid's Soul* while in junior high. Kerri earned a Ph.D. in cell biology and is currently doing research at Harvard Medical School, studying heart formation and rhythm generation.

Sandra Warren is an author, educational consultant and publisher. She has authored books, poetry, reader's theatre, video and audio scripts including *Arlie the Alligator,* a story-song picture book for children. Contact Sandra at P.O. Box 360933, Strongsville, OH, 44136, or via e-mail at *arlieentwarren@juno.com*

We would also like to thank the following contributors: From Costa Mesa, California: **Lauren Aitch; Mike Curtis; Evan de Armond; Tania Garcia; Elisabeth Hansen; Elvis Hernandez; Stephanie Lane; David Neira; Nedim Pajevic; Ashley Parole; Karen Perdue; Amanda Smith; Hayley Valvano;** and **Roman Zaccuri.** From Newport Beach, California: **Katie Adnoff; Natalie Citro; Marleigh Dunlap; Philip Maupin; Brittany Miller; Mikie Montmorency; Geoffrey Rill; Raelyn Ritchie; Corey Schiller;** and Erika Towles. Also, **Danielle Uselton** from Cleveland, TN; **Martina Miller** from Reidville, SC; **Sarah Bennett** from St. Petersburg, FL; **Meghan Gilstrap** and **MeShelle Locke** from Lacey, WA; **Molly Oliver** from Cincinatti, OH; **Jessica Ann Farley** from Hartly DE; **Jorge Prieto** from El Paso, TX; **Leah Hatcher** from Cloverdale, VA; **Megan Preizer** from Rushville, IN; **Angie Porter** from Stendal, IN; **Renny Usbay** from Sunnyside, NY; **Eun Joo Shin** from Woodside, NY; **Gina Pozielli** from Gibbstown, NJ; **Ronnie Evans; Katie Fata; Samantha Jean Fritz; Ashlee Gray; Ben Hall; Michelle Nicole Rodgers; Maria McLane;** and **Benjamin Mitchell** from Lansing, MI; **Andrea Gwyn** from Midlothian, VA; **Becky Rymer** from Greensboro, NC; **Pat Wheeler's** fourth grade class from Paducah, KY and Tracey Alvey's fourth grade class from Paducah, KY; and **Alle Vitrano** from Windsor, CA.

Permissions

We would like to acknowledge the many publishers and individuals who granted us permission to reprint the cited material. (Note: The stories that were penned anonymously, that are in the public domain, or that were written by Jack Canfield, Mark Victor Hansen, Patty Hansen or Irene Dunlap are not included in this listing.)

Book. Reprinted by permission of Jessica McCain and Nancy McCain. ©1998 Jessica McCain and Nancy McCain.

Is That When You Know? Reprinted by permission of Candice Hanes and Janine Ann Thomas. ©1998 Candice Hanes and Janine Ann Thomas.

Discovery. Reprinted by permission of Jesse Damazo and Becky Damazo. ©1998 Jesse Damazo and Becky Damazo.

Love. Reprinted by permission of Stephanie Lee and Hwa Sook Park. ©1998 Stephanie Lee and Hwa Sook Park.

Kelly, The Flying Angel. Reprinted by permission of Louise R. Hamm. ©1998 Louise R. Hamm.

The Tower. Reprinted by permission of Robert J. Fern. ©1998 Robert J. Fern.

Uncle Charlie. Reprinted by permission of Patty Hathaway-Breed. ©1998 Patty Hathaway-Breed.

The Game of Love. Reprinted by permission of Lou Kassem. ©1998 Lou Kassem.

"Where's My Kiss, Then?" Granted permission by Ann Landers and Creators Syndicate. Reprinted by permission of M. A. Urquhart. ©1998 M. A. Urquhart.

The Visit. Reprinted by permission of Debbie Herman. ©1998 Debbie Herman.

The Fire Truck. Reprinted by permission of Lori Moore. ©1998 Lori Moore.

Merry Christmas, My Friend. Reprinted by permission of Christa Holder-Ocker. ©1998 Christa Holder-Ocker.

There's An Alien on the Internet. Reprinted by permission of Joanne Peterson. ©1998 Joanne Peterson.

Seeing, Really Seeing. Reprinted by permission of Marie P. McDougal. ©1998 Marie P. McDougal.

Kim Li, The Great. Reprinted by permission of Berniece Rabe. ©1998 Berniece Rabe.

Edna Mae: First Lesson in Prejudice. Reprinted by permission of Sandra Warren. ©1998 Sandra Warren.

The Connection. Reprinted by permission of Joel Walker and Laurie J. Walker. ©1998 Joel Walker.

The Favorite Vase. Reprinted by permission of Belladonna Richuitti and Alicia

No Home. Reprinted by permission of Elizabeth A. Gilbert-Bono. ©1998 Elizabeth A. Gilbert-Bono.

Baby's Ears. Reprinted by permission of Valerie Allen. ©1998 Valerie Allen.

Kindness is Contagious. Reprinted by permission of Kristin Seuntjens. ©1998 Kristin Seuntjens.

Do You Have Your Wallet? Reprinted by permission of Laksman Frank and Mitchell Frank. ©1998 Laksman Frank.

Small Talk. Reprinted by permission of the authors. ©1998 Vanessa Breeden and Stuart Breeden. ©1998 Lois Wooster Gopin. ©1998 Meg Conner. ©1998 Bader Alshammeri and Norma Alshammeri. ©1998 Elizabeth Cornish and Barbara Cornish. ©1998 Melanie Hansen and Patricia J. Hansen. ©1998 Erin Althauser and Sheryl Althauser. ©1993 Dr. Sherry L. Meinberg. ©1998 Joshua Cantrell and William Cantrell. ©1998 Mark Victor Hansen.

The Day I Figured Out That No One Is Perfect. Reprinted by permission of Ellie Logan and Clare S. Logan. ©1998 Ellie Logan.

The Little Notice. Reprinted by permission of Kenan Thompson. ©1998 Kenan Thompson.

Teenagers. Reprinted by permission of Melissa Mercedes and Reina Mercedes. ©1998 Melissa Mercedes.

My Guardian Angel. Reprinted by permission of Travis Ebel and Melissa J. Ebel. ©1998 Travis Ebel.

Grandpa's Bees. Reprinted by permission of Barbara Allman. ©1998 Barbara Allman.

The Flying Fish. Reprinted by permission of Megan Niedermeyer and Patricia Niedermeyer and Killeen Anderson. ©1998 Megan Niedermeyer and Killeen Anderson.

Mother Says. . . . Reprinted by permission of Martha Bolton. ©1996 Martha Bolton.

What I've Learned So Far. Reprinted by permission of the authors. ©1998 Andrea Gwyn, Samantha Jean Fritz, Michelle Nicole Rodgers, Katie Adnoff, Natalie Citro, Alle Vitrano, Amanda Smith, Ashlee Gray, Katie Fata, Ronnie Evans, Ben Hall, Maria McLane, Benjamin Mitchell, Pat Wheeler's fourth-grade class, Tracey Alvey's fourth-grade class, Ashley Parole, Nedim Pajevic, Becky Rymer, Karen Perdue, Philip Maupin, Elvis Hernandez, Erika Towles, Geoff Rill, Corey Schiller, David Neira, Lauren Aitch, Evan de Armond, Mikie Montmorency, Raelyn Ritchie.

An Act of Co-Creation. Reprinted by permission of James E. Conner. ©1998 James E. Conner.